Competition Law in Canada

Competition Law in Canada

Second Edition

Susan M. Hutton

This book was originally published as a monograph in the International Encyclopaedia of Laws/Competition Law.

General Editors: Roger Blanpain, Frank Hendrickx
Volume Editors: Francesco Denozza, Alberto Toffoletto

Wolters Kluwer

Published by:
Kluwer Law International
PO Box 316
2400 AH Alphen aan den Rijn
The Netherlands
Website: www.wklawbusiness.com

Sold and distributed in North, Central and South America by:
Aspen Publishers, Inc.
7201 McKinney Circle
Frederick, MD 21704
United States of America
Email: customer.service@aspenpublishers.com

Sold and distributed in all other countries by:
Turpin Distribution Services Ltd.
Stratton Business Park
Pegasus Drive, Biggleswade
Bedfordshire SG18 8TQ
United Kingdom
Email: kluwerlaw@turpin-distribution.com

ISBN 978-90-411-6640-1

This title is available on www.kluwerlawonline.com

The Author

Susan Hutton is a senior partner in Stikeman Elliott's Competition and Foreign Investment and the International Trade practice groups. She has provided *Competition Act* and *Investment Canada Act* advice in respect of numerous recent complex mergers and acquisitions, for example: Forest/Actavis, Lenovo/IBM x86 servers, MTS Allstream/ Accelero, CNOOC/Nexen, Astral/BCE, Motorola Mobility/Google, Johnson & Johnson/Synthes, Potash Corp/BHP Billiton, and United/Continental. She has guided clients through civil and criminal investigations as well as complaints under the *Competition Act*, and provides ongoing compliance advice to many clients. She also has particular expertise in complex net benefit and national security reviews under the *Investment Canada Act*. She has successfully represented complainants and exporter/importers in dumping and countervailing duty actions and also advises with respect to anti-corruption compliance.

Global Competition Review has noted Ms Hutton as 'among the most talented and well-regarded in the country'. Also recognized by Chambers & Partners as a leading individual in The World's Leading Lawyers for Business. Repeatedly recommended by The Canadian Legal Lexpert® Directory and as one of The Best Lawyers in Canada for competition. Chair of the National Competition Law Section of the CBA (2015/16); Chair of the Editorial Board of the Canadian Competition Law Review (2010-2015). Active in the antitrust sections of the ABA and the IBA. Publishes and speaks frequently in her fields.

Ms Hutton worked in the field of economic research including econometric modelling with the Bank of Canada prior to entering law. She has worked in Bangkok and Singapore, has advised the Government of Vietnam regarding the development of its competition law, and is a member of Stikeman Elliott's China Task Force.

Representative Work

- Counsel to Actavis with respect to its USD 28 billion acquisition of Forest.
- Counsel to Lenovo with respect to its USD 2.1 billion acquisition of the x86 server business of IBM.
- Counsel to MTS Allstream with respect to its proposed CAD 520 million sale of Allstream to Accelero.

The Author

- Counsel to China National Offshore Oil Company (CNOOC) with respect to its USD 19.5 billion acquisition of Nexen Inc.
- Counsel to Motorola Mobility Holdings, Inc. with respect to its USD 12.5B acquisition by Google Inc.
- Counsel to Johnson & Johnson in respect of its USD 21.3B acquisition of Synthes, Inc.
- Counsel to PotashCorp in its defence of BHP Billiton's USD 38.6B unsolicited take-over bid, with the bid being subsequently withdrawn after the key decision of Investment Canada to reject the proposal.
- Counsel to United Airlines with respect to its USD 8B merger with Continental Airlines.

Education

Ms Hutton is a graduate of the University of Toronto (LL.B. 1991, Bronze Medal) and of McGill University (Honours BA economics 1985, Faculty of Arts Gold Medal). She was called to the Bar of Ontario in 1993.

Table of Contents

Table of Contents

List of Abbreviations

AMPs	Administrative Monetary Penalties
ARC	Advance Ruling Certificate
CCGs	Competitor Collaboration Guidelines
DPP	Director of Public Prosecutions
GDP	Gross Domestic Product
ICA	*Investment Canada Act*
IPEG	Intellectual Property Enforcement Guidelines
IPRs	Intellectual Property Rights
MEGs	Merger Enforcement Guidelines
MLATs	Mutual Legal Assistance Treaties
MOU	Memorandum of Understanding
MRPG	Merger Review Process Guidelines
OECD	Organization for Economic Cooperation and Development
RCD	Regulated Conduct Defence
TREB	Toronto Real Estate Board
WTO	World Trade Organization

List of Abbreviations

General Introduction

§1. General Background of the Country

1. Canada is a federal parliamentary democracy comprising most of the northern half of North America. Canada is the second largest country geographically after Russia. Most of Canada's 35.8 million people[1] live in the southern third of the country. Canada has ten constitutionally established provinces and three federally authorized territories. In descending order, the most populous provinces are Ontario, Quebec, British Columbia and Alberta. Canada's most populous city is Toronto, Ontario. Toronto is often regarded as Canada's commercial and financial centre. Montreal, Quebec and Vancouver, British Columbia are also large and economically important cities. The capital of the country is Ottawa, Ontario.

2. A constitutional monarchy under the Commonwealth sovereign, Canada became a self-governing and largely independent state in 1867. Historically, Europeans first began exploring Canada around 1500. Until 1763, most of contemporary Quebec and Ontario were under French control, but British dominance increased after 1759 following the British victory over the French at the Plains of Abraham in Quebec City. Eventually the entire colonial territory came under British control. However, the *Quebec Act* of 1774 established a legal framework to maintain Quebec's distinct language, culture and legal system. As a result, Canada has a bijural legal system. Civil law applies at the provincial level in Quebec and common law applies federally and in all other provincial jurisdictions. The entire country remains officially bilingual. French is the dominant language in Quebec and parts of New Brunswick, while English is the dominant language in most other parts of Canada. Approximately 67% of Canada's population speaks English only; 13% speaks French only; and 17% of Canadians are bilingual.[2] Also important, Canada is now highly multicultural and has a substantial aboriginal population.

3. Canada took its first major step towards independent governance in 1867. The province of Canada – consisting of Upper Canada (modern day Ontario) and Lower Canada (modern day Quebec) – united with the colonial provinces of Nova Scotia

1. Statistics Canada, *Population by year, by province and territory*, http://www.statcan.gc.ca/tables-tableaux/sum-som/l01/cst01/demo02a-eng.htm (29 Sep. 2015).
2. Office of the Commissioner of Official Languages, *Statistics*, http://www.ocol-clo.gc.ca/html/canada_06_e.php (20 Oct. 2009).

and New Brunswick to form the Dominion of Canada. The British Parliament recognized and granted partial independence to this new federation by enacting the *British North America Act*. This event is known to Canadians as Confederation. In subsequent years, Canada grew westward to eventually include British Columbia on the Pacific coast. The tenth province, Newfoundland & Labrador, joined Canada in 1949, after the Second World War. The Canadian arctic remains under federal control and is divided into three territories: Yukon, Nunavut and the Northwest Territories.

4. In 1931, Canada achieved greater independence with the enactment of the *Statute of Westminster*, which authorized Canada to unilaterally pursue foreign relations. Canada officially achieved constitutional independence in 1982 when the United Kingdom relinquished its remaining constitutional authority over Canada. At this time, the *British North America Act* was renamed the *Constitution Act, 1867*.[3] Together with the *Canadian Charter of Rights and Freedoms*, the *Constitution Act, 1867* represents the most important part of the Constitution of Canada.[4]

§2. Economic System

5. Canada's economy is a mixed market – meaning it combines private and governmental controls – but overall the Canadian economy operates as one of the freest markets in the world. Most businesses are privately owned, though the government plays a significant role in providing healthcare and overseeing vital services like transportation and utility services. Canada is a G7 country and a member of the Organization for Economic Cooperation and Development (OECD).

6. The largest sector of the Canadian economy is the service sector. Other important sectors include manufacturing (particularly of automobiles), construction, agriculture, oil and gas, and mining.[5] In 2014, Canadian exports totalled over CAD 528 billion, while imports totalled nearly CAD 524 billion. The United States is by far Canada's largest trading partner. The European Union, the United Kingdom and China also account for a significant portion of Canada's exports and imports.[6]

§3. Legal System

7. Canada is both a constitutional monarchy and a federal parliamentary democracy. As a constitutional monarchy, Canada's official head of state is the British

3. 30 & 31 Victoria, c. 3. (U.K.) [*Constitution Act*].
4. *Constitution Act, 1982*, being Schedule B to the *Canada Act 1982*, 1982 c. 11 (U.K.) [*Charter*].
5. Statistics Canada, *CANSIM table 282-0008*, http://www5.statcan.gc.ca/cansim/a26?lang=eng&retrLang=eng&id=2820008&&pattern=&stByVal=1&p1=1&p2=37&tabMode=dataTable&csid= (5 Oct. 2015).
6. Statistics Canada, *CANSIM table 228-0058*, http://www.statcan.gc.ca/tables-tableaux/sum-som/l01/cst01/gblec02a-eng.htm (5 Oct. 2015).

monarch. In practice, though, the Queen's role is purely symbolic. Her representative in Canada, the Governor General, performs her ceremonial functions. The Prime Minister of the day selects the Governor General and is the de facto leader of Canada. The legislative branch of Canada's government comprises the House of Commons and the Senate. Canadian citizens elect representatives to the House of Commons, who are called Members of Parliament (MPs). The Prime Minister appoints Senators to the Senate, but their role in the legislative process is minimal as compared to the role of MPs. There are 308 MPs[7] (increasing to 338 for the 2015 election).[8] Each represents a geographic riding and is usually a member of a political party. The leader of the party (or coalition) with a majority of elected MPs becomes the Prime Minister. The Prime Minister heads the executive branch of government and appoints people (usually MPs from his political party) to serve as members of the federal cabinet, which is called the Governor in Council.

8. Sections 91 and 92 of the *Constitution Act, 1867* divide governmental powers between the federal and provincial jurisdictions. Cases dealing with jurisdiction can be complex. In general, however, the Constitution grants the federal government authority over matters of national and international importance, whereas the provinces have jurisdiction over more localized matters. Objects of the federal government's authority include trade and commerce, criminal law, intellectual property and competition law. Provincial governments control most private law issues in their jurisdiction, including property and contracts. The common law system applies to matters within federal jurisdiction, as well as to provincial jurisdictions with the exception of Quebec. In Quebec, the civil law system applies to matters of a provincial nature. Hence, property and contract law in Quebec are governed by the *Civil Code of Quebec*.

9. All Canadian judges are appointed. The appointment of most Canadian judges falls within federal jurisdiction. Provinces possess the authority to appoint judges who serve in lower level courts of limited jurisdiction that are known as inferior courts. The federal government appoints judges to provincial courts of inherent jurisdiction, called superior courts. Each province has its own court system. There is also a Federal Court system that hears some matters falling exclusively within federal jurisdiction, such as intellectual property and non-criminal competition law cases. The Supreme Court of Canada is the final court of appeal for all provinces, as well as for all federal courts. Like other high-level judges in Canada, members of the Supreme Court are officially appointed by the Governor General, though in practice, the decision is made by the Prime Minister. All judges are appointed to serve for life or until they reach a mandatory retirement age of 70 or 75.[9]

---

7. Parliament of Canada, *Current Members of Parliament,* http://www.parl.gc.ca/Parliamentarians/en/members (5 Oct. 2015).
8. Elections Canada, *New House of Commons Seat Allocation,* http://www.elections.ca/content.aspx?section=med&document=dec1911&dir=pre&lang=e (19 Dec. 2011).
9. For more on Canada's court system, see Department of Justice, *Canada's Court System*, http://www.justice.gc.ca/eng/dept-min/pub/ccs-ajc/pdf/courten.pdf (2005).

§4. Historical Background of Competition Law in Canada

10. Canada's federal government first enacted competition legislation in 1889, making it the first western industrialized country to do so.[10] The legislation, called *An Act for the Prevention and Suppression of Combinations in Restraint of Trade*,[11] was enacted with the aim of creating criminal prohibitions against conspiracies, combinations, and agreements or arrangements aimed at lessening competition.[12] Despite Canada's early adoption of competition legislation, developments in the area came very slowly. The early legislation was difficult to implement, in part because it relied exclusively on criminal enforcement at a time when arrangements among competitors were still commonplace. Criminal enforcement, of course, requires proof beyond a reasonable doubt.

11. In 1919, the federal government replaced earlier legislation with the *Board of Commerce Act*[13] and the *Combines and Fair Prices Act, 1919.*[14] This new legislation marked a shift in competition law from the criminal law model to the regulatory approach. The legislation created the Board of Commerce, which had the power to investigate anti-competitive behaviour, issue orders based on its findings, and regulate the production and price of goods.[15] However, the law's development took a step backwards two years later when the Privy Council of the House of Lords in the UK (then still Canada's highest court of appeal) declared the Acts to be unconstitutional because they infringed on the provincial governments' jurisdiction over property and civil rights.[16]

12. Consequently, competition law reverted to its criminal roots for several decades. In 1935, the federal government expanded the *Combines Investigation Act*[17] to include discriminatory discounts, territorial price discrimination and predatory pricing.[18] The new legislation also created a commission to administer the Act and to recommend prosecution under the *Criminal Code.*[19] In 1952, the statute's scope expanded to criminalize resale price maintenance. Further, the office of the modern day Commissioner of Competition – then called the office of the Director of Investigation and Research – came into being.[20] Despite these changes, serious

---

10. B. Facey & D. Assaf, *Competition and Antitrust Law: Canada and the United States* 2 (Lexis Nexis Butterworths 2006).
11. R.S.C. 1889, c. 41.
12. Facey & Assaf, *supra* n. 10 at 3.
13. S.C. 1919, c. 37.
14. S.C. 1919, c. 45.
15. W.T. Stansbury, *The Legislative Development of Canadian Competition Policy, 1888-1981*, 2 Canadian Competition Policy Rec. 1 (1981).
16. See *In Re Board of Commerce Act, 1919 and Combines and Fair Prices Act, 1919*, [1922] 1 A.C. 191 (P.C.).
17. S.C. 1923, c. 9.
18. S. Walker and M. Kilby, *Fundamentals of Canadian Competition Law 2015* (J. Musgrove, J. Macneil & M. Osborne eds., Thomson Carswell 2015).
19. R.S. 1985, c. C-46, as amended [*Criminal Code*].
20. Walker, *supra* n. 18 at 16.

deficiencies remained. The legislation was relatively ineffective at regulating mergers, monopolies, price discrimination and predatory pricing.[21] Furthermore, convictions for conspiracy remained difficult to secure.[22]

13. In 1969, the Economic Council of Canada issued a report that led to the reshaping of Canadian competition law. Vitally, the Council recommended the division of the *Combines Investigation Act* into criminal and civil sections.[23] The first stage of reform occurred in 1976. The *Combines Investigation Act* expanded to apply to services. Bid rigging became per se illegal. Refusal to supply, tied selling, exclusive dealing, and market restriction became civilly reviewable practices.[24] The amendments also created a limited private right of action for damages incurred as a result of criminal infractions. In *City National Leasing Ltd. v. General Motors of Canada Ltd.*,[25] the Supreme Court of Canada upheld the constitutionality of the legislation – including the private right of action – confirming that the federal government has the constitutional authority to regulate competition by virtue of its jurisdiction over trade and commerce.

14. The second stage of major reform occurred in 1986 when Parliament amended the *Combines Investigation Act* and renamed it the *Competition Act*[26] (the Act). Various amendments strengthened the Act's criminal provisions regarding conspiracies, price maintenance, bid rigging, predatory pricing, price discrimination, promotional allowances and misleading advertising.

15. The 1986 reforms also created the Competition Tribunal (the Tribunal). The *Competition Tribunal Act*[27] authorized the Tribunal to hear applications related to deceptive marketing practices and restrictive trade practices. Hence, the Tribunal could rule on applications regarding refusal to supply, exclusive dealing, tied selling, market restriction, abuse of dominant position, delivered pricing, and mergers.[28] These legislative changes resulted in the Competition Bureau taking a more administrative, less adversarial, approach to enforcement of the Act.[29] This approach has continued to date with respect to the Act's non-criminal provisions.

21. M.J. Trebilcock, *Law and Economics of Competition Policy* 3 (F.J. Mathewson et al. eds., Fraser Inst. 1990).
22. Walker, *supra* n. 18 at 17. For examples of unsuccessful conspiracy prosecutions see, *Atlantic Sugar Refineries Co. v. Canada (Attorney General)*, [1980] 2 S.C.R. 644, 53 C.P.R. (2d) [*Atlantic Sugar*] (conformity of prices was insufficient to find a conspiracy absent evidence of collusion); *R. v. Aetna Insurance Co.* (1977), [1978] 1 S.C.R. 731 (despite a rate-setting agreement there was no 'undue' lessening of competition to find conspiracy).
23. Economic Council of Canada, *Interim Report on Competition Policy* (Info. Canada 1969).
24. *An Act to amend the Combines Investigation Act and the Bank Act and to repeal an Act to amend the Combines Investigation Act and the Criminal Code*, S.C. 1974-75-76, c. 76.
25. [1989] 1 S.C.R. 641 [*City National Leasing*].
26. R.S.C. 1985, c. C-34, as amended [*Competition Act*].
27. R.S., 1985, c. 19 (2nd Supp.), as amended [*Competition Tribunal Act*].
28. See Competition Tribunal, *Mandate*, http://www.ct-tc.gc.ca/Tribunal/Mandate-eng.asp (20 May 2011).
29. Walker, *supra* n. 18 at 10.

16. Parliament did not amend either the *Competition Act* or the *Competition Tribunal Act* again until 1999. Since then there have been several changes to competition-related legislation, though the basic substance and structure of the two Acts have remained relatively consistent. Notable developments have included the conversion of non-egregious misleading advertising into non-criminal conduct;[30] the addition of misleading telemarketing as a criminal offence;[31] the addition of protections for whistleblowers who facilitate investigation and enforcement of the Act;[32] and the addition of provisions to facilitate the Bureau's cooperation with international bodies.[33]

17. The most significant changes since the reforms of the 1970s and 1980s occurred in March 2009 with the passage of Bill C-10.[34] The 2009 legislation created a two-track approach for dealing with anti-competitive arrangements between competitors: criminal sanctions for hardcore cartels, versus civil review for agreements that substantially lessen or prevent competition. C-10 also created administrative monetary penalties (AMPs) for abuse of dominance. Offenders can now pay up to CAD 10 million for a first order and CAD 15 million for subsequent orders. C-10 also decriminalized predatory pricing, price discrimination, promotional allowances and price maintenance. Yet C-10 significantly increased criminal penalties and civil remedies for deceptive marketing practices (i.e., misleading advertising). For instance, restitution is now available as a remedy to affected purchasers. In addition, C-10 increased a key pre-merger notification threshold which is indexed annually to Canada's gross domestic product (GDP) (CAD 86 million for the 'size of target' in 2015)[35] and introduced an American-style two-stage merger review process.[36]

---

30. *An Act to amend the Competition Act and to make consequential and related amendments to other acts*, S.C. 1999, c. 2., s. 12.
31. *Ibid.*, at ss 13 and 47.
32. *Ibid.*, at s. 19.
33. *An Act to Amend the Competition Act and the Competition Tribunal Acts*, S.C. 2002, c. 16, s. 3 [Bill C-23].
34. *An Act to implement certain provisions of the budget and related fiscal measures*, S.C. 2009, c. 2 [Bill C-10].
35. Government of Canada, *Canada Gazette*, Vol. 149, No. 6, 'Revised Competition Act pre-merger notification transaction-size threshold for 2015', http://www.gazette.gc.ca/rp-pr/p1/2015/2015-02-07/pdf/g1-14906.pdf (7 Feb. 2015).
36. See D.J. Brown & K. Rushton, *Bill C-10 Competition Act and Investment Canada Act Amendments Enacted*, http://www.stikeman.com/cps/rde/xchg/se-en/hs.xsl/12302.htm (13 Mar. 2009); Competition Bureau, *Frequently Asked Questions – Amendments to the Competition Act*, http://www.competitionbureau.gc.ca/eic/site/cb-bc.nsf/eng/03046.html (4 Oct. 2011).

Part I. Structure of Competition Law and Its Enforcement

Chapter 1. Sources of Antitrust Law

§1. National Sources

18. Canadian competition law is statute-based. While all Canadian legislation is subject to the constitutional limits set out in Canada's *Constitution Act,*[37] there is no specific provision or principle within the Canadian constitutional framework relating to consumer welfare or competition. Laws relating to the promotion of competition or the protection of social welfare in the marketplace have only attracted constitutional review once (*Tervita* – see Concentrations), other than in respect of jurisdictional disputes concerning the exercise of federal or provincial powers.[38] That being said, the *Competition Act* does include a purpose clause, which includes a number of economic and/or social goals:

> The purpose of this Act is to maintain and encourage competition in Canada in order to promote the efficiency and adaptability of the Canadian economy, in order to expand opportunities for Canadian participation in world markets while at the same time recognizing the role of foreign competition in Canada, in order to ensure that small and medium-sized enterprises have an equitable opportunity to participate in the Canadian economy and in order to provide consumers with competitive prices and product choices.[39]

19. The Act is broad in scope and provides for both criminal and civil enforcement of its provisions. Part II of the Act sets out the administrative framework. It vests the Commissioner of Competition with the primary authority to administer the Act.[40] Part III of the Act establishes provisions to facilitate international cooperation between Canadian and international officials with respect to investigatory and enforcement processes. Part IV of the Act provides remedies for violations of the Act. Notable provisions include sections 33 and 34. These sections allow courts to grant injunctions or issue prohibitions in response to potential violations of the Act.

37. *Constitution Act, supra* n. 3.
38. See paras. 11–13; *Tervita Corp. v. Canada (Commissioner of Competition),* 2015 SCC 3, [2015] S.C.J. No. 3.
39. *Competition Act, supra* n. 26 at s. 1.1.
40. *Ibid.*, at s. 7(1).

Section 36 creates a private right of action for those who have been harmed by criminal violations of the Act.

20. Parts VI and VII deal with criminal offences. Specific offences include conspiracies and agreements to fix prices, allocate sales, or limit the supply of products (section 45); conspiracies related to professional sports and federal financial institutions (sections 48 and 49); bid rigging (section 47); intentional or reckless misleading representations (section 52); deceptive telemarketing (section 52.1); deceptive notice of winning a prize (section 53); double ticketing (section 54); multi-level marketing that does not comply with the disclosure requirements of the Act (section 55); and pyramid schemes (section 55.1). Potential punishments vary by offence, but all offences entail the possibility of lengthy jail terms and significant fines. Generally, Part VII of the Act deals with criminal procedural issues under the Act. Part VII also creates offences for interfering with or obstructing enforcement of the Act, as well as for failure to comply with orders made pursuant to certain sections of the Act.

21. Parts VII.1 and VIII deal with practices that, while not illegal, are civilly reviewable and may be sanctioned by the Competition Tribunal.[41] Practices are reviewable on application by the Commissioner or, in some cases, on application by a private party.[42] Affected parties can achieve resolution in one of two ways: first, through a Consent Agreement between the Commissioner and the parties; second, through formal adjudication before the Competition Tribunal. In the latter case, the applicant acts as the prosecutor. Reviewable practices under the Act include some misleading marketing practices (section 74.01); refusal to deal (section 75); price maintenance (section 76); exclusive dealing, tied selling and market restriction (section 77); abuse of dominance (section 79); delivered pricing (section 80); and anti-competitive agreements between competitors (other than cartels) (section 90.1). In most cases, remedies must take the form of injunctions. However, AMPs are available for abuse of dominance and civilly reviewable misleading advertising offences.

22. Mergers are reviewable by the Tribunal upon the Commissioner's recommendation. If the Tribunal finds that a merger or proposed merger is likely to substantially prevent or lessen competition, then the Tribunal may issue various orders. Options include the dissolution of a completed merger or the prohibition of a proposed merger.[43] Part IX of the Act sets out the procedure and conditions for notification of the Commissioner in advance of certain proposed transactions. The Tribunal's jurisdiction extends to all mergers (even non-notifiable) and lasts for one year following substantial completion of the transaction.

---

41. Deceptive marketing is unique in that it is also civilly reviewable, upon recommendation of the Commissioner, by a superior court of a province (*ibid.*, at secs 74.09 and 74.1). Non-criminal agreements between competitors may also be reviewed civilly by the Competition Tribunal if they have a substantially anti-competitive effect (*ibid.,* at sec. 90.1).

42. *Ibid.*, at s. 103.1. Private parties can bring applications with regard to ss 75 (refusal to deal), 76 (price maintenance) and 77 (exclusive dealing, tied selling and market restriction).

43. *Ibid.*, at s. 92.

23. The final part of the Act, Part X, confers additional powers and obligations to the Commissioner. For example, the Commissioner may issue binding written opinions to individuals who request such an opinion,[44] and the Commissioner may pose reference questions to the Tribunal.[45] As well, there are provisions dealing with the Commissioner's interaction with Parliament and other boards and tribunals.[46]

24. The Competition Bureau also has jurisdiction to enforce some industry specific legislation. These statutes include the *Consumer Packaging and Labelling Act*,[47] which prescribes labelling requirements for pre-packaged, non-food products; the *Textile Labelling Act*,[48] which establishes requirements for the content of clothing labels; and the *Precious Metals Marking Act*,[49] which stipulates what information must be available to consumers regarding precious metals.

25. Another important statutory source of competition law is the *Competition Tribunal Act*. The *Competition Tribunal Act* does not create any substantive rules. Rather, it sets the composition and powers of the Tribunal and stipulates the general rules and procedures for Tribunal operations. In addition, it establishes the Tribunal's jurisdiction to hear matters referred to it under certain provisions of the *Competition Act*.[50]

26. The *Investment Canada Act*[51] (the *ICA*) has implications for competition law as well. The *ICA* sets requirements for foreigners investing in Canadian businesses. Foreign-controlled investors who seek, directly or indirectly, to acquire control of an existing Canadian business must file either a notification or an application for review under the *ICA*. The particular requirement depends on the size of the Canadian business and the nationality of the investor. Investments to establish new Canadian businesses require only the filing of a notification.[52]

27. If review is required, it is usually undertaken by the Minister of Industry (the exception is for review of cultural businesses: see below). By law, the Minister approves the transaction only if he or she determines that the transaction is likely to be of 'net benefit' to Canada (although a transaction may also be blocked or subjected to conditions on national security grounds – see below).[53] In deciding whether an investment is likely to be of net benefit to Canada, the Minister must consider several factors:

---

44. *Ibid.*, at s. 124.1.
45. *Ibid.*, at s. 124.2.
46. *Ibid.*, at ss 125–127.
47. R.S.C. 1985, c. C-38.
48. R.S.C. 1985, c. T-10.
49. R.S.C. 1985, c. P-19.
50. *Competition Tribunal Act*, *supra* n. 27 at s. 8.
51. R.S.C. 1985, c. 28 (1st Supp.) [*Investment Canada Act (ICA)*].
52. For more information on threshold requirements and the notification and review processes see Industry Canada, *An Overview of the Investment Canada Act (FAQs)*, http://www.ic.gc.ca/eic/site/ica-lic.nsf/eng/home (8 Mar. 2013) [Investment Canada FAQ].
53. *ICA*, *supra* n. 51 at s. 16(1).

(a) the effect of the investment on the level and nature of economic activity in Canada, including, without limiting the generality of the foregoing, the effect on employment, on resource processing, on the utilization of parts, components and services produced in Canada and on exports from Canada;
(b) the degree and significance of participation by Canadians in the Canadian business or new Canadian business and in any industry or industries in Canada of which the Canadian business or new Canadian business forms or would form a part;
(c) the effect of the investment on productivity, industrial efficiency, technological development, product innovation and product variety in Canada;
(d) the effect of the investment on competition within any industry or industries in Canada;
(e) the compatibility of the investment with national industrial, economic and cultural policies, taking into consideration industrial, economic and cultural policy objectives enunciated by the government or legislature of any province likely to be significantly affected by the investment; and
(f) the contribution of the investment to Canada's ability to compete in world markets.[54]

The Minister typically conditions approval on the investor's agreement to legally binding terms (undertakings) that govern the conduct of the Canadian business for several years following acquisition.[55] Special considerations apply to state-owned investors.

28. If the Canadian business has a 'cultural' aspect (no matter how trivial) and its assets exceed CAD 5 million in book value, the Minister of Canadian Heritage conducts a 'net benefit' review of all direct acquisitions of control of the Canadian business. The threshold increases to CAD 50 million for review of indirect acquisitions of control – still much lower than applicable thresholds for non-cultural businesses acquired by World Trade Organization (WTO) investors (CAD 369 million (direct)/non-reviewable (indirect) in 2015 for state-owned enterprises (SOEs), based on the book value of the assets of the Canadian business; CAD 600 million based on its 'enterprise value' for non-SOEs).[56] A cultural business is a Canadian business that conducts any of the following activities:

(a) the publication, distribution or sale of books, magazines, periodicals or newspapers in print or machine readable form, other than the sole activity of printing or typesetting of books, magazines, periodicals or newspapers;

---

54. *Ibid.*, at s. 20.
55. See S. Neylan & M. Kilby, 'Foreign Investment Review under the Investment Canada Act', in *2015 Competition Act and Commentary* 193-194 (D.J. Brown ed., Lexis Nexis Canada Inc. 2014).
56. Government of Canada, *Canada Gazette*, Vol. 149, No. 6, '*Investment Canada Act* Amount for the year 2015', http://www.gazette.gc.ca/rp-pr/p1/2015/2015-02-07/pdf/g1-14906.pdf (7 Feb. 2015); Government of Canada, *Canada Gazette*, Vol. 149, No. 6, '*Regulations* amending the *Investment Canada Regulations*', http://www.gazette.gc.ca/rp-pr/p2/2015/2015-03-25/pdf/g2-14906.pdf (25 Mar. 2015). The SOE threshold is indexed annually for inflation; the non-SOE threshold will increase gradually over a few years to CAD$1 billion.

(b) the production, distribution, sale or exhibition of film or video recordings;
(c) the production, distribution, sale or exhibition of audio or video music recordings;
(d) the publication, distribution or sale of music in print or machine readable form; or
(e) radio communication in which the transmissions are intended for direct reception by the general public, any radio, television and cable television broadcasting undertakings and any satellite programming and broadcast network service.[57]

The Minister considers whether the investment under review is compatible with Canadian cultural policies. Such policies, available on the Canadian Heritage website, largely preclude foreign acquisition of control of Canadian newspapers and magazines, for example. Other legislation may also apply. See, for instance, Ontario's *Paperback and Periodicals Distributors Act*.[58]

29. Since 2009, the *ICA* has empowered the federal Cabinet to review any investment by non-Canadians that may injure Canada's national security.[59] A review on national security grounds is possible for any investment, regardless of magnitude, in a business with either assets, employees or a place of business in Canada. In contrast, a benefit review requires that a business have all three features: assets, employees and a place of business in Canada. 'National security' is undefined and there is no illustrative list of industries of concern. Hence, the formal hurdles for a national security review seem very low. However, the weighty and potentially politicized procedural requirements for a national security review temper this concern. The federal cabinet must order a review on the recommendation of the Minister of Industry after consultation with the Minister of Emergency Preparedness. In practice, this procedure means that the cabinet orders relatively few reviews. Since 2013, however, the telecom industry has been under scrutiny, and had two (effectively) blocked transactions in that year. These include the proposed acquisition by Russia's (formerly Egypt's) Vimplecom, via its subsidiary (Orascom), of Wind Mobile in June 2013, and the proposed acquisition by Accelero Capital Holdings S.a.r.l. of Manitoba Telecom's Allstream business telecommunications division in October 2013. Although the former proposed transaction was not officially rejected on national security concerns, Vimplecom withdrew its application to acquire control of Wind Mobile following reports that its application was being delayed on national security concerns,[60] while, in contrast, the Government of Canada formally rejected the latter proposed acquisition citing national security concerns.[61] On 9 July 2015, the Government of Canada ordered Chinese company O-Net Communications Group Ltd. ('O-Net'), an optical networking component developer, to divest

57. *ICA, supra* n. 51 at s. 14.1(6).
58. RSO 1990, c P-1.
59. *ICA, supra* n. 51 at s. 25.2.
60. 'Wind Mobile's backers shelve bid' (19 Jun. 2013), *The Globe and Mail*.
61. 'Ottawa rejects MTS Allstream takeover deal, citing unspecified security concerns' (7 Oct. 2013), *The Globe and Mail*.

recently acquired ITF Technologies Inc. due to national security concerns. In response, O-Net filed an application for judicial review, seeking to quash the decision requiring divesture of ITF. At the time of writing, the application for judicial review was ongoing.[62]

30. An order for a national security review begins a process that may last as long as 155 days (and in practice, can be extended indefinitely). This timeline assumes the preliminary issuance of a notice of possible review. The Minister has a limited time to issue such a notice. If the particular investment requires a 'net benefit' notification or review under the *ICA*, then the Minister may issue a notice of a potential national security review within 45 days of the investor's notice or review application filing (with additional time to deliver the notice). If the investment does not require a notification or review for change of control reasons, then the time-period runs from the time that the transaction comes to the attention of the Minister of Industry or is completed. A foreign-controlled investor may therefore formally write to the Minister to put him or her on notice of the transaction in advance of an investment to remove the risk of a post-closing national security review.

§2. International Sources

31. There are no binding sources of international competition law in Canada. However, Canada played a significant role in establishing the International Competition Network, and the Commissioner of Competition has expressed the Bureau's commitment to cooperate formally and informally with other countries for enforcement purposes.[63] The Bureau is also active in developing and promoting coordinated competition guidelines through the OECD.[64] Furthermore, Canada has a National Contact Point, which is an interdepartmental committee chaired by the Department of Foreign Affairs, Trade and Development. The committee's mandate is to promote the OECD Guidelines for Multinational Enterprises[65] in Canada.[66] These guidelines deal with multinational enterprises generally, but they feature a section on competition law.

62. 'Chinese Co. Fights Canada On Security Risks Of Tech Co. Buy' (15 Jul. 2015), *Law360*; *O-Net Communications Ltd. v. Canada (Attorney General),* Federal Court, T-1319-15.
63. See Competition Bureau, *Remarks by John Pecman, Commissioner of Competition, to The Indian Institute of Management,* http://www.competitionbureau.gc.ca/eic/site/cb-bc.nsf/eng/03630.html (20 Nov. 2013).
64. See Competition Bureau, *International Efforts– International Organizations*, http://www.competitionbureau.gc.ca/eic/site/cb-bc.nsf/eng/03763.html#tab3 (27 Aug. 2014) [International Efforts].
65. *OECD Guidelines for Multinational Enterprises, http://mneguidelines.oecd.org/text/* (Org. Econ. Co-operation & Dev. 2011).
66. Foreign Affairs, Trade and Development Canada, *Canada's National Contact Point (NCP) for the OECD Guidelines for Multinational Enterprises (MNEs)*, http://www.international.gc.ca/trade-agreements-accords-commerciaux/ncp-pcn/index.aspx?lang=eng&menu_id=1&menu=R (14 Nov. 2014).

32. Canada is a member of the WTO. As such, the *ICA* has different thresholds for direct acquisitions of control by WTO nationals (or from non-Canadian, WTO nationals) versus non-WTO nationals.[67] As well, there is no review of indirect investments by or from WTO nationals assuming that the Canadian business has no 'cultural' aspect. The presence of a 'cultural' aspect, however, reduces the WTO nationals' investment thresholds to CAD 5 million for direct and CAD 50 million for indirect acquisitions of control. The distinctions between WTO and non-WTO investors exist in order for Canada to comply with its obligations under the WTO agreement.[68]

33. Finally, Canada has competition-specific cooperation agreements with several countries. These agreements exist as bilateral treaties at the state level, or as agreements between the Commissioner and a foreign competition law authority.[69] In the criminal context, Canada has Mutual Legal Assistance Treaties with many foreign states. These treaties facilitate the sharing of information during criminal investigations generally, including criminal investigations under the *Competition Act*.[70] Importantly, none of these agreements create competition law. Rather, they facilitate enforcement at the international level and, in some cases, create legal obligations with regard to information sharing between the Canadian government and foreign states.

§3. Secondary Sources

I. Regulations

34. The *Competition Act*, like many Canadian statutes, provides that the Governor in Council (i.e., the federal cabinet) may make regulations under the Act.[71] The only regulations in existence under the Act are the *Notifiable Transactions Regulations*.[72] These regulations provide information on how to calculate assets and revenues for notification thresholds. They also list the information that must be provided to the Commissioner in the case of a notifiable transaction.

---

67. The non-WTO threshold for 2015 for direct acquisitions of control is CAD 5 million based on book value, versus CAD 600 million based on enterprise value for non-SOE WTO investors (the latter amount will eventually increase to CAD 1 billion, per the 2015 amendments to the regulations). The threshold for non-cultural review for SOE WTO investors is CAD $369 million in 2015, indexed annually.
68. See Investment Canada FAQ, *supra* n. 52.
69. For a list of Canada's cooperation agreements, see International Efforts, *supra* n. 64.
70. To access a current list of Canada's MLATs visit, Canada Treaty Information, *Search*, http://www.treaty-accord.gc.ca/index.aspx.
71. *Competition Act*, *supra* n. 26 at s. 24(1).
72. SOR/87-348 [*Notifiable Transactions Regulations*]. There is also a set of regulations called the *Regulations Respecting Anti-Competitive Acts of Persons Operating a Domestic Service*, SOR/2000-324. However, these regulations are no longer relevant because they define terms that were repealed from the *Competition Act* in 2009.

35. The only regulations in existence pursuant to the *Competition Tribunal Act* are the *Tribunal Rules.*[73] They provide procedural guidance for Tribunal members and for individuals or corporations appearing before the Tribunal.

36. There are two sets of regulations enacted under the *ICA*. The *Investment Canada Regulations*[74] provide information on how to calculate assets and enterprise values for review thresholds. They also set out what information must be provided to the Minister for transactions requiring notice or review. The *National Security Review of Investments Regulations*[75] detail the procedural steps that the Minister follows when reviewing an investment pursuant to Part IV.I of the *ICA*.

II. Guidelines

37. The Competition Bureau publishes numerous bulletins and enforcement guidelines dealing with various provisions under the *Competition Act*, the *Consumer Packaging and Labelling Act*, the *Textile Labelling Act* and the *Precious Metals Marking Act*. These documents are not legally binding. However, they often provide valuable information about how the Bureau interprets and applies provisions of the relevant legislation. All documents published by the Bureau are available on its website.[76] The Competitor Collaboration Guidelines (CCGs) are an example of an enforcement guideline published by the Bureau which may be updated periodically as the jurisprudence develops or as amendments to the *Competition Act* are brought into force. The CCGs and other enforcement guidelines are available on the Bureau's website while guidelines applicable to ICA enforcement are available on the Industry Canada website.[77]

§4. Sources' Relation and Hierarchy

38. All Canadian legislation must comply with the Constitution of Canada, which comprises the *Constitution Act, 1867* and the *Canadian Charter of Rights and Freedoms* (the *Charter*).[78] Various provisions of the *Competition Act* have been challenged on the basis of their constitutional validity. In 1988, the Supreme Court of Canada upheld the validity of the Act as federal legislation.[79] Provisions of the

73. SOR/2008-141 [*Tribunal Rules*].
74. SOR/85-611.
75. SOR/2009-271.
76. See Competition Bureau, *Publications*, http://www.competitionbureau.gc.ca/eic/site/cb-bc.nsf/eng/h_00139.html (18 Feb. 2013). This monograph deals in detail with specific publications, as relevant.
77. See http://www.competitionbureau.gc.ca/eic/site/cb-bc.nsf/eng/h_00168.html, and http://www.ic.gc.ca/eic/site/ica-lic.nsf/eng/lk00064.html.
78. Section 33 of the *Charter*, *supra* n. 4, provides an exception where the legislature can expressly declare that a particular law shall operate notwithstanding the *Charter*. However, use of this provision is extremely rare.
79. *City National Leasing*, *supra* n. 25.

Act dealing with enforcement and punishment have been repeatedly challenged under the *Charter.*[80]

39. After the Constitution, the most authoritative source of law in Canada is legislation, including statutes and regulations. Federal legislation and provincial legislation are equally binding. However, where valid federal and provincial legislation conflict, the federal legislation prevails in accordance with the paramountcy doctrine. The paramountcy doctrine provides that provincial legislation will be inoperative insofar as it conflicts with federal legislation.[81] In competition law, though, a limited exception to the federal paramountcy doctrine has developed. This exception covers conduct regulated by a province pursuant to its constitutional jurisdiction over private and civil rights. Generally, the regulated conduct exception precludes review under the Act if the conduct at issue is authorized or required by a public body validly exercising its authority under a provincial statute.[82]

40. While competition law is primarily statute-based, judicial decisions are important as interpretations of the relevant legislation. In some instances, important principles have also developed at common law.[83] Further, areas of law relevant to competition-related proceedings – such as the law of evidence – have developed jurisprudentially.

41. Other sources of law, such as statements and guidelines published by the Bureau, are not legally binding. However, they may provide insight and guidance into the Bureau's approach to statutory interpretation and application. Indeed, the jurisprudence often cites Bureau publications, suggesting an institutional emphasis on cohesion.

§5. Role and Authority of Precedents

42. Canada's legal system is primarily a common law system. Accordingly, the principle of stare decisis obtains, requiring judges to stand by past decisions of superior courts. Within a given jurisdiction, decisions of higher-level courts bind

80. See *R v. Wholesale Travel Group Inc.*, [1991] 3 S.C.R. 154 (a reverse onus provision regarding deceptive marketing was held to violate s. 11(d) of the *Charter* and a requirement for timely retraction in order to show due diligence violated s. 7 of the *Charter*); *Thomson Newspapers Ltd. v. Canada (Director of Investigation and Research, Restrictive Trade Practices Commission)*, [1990] 1 S.C.R. 425 (provisions of the *Combines Investigation Act* providing for oral examinations and the production of documents did not violate s. 8 of the *Charter*); *Ravenshoe Services Ltd. v. Canada (Commissioner of Competition)* (2001), 15 C.P.R. (4th) 543 (s. 11 of the Act, allowing the Commissioner to request evidence, was held not to violate s. 8 of the *Charter*); *R. v. Durward,* 2014 ONSC 4194 (s. 69(2) of the Act, requiring trier of fact to accept that documents introduced into evidence pursuant to s. 69(2) of the Act are prima facie in knowledge of accused, effectively reversing the onus of proof onto the accused, were held to violate section 7 and 11(d) of the *Charter.*).
81. See *Multiple Access Ltd. v. McCutcheon*, [1982] 2 S.C.R. 161.
82. For a detailed discussion of the regulated conduct exception, see 'Part 1: Chapter 2: §2. Special Sectors'.
83. See, for example, the regulated conduct exception.

lower-level courts and administrative boards and tribunals. Consequently, decisions of the Supreme Court of Canada bind all Canadian courts. Additionally, unless later overruled by the Supreme Court, decisions of the British Privy Council pre-1949 also bind all Canadian courts.[84] Decisions of the Federal Court of Appeal bind trial-level federal courts. Appellate-level provincial decisions bind all courts in the same province. Generally, a court's past decisions are not self-binding, but they are highly persuasive. The Supreme Court has repeatedly expressed that it does not consider itself bound by its past decisions if there is a compelling reason to overturn a past decision.[85]

43. Precedents from courts in other jurisdictions – including other Canadian provinces and foreign countries – do not bind Canadian courts. This means that appellate-level decisions in one province do not bind trial courts in other provinces, nor do decisions of the Federal Court of Appeal bind provincial courts. However, these precedents may be very persuasive. Factors that shape the persuasive force of a holding include the size of the jurisdiction, the level of the court, and the age of the precedent. Internationally, Canadian courts tend to favour British precedents. However, American competition law has influenced Canadian competition law such that the underlying principles and structures are broadly similar.[86] Consequently, some American precedents may be contextually persuasive in Canadian competition law.

84. Until 1949, the British Privy Council was Canada's final Court of Appeal.
85. See *Minister of Indian Affairs and Northern Development v. Ranville* et al., [1982] 2 S.C.R. 518 at 527; *Capital Cities Communications Inc. v. Canadian Radio-Television Commission*, [1978] 2 S.C.R. 141 at 161; *Re Farm Products Marketing Act*, [1957] S.C.R. 198 at 212 [*Re Farm*].
86. Facey & Assaf, *supra* n. 10 at 3.

Chapter 2. Scope of Application

§1. Territorial Reach

44. Federally enacted competition law applies across Canada. However, the Bureau interprets the Act to apply to all behaviour affecting competition within Canadian territory. This 'effects-based' interpretation suggests the possibility of extra-territorial application of the Act to conduct and entities beyond Canada's borders.

§2. Special Sectors

45. The *Competition Act* is a statute of general application, meaning it applies to all sectors unless there is a specific statutory or judicially created exemption.

46. The Act provides statutory exemptions for collective bargaining,[87] fisheries-related arrangements,[88] and amateur sports.[89] There is also an exemption for certain conduct of underwriters of securities.[90] In addition, while the Commissioner of Competition plays a role in reviewing some mergers involving transportation or finance, the authority to approve or reject certain transactions in these sectors ultimately lies with the Minister of Transportation or the Minister of Finance, respectively.[91] The *Shipping Conferences Exemption Act, 1987*[92] also provides that the Act does not apply to certain agreements among international shipping conferences.

47. Some provisions of the Act apply only to certain activities within specific sectors. Special provisions govern arrangements of federal financial institutions;[93] conspiracies related to professional sports;[94] and conspiracies and arrangements related solely to exports.[95]

48. The communications and transportation industries are not specifically exempted from the general application of the *Competition Act*.[96] However, both these industries are heavily regulated at the federal level. The Canadian Radio-television and Telecommunications Commission oversees the communications

87. *Competition Act, supra* n. 26 at s. 4(1)(a).
88. *Ibid.,* at s. 4(1)(b).
89. *Ibid.,* at s. 6.
90. *Ibid.,* at s. 5.
91. See generally: *Canada Transportation Act,* S.C. 1996, c. 10; *Bank Act,* S.C. 1991, c. 46; *Cooperative Credit Associations Act,* S.C. 1991, c. 48; *Insurance Companies Act,* S.C. 1991, c. 47 and *Trust and Loan Companies Act,* S.C. 1991, c. 45.
92. R.S.C. 1985, c. 17 (3rd Supp.), s. 4.
93. See *Competition Act, supra* n. 26 at s. 49.
94. *Ibid.,* at s. 48.
95. *Ibid.,* at s. 45(5).
96. The only exception to this is the Minister of Transportation's ability to review mergers, as discussed above.

industry and enforces the *Broadcasting Act*[97] and the *Telecommunications Act.*[98] Together with other federal legislation, the *Canada Transportation Act*[99] governs some parts of the transportation industry. Provincial legislation governs intra-provincial road transport. The *Competition Act* may come into conflict with these regulatory regimes. In the event of a conflict, the courts may apply the Regulated Conduct Defence (RCD), as discussed below.

49. The situation is similar in the energy industry. The sector is not generally exempt from the application of the *Competition Act*, but affected parties may avail themselves of the RCD in instances of conflict. Also, note that the *Energy Supplies Emergency Act*[100] – intended to conserve energy during national emergencies – permits the Energy Supplies Acquisition Board to grant an exemption from the *Competition Act*. An exemption can cover an agreement or course of action ordered by the Minister of Natural Resources.

50. To deal with conflicts between competition law and regulated industries or professions, Canadian courts have recognized the RCD. The RCD precludes review under the Act where the conduct at issue is authorized or required by a public body validly exercising its authority under a provincial statute. The RCD applies to criminal sanctions under the Act. The defence probably also applies to civilly reviewable conduct under the Act.[101]

51. The RCD began as a defence to criminal charges under the *Combines Investigation Act*. The courts generally applied the RCD in the context of provincial agricultural schemes.[102] The leading modern case on the defence is *A.G. Can. v. Law Society of B.C.*[103] On the facts, a British Columbia lawyer challenged the Law Society's ban on most advertising as an alleged violation of the *Combines Investigation Act* (since replaced by the *Competition Act*). The Supreme Court of Canada held that the rules created by the Law Society were not subject to review under the Act. The Court reasoned that the Law Society, in promulgating the ban on advertising, was exercising the broad powers conferred to it by the legislature to define conduct unbecoming to its members. The Court explained that the language of the *Combines Investigation Act* was not 'apt to describe the deliberations of persons holding

97. S.C. 1991, c. 11.
98. S.C. 1993, c. 38.
99. *Transportation Act*, *supra* n. 91.
100. R.S.C. 1985, c. E-9.
101. Facey & Assaf, *supra* n. 10 at 425.
102. D.J. Brown, *2015 Competition Act and Commentary* 2-3 (D.J. Brown ed., Lexis Nexis Canada Inc. 2014). For relevant case law see *Rex v. Chung Chuck*, [1929] 1 D.L.R. 756 (B.C.C.A.); *Rex v. Simoneau*, [1936] 1 D.L.R. 143 (Montreal Ct. of Sess. of the Peace); *Cherry v. The King*, [1938] 1 D.L.R. 156 (Sask. C.A.); *Ontario Boys Wear Ltd. v. Ontario (Advisory Committee, Industrial Standards Act)*, [1944] S.C.R. 349; and*Re Farm*, *supra* n. 85.
103. [1982] 2 S.C.R. 307.

office under provincial legislation … [rather] it describes voluntary private agreements'.[104]

52. Whether the RCD applies depends on two factors: first, whether the wording of the *Competition Act*'s provision allows for the possibility of the defence; second, whether there is actually a conflict between the Act and the regulatory scheme in question. The first requirement was discussed by the Supreme Court in *Garland v. Consumers' Gas Co.*,[105] which was not a competition case but applies nonetheless. The Court in *Garland* explained that the RCD will not be available where the provision creates a per se offence. Rather, the statute must provide for some 'leeway'. For example, a provision that creates an offence may include phrases such as 'unduly' or in 'the public interest'.[106] The second requirement – genuine statutory conflict – exists because the purpose of the RCD is to preserve regulatory regimes where conduct that would otherwise be contrary to the *Competition Act* is in the public interest.[107] If there is no conflict, there is no need to save the regulatory regime from the application of the *Competition Act*.

53. The 2009 amendment of the Act gave statutory recognition to the RCD in the context of conspiracies, agreements or arrangements between competitors. The Act now reads:

> The rules and principles of the common law that render a requirement or authorization by or under another Act of Parliament or the legislature of a province a defence to a prosecution under subsection 45(1) of this Act, as it read immediately before the coming into force of this section, continue in force and apply in respect of a prosecution under subsection (1).[108]

Thus, the RCD will apply in the context of a prosecution under section 45 in respect of cartels, provided there is a conflict between the Act and the impugned regulatory regime.

54. In 2010, the Bureau issued a *Bulletin on Regulated Conduct*, in which it took the view that a 'cautious' approach to the application of the RCD was warranted.[109] The bulletin explained that, in deciding whether to review regulated conduct, the Bureau would carefully weigh several considerations:

> [T]he purpose of the Act and any other law said to be applicable to the conduct, the interests sought to be protected by both laws, the impugned conduct,

104. *Ibid.,* at 357. Also, see *Industrial Milk Producers* et. al. *v. Milk Board* et al. (1988), 47 D.L.R. (4th) 710 (confirmed that regulated exemption jurisprudence developed under the *Combines Investigation Act* applied to the *Competition Act*).
105. [2004] 1 S.C.R. 629.
106. *Ibid.,* at para. 75.
107. *Alex Couture Inc. v. Canada (Attorney General)*, [1991] A.Q. no 1604, 38 C.P.R. (3d) 293 (C.A.), leave to appeal to the Supreme Court refused [1992] 2 S.C.R.
108. *Competition Act, supra* n. 26 at s. 45(7).
109. Competition Bureau, *Bulletin on 'Regulated' Conduct* (Competition Bureau Canada, 2010).

> the potentially applicable provision(s) of the Act and of the other law, the parties involved, and the principles of statutory interpretation applicable to the case.[110]

The Bulletin also confirmed that the Bureau would apply the RCD to both regulators and regulated parties, but that greater scrutiny may be given to the activities of regulated parties.[111]

§3. State-Owned Enterprises and Public Utilities

55. In Canada, state-owned corporate entities are called crown corporations. Crown corporations are not exempt from application of the Act. Crown immunity, a common law principle, provides for government immunity from legislation unless the relevant legislation specifies otherwise.[112] In order to avoid the common law rule, the Act therefore provides:

> [It] is binding on and applies to an agent of Her Majesty in right of Canada or a province that is a corporation, in respect of commercial activities engaged in by the corporation in competition, whether actual or potential, with other persons to the extent that it would apply if the agent were not an agent of Her Majesty.[113]

Consequently, corporate agents of the Crown that engage in commerce, such as Canada Post, are subject to the same competition rules as non-government actors. However, note that Crown immunity still applies such that the Act is not binding on the federal or provincial governments in respect of their non-commercial activities.[114]

§4. Sensible Effect and *De Minimis*

56. The Act does not include an explicit *de minimis* provision. Indeed the 2009 amendments to the cartel provision removed the requirement that cartel activities 'unduly' lessen or prevent competition. Other provisions, however, require proof of

---

110. *Ibid.*, at 1.
111. *Ibid.*, at 6.
112. *R. v. Eldorado Nuclear Ltd.; R. v. Uranium Can. Ltd.*, [1983] 2 S.C.R. 551 [*Eldorado Nuclear Ltd.*]. In this case two crown corporations were acquitted, by virtue of Crown immunity, of an alleged conspiracy to restrict competition. Section 2.1 was subsequently added to the *Competition Act* to preclude such a result in future.
113. *Competition Act*, *supra* n. 26 at s. 2.1.
114. See *Eldorado Nuclear Ltd.*, *supra* n. 112 (the addition of s. 2.1 did not affect this aspect of the decision); and *West Van Cab Ltd. v. British Columbia*, 2009 BCCA 47, 2009 CarswellBC 312 (B.C.C .A.); affirmed (2007), 2007 CarswellBC 1521 (B.C.S.C.) (the *Competition Act* was held not to apply to the British Columbia legislature).

an impact on competition. Moreover, the Bureau employs case selection criteria that include the impact on competition, as well as a 'compliance continuum', which involves openness to remedies short of prosecution, particularly if the impact on competition is small and other factors favour a less formal resolution. For more information, see Chapter 4, § 5 'Restriction of Competition'.

Chapter 3. Overview of Substantive Provisions

§1. Restrictive Agreements

57. Restrictive agreements among actual or likely competitors can be subject to criminal prosecution or civil review. Section 45 of the Act addresses criminal conspiracies, the most obvious type of anti-competitive agreement between competitors. Section 45 prohibits agreements to fix prices; agreements to allocate sales, customers, territories or markets; and agreements to limit production. Section 47 of the Act criminalizes bid rigging agreements. Additional provisions deal with anti-competitive agreements in specialized areas.[115] Section 90.1 provides for civil review of any agreement between actual or likely competitors that 'is likely to prevent or lessen, competition substantially in a market'. For a detailed overview of these sections and the relevant concepts of interpretation and application, see '§4. Agreements and Concerted Practices' in the next chapter. Part II: Chapter 1 discusses the application of these sections to specific kinds of competitor agreements.

§2. Dominant Undertakings

58. Section 79 of the Act makes abuse of dominance a reviewable practice. The Tribunal has the authority to issue prohibition orders and impose AMPs of up to CAD 10 million for a first order and CAD 15 million for a subsequent order against the same party.[116] The Tribunal can issue these orders if it finds that a party (or parties) with market power has engaged in a practice of anti-competitive acts that has caused, or is likely to cause, a substantial lessening or prevention of competition. A party has market power if that party 'substantially or completely controls a class or species of business'. The Act does not exhaustively define abuse of dominance, though section 78 provides examples of practices that may be considered anti-competitive. Hence, there is no defined limit to conduct that could constitute abuse of dominance. For a discussion of the substantive test for abuse of dominance, see '§6. Monopolization and Abuse of Dominance', in the following chapter. Part II: Chapter 2 discusses specific anti-competitive behaviours.

59. The Act contains several other provisions regarding unilateral conduct. Section 75 concerns refusal to supply. Section 76 addresses resale price maintenance. Section 77 deals with tied selling, exclusive dealing and market restriction. Sections 80 and 81 deal with delivered pricing. With leave, private parties may bring cases before the Tribunal under these sections, provided that the Commissioner is not investigating and has not settled the dispute. Only the Commissioner can bring an 'abuse' case under section 79. Additionally, the Tribunal does not have the authority to issue AMPs under any of these sections, other than in respect of abuse of dominance. That said, even where behaviour is covered by one of these sections,

---

115. See *Competition Act*, *supra* n. 26 at ss 48 (dealing with professional sports) and 49 (dealing with federal financial institutions).

116. *Ibid.*, at s. 79(3.1).

the Commissioner can still challenge it as an abuse of dominance under section 79. That is, if part of a practice of anti-competitive acts, behaviour under these sections may rise to abuse of dominance.

§3. Concentrations (Mergers)

60. 'Concentrations' are known as 'mergers' in Canadian competition law. Mergers are civilly reviewable by the Tribunal under the Act. Section 91 of the Act defines 'merger' broadly:

> '[M]erger' means the acquisition or establishment, direct or indirect, by one or more persons, whether by purchase or lease of shares or assets, by amalgamation or by combination or otherwise, of control over or significant interest in the whole or a part of a business of a competitor, supplier, customer or other person.

61. The Commissioner can apply to the Tribunal to challenge a completed or proposed merger under section 92. The application succeeds if the merger is likely to result, or has resulted, in a substantial prevention or lessening of competition. The Tribunal can totally or partially (through divestitures) dissolve a completed merger or prohibit a proposed merger. The Tribunal can also allow the merger with conditions, such as the divestiture of assets or shares. Section 93 of the Act lists a number of factors that the Tribunal should consider in assessing the competitive effects of a merger or proposed merger. Section 96 contains an efficiency defence to an otherwise anti-competitive merger.

62. As noted in section 92, the Tribunal has the authority to block a merger or proposed merger in cases where the merger 'prevents or lessens, or is likely to prevent or lessen, competition substantially'.[117] The first merger case to be challenged for an alleged 'prevention' of competition as opposed to 'lessening' was *The Commissioner of Competition v. CCS Corporation* et al. (CCS). This case involved CCS' acquisition of Complete Environmental Inc., which owned the rights to the Babkirk Secure Landfill in Northern B.C. (see paragraph 333 for details). The Commissioner's theory of harm in this case was founded on a likely 'prevention' rather than 'lessening' of competition, which is typically harder to prove. According to the Application filed by the Commissioner, '[t]he Merger [was] likely to prevent competition substantially in the Relevant Market owing to elimination of Complete as a likely vigorous and effective competitor'.[118] The case is also notable for the fact that the Commissioner was seeking to have the merger dissolved in its entirety

117. *Competition Act, supra* n. 26, s. 92.
118. *Commissioner of Competition v. CCS Corporation, Complete Environmental Inc., Babkirk Land Services Inc., Karen Louise Baker, Ronald John Baker, Kenneth Scott Watson, Randy John Wolsey, and Thomas Craig Wolsey* (24 Jan. 2011) CT-2011-002 [*CCS*].

(albeit, requesting in the alternative a divestiture of assets to an approved purchaser). Interestingly, the Commissioner's section 92 challenge came after the transaction closed. CCS (now called 'Tervita') and the other parties involved in the transaction appealed the Tribunal's decision to the Federal Court of Appeal. The Federal Court of Appeal upheld the Tribunal's decision.[119] In its decision, the Court of Appeal affirmed that, in the context of a merger's likely prevention of competition, poised entry should be determined within a reasonable period of time and the new entrant need not be poised to do so at the date of the merger.[120] The Court of Appeal also took the opportunity to clarify the objective nature of the efficiencies defence.[121] The Court of Appeal's decision was appealed to the Supreme Court of Canada.[122] The Supreme Court upheld the Court of Appeal's treatment of likely future entry in cases involving 'prevention' of competition, but overturned its ruling as to the application of the efficiencies defence (see paragraph 348 for details).[123]

63. Ostensibly, the Commissioner can challenge any merger with anti-competitive effects in Canada, even if neither party has a presence in Canada (though this has never been tested). However, only transactions involving at least one party with assets in Canada require notification to the Commissioner in advance of closing (if certain thresholds are exceeded). Part IX of the Act deals with notification.

64. Part II: Chapter 3 of this monograph deals in detail with substantive merger review. Part III: Chapter 2 discusses notification requirements and timelines.

§4. Other Prohibitions

65. In Canada, deceptive marketing practices lie within the scope of the competition law regime. The criminal provisions of the Act punish the most egregious offences – including those committed knowingly or recklessly. In practice, instances of misleading marketing are more often dealt with through the civil regime.

66. Part VII.1 of the Act includes the civil provisions dealing with deceptive marketing practices. Section 74.01 provides that a person engages in reviewable conduct where, for the purpose of promoting, directly or indirectly, the supply or use of a product or any business interest, the person: (i) makes a representation to the public that is false or misleading in a material respect; (ii) makes a representation to the public in the form of a statement, warranty or guarantee of the performance, efficacy or length of life of a product that is not based on an adequate and proper test thereof; (iii) makes a representation to the public in a form that purports

119. *Tervita Corporation, Complete Environmental Inc. and Babkirk Land Services Inc. v. Commissioner of Competition, Karen Louise Baker, Ronald John Baker, Kenneth Scott Watson, Randy John Wolsey, and Thomas Craig Wolsey,* 2013 FCA 28 [*Tervita*].

120. *Ibid.*, at paras. 88–91.

121. *Ibid.*, at para. 147.

122. *Tervita, supra* n. 119.

123. *Tervita, supra* n. 38.

to be a warranty or guarantee of a product, or a promise to replace, maintain or repair an article or any part thereof or to repeat or continue a service until it has achieved a specified result, if the form of purported warranty or guarantee or promise is materially misleading or if there is no reasonable prospect that it will be carried out; or (iv) makes a misleading ordinary price claim.[124] The Commissioner does not need to establish that anyone was misled by the representation.[125] It is also reviewable conduct to engage in bait and switch selling[126] or to sell above an advertised price.[127] In the case of promotional contests, reviewable conduct occurs where: (i) adequate and fair disclosure is not made of the number and approximate value of the prizes, of the area or areas to which they relate and of any fact within the knowledge of the person that affects materially the chances of winning; (ii) distribution of the prizes is unduly delayed; or (iii) selection of participants or distribution of prizes is not made on the basis of skill or on a random basis in any area to which prizes have been allocated.[128]

67. Private parties do not have standing to bring an application to the Tribunal under Part VII.1 of the Act. Only the Commissioner may bring an application to the Tribunal in respect of conduct reviewable under this part. That being said, section 9 of the Act allows for any six Canadian residents who are of the age of majority to apply to the Commissioner for an inquiry if they are of the opinion that a person has contravened an order made pursuant to Part VII.1 or that grounds exist for the making of an order under Part VII.1. Once an application is made, section 10 requires the Commissioner to launch an inquiry. For details on the substance of such an inquiry, please see Chapter 1, § 1 III 'Complaints'.

68. Unlike other reviewable practice provisions, the deceptive marketing provisions allow the Commissioner to bring an application to the Tribunal, the Federal Court, or a provincial superior court. There is also a wider range of possible remedies than under most other reviewable conduct sections.[129] The Tribunal or court can issue prohibition orders and can force the party under review to publicly disseminate notice of its misleading advertising. Furthermore, the Tribunal or court can issue AMPs of up to CAD 750,000 for an individual and up to CAD 10 million for a corporation. For subsequent orders, the maximums increase to CAD 1 million and CAD 15 million respectively. Finally, the Tribunal or court can order the party to

124. An ordinary price claim is misleading where: (i) there has not been a sale of a substantial volume of the product at the advertised price or a higher price within a reasonable period of time before or after the making of the claim, as the case may be; and (ii) the product has not been offered at that price or a higher price in good faith for a substantial period of time recently before or immediately after the making of the representation, as the case may be (s. 74.01(2)).

125. *Competition Act*, *supra* n. 26 at s. 74.03(4).

126. *Ibid.*, at s. 74.04. Bait and switch selling occurs where a product is advertised at a bargain price but is not actually available in reasonable quantities.

127. *Ibid.*, at s. 74.05.

128. *Ibid.*, at s. 74.06.

129. See *ibid.*, at s. 74.1(1).

pay restitution to customers, measured by the amount paid for the product. However, if a party was duly diligent in preventing the misleading practice, the Tribunal or court may only issue prohibition orders.[130]

69. A 2012 decision by the Ontario Superior Court of Justice highlights the relatively large monetary penalties that may be imposed for deceptive marketing practices notwithstanding the fact that the prohibitions in section 74.01 are civil rather than criminal. In *The Commissioner of Competition v. Yellow Page Marketing B.V. et al.* the Superior Court considered an application by the Commissioner which alleged that the respondents, Yellow Page Marketing et al. (YPM) engaged in a scheme of false and misleading representations that induced businesses, individuals, and other organizations to erroneously believe that the corporate respondents were the well-known 'Yellow Pages Group'.[131] The Commissioner alleged that the scheme cost Canadians an estimated CAD 7 million. The Superior Court found that unsolicited YPM faxes were intentionally designed to mislead consumers. In addition to a prohibition order, the Court ordered that the respondents publish corrective notices, pay restitution to customers that fell victim to its scheme, and imposed AMPS in the amount of CAD 8 million for the corporate respondents and CAD 500,000 on each of the respective companies' two principals. One of the aggravating factors in this case was that the respondents had deliberately engaged in identical conduct in other jurisdictions, including in Australia where the Federal Court imposed an AUD 2.7 million AMP. The decision was appealed to the Ontario Court of Appeal, which affirmed the ruling.[132]

70. Section 52 of the Act creates a parallel criminal offence for materially false or misleading advertising that parties engage in knowingly or recklessly. As with the civil track, there is no need to prove that anyone was actually misled by the representation. Whether a representation is materially false or misleading depends on two factors: first, the representation's literal meaning and, second, the general impression it conveys when viewed as a whole.[133] On indictment, a conviction is punishable by up to fourteen years in jail. The court also has the discretion to impose a fine in addition to, or in lieu of, jail time. On summary conviction, the maximum prison sentence is one year and the maximum fine is CAD 200,000.[134]

71. Section 52.1 of the Act addresses deceptive telemarketing. The Act defines 'telemarketing' as 'the practice of communicating orally by any means of telecommunication for the purpose of promoting, directly or indirectly, any business interest or the supply or use of a product'.[135] This section requires telemarketers to make certain disclosures at the beginning of a conversation. These disclosures include the

---

130. *Ibid.*, at s. 74.1(3).
131. *The Commissioner of Competition v. Yellow Page Marketing*, 2012 ONSC 927, [2012] O.J. No. 998.
132. *The Commissioner of Competition v. Yellow Page Marketing,* 2013 ONCA 71, [2013] O.J. No. 455.
133. *Competition Act*, *supra* n. 26 at s. 52(4).
134. *Ibid.*, at s. 52(5).
135. *Ibid.*, at s. 52.1(1).

identity of the person behind the communication, the nature of the product or business interest being promoted, and the purposes of the communication. The section prohibits any false or misleading representation that occurs through telemarketing. Upon conviction for this criminal offence, the potential punishment is the same as for criminal misleading advertising under section 52 (see above).

72. The Act also prohibits several specific deceptive marketing tactics.[136] Section 53 prohibits deceptive notices of winning a prize. A deceptive notification occurs if a marketer first falsely leads a person to believe they have or will win a prize, and then asks the person to give money or incur some cost to claim the prize. Section 54 prohibits double ticketing. Double ticketing is the supply of a product at the higher of two prices advertised in association with the product. Deceptive notice of winning a prize is punishable, on indictment, with up to fourteen years in prison and/or a fine at the discretion of the court. On summary conviction, the maximum penalty is one year in prison and a CAD 200,000 fine.[137] Double ticketing is not an indictable offence, and the maximum penalty for a summary conviction is one year in prison and/or CAD 10,000.[138]

73. Finally, sections 55 and 55.1 prohibit misleading multi-level marketing and pyramid schemes. The Act defines multi-level marketing as 'a plan for the supply of a product whereby a participant in the plan receives compensation for the supply of the product to another participant in the plan who, in turn, receives compensation for the supply of the same or another product to other participants in the plan'.[139] These plans are not necessarily illegal, but they become illegal where misleading representations distort the compensation that participants will or are likely to receive. These plans also become illegal if the marketer fails to disclose prescribed information.[140] A multi-level marketing plan is also illegal if it is a 'pyramid scheme' under section 55.1. A pyramid scheme occurs if one of several conditions obtains: (i) a participant must pay for the right to recruit new participants, who in turn must pay for the right to recruit new participants; (ii) a participant must, in order to participate in the plan, buy specific quantities of product other than those bought at the seller's cost price for the purpose of facilitating sales; (iii) a participant must buy unreasonable quantities of the product or products; or (iv) a participant cannot return products on reasonable terms or is not informed of this right.[141] Offences under these sections are punishable on indictment by up to five years in prison along with the possibility of a fine at the court's discretion. On summary conviction, the maximum jail sentence is one year and/or a maximum fine of CAD 200,000.[142]

136. See *ibid.*, at s. 52.1(3).
137. *Ibid.*, at ss 52.1(9) and 53(6).
138. *Ibid.*, at s. 54(2).
139. *Ibid.*, at s. 55(1).
140. *Ibid.*, at s. 55(2).
141. *Ibid.*, at s. 55.1(1).
142. *Ibid.*, at ss 55(3) and 55.1(3).

§5. TESTS OF ILLEGALITY

74. Most of the Act's reviewable conduct sections require that there be a substantial prevention or lessening of competition, though the wording of specific sections varies somewhat. Generally, this requirement entails an analysis of whether the impugned behaviour has or is likely to create, maintain, or enhance market power. Market power is the ability of a firm, or group of firms, to behave independently of the market. In effect, market power is the ability to maintain prices above the competitive rate. For more, see the next Chapter '§3. Market Power/Dominant Position'. The concept of market power also appears periodically in this monograph when relevant.

I. Per Se Prohibitions and Naked Restraints

75. The Act's only per se prohibitions exist with regard to the criminal prohibitions against conspiracy, bid rigging and certain marketing practices. Until 2009, the conspiracy provisions required the Crown to prove that an agreement among competitors would 'unduly' prevent or lessen competition. This stipulation required a complex factual, legal and economic analysis to demonstrate beyond a reasonable doubt that there had been, or was likely to be, economic harm. Since 2009, however, per se prohibitions have existed against agreements to fix prices; agreements to allocate sales, customers, territories or markets; agreements to limit production of a product; and bid rigging. The legislature at that time also repealed previous per se criminal provisions dealing with price discrimination, predatory pricing, and price maintenance. Price maintenance remains a reviewable practice whereas predatory pricing and price discrimination no longer are the subject of separate provisions of the Act and, as such, are actionable only if part of an abuse of a dominant position.

II. Balancing Tests

76. Generally speaking, the Act embodies economic principles and eschews other public interest concerns. The only balancing test in the Act exists in relation to the efficiencies defence. The efficiencies defence applies in the context of substantive merger review and civilly reviewable competitor agreements. In both cases, gains in efficiency preclude the Tribunal from making an order if the gains 'will be greater than, and will offset, the effects of any prevention or lessening of competition that will result or is likely to result from the agreement or arrangement, and that the gains in efficiency would not have been attained if the order had been made or would not likely be attained if the order were made'[143] In the context of mergers, the Federal Court of Appeal has said that this assessment must involve a balancing approach. The finder of fact must weigh all of the anti-competitive effects of the

143. *Ibid.*, at ss 90.1(4) and 96(1).

arrangement against all of the resultant quantitative and qualitative efficiencies.[144] An analysis of a section 90.1 agreement would require a similar approach. Section 86 of the Act allows for the registration of specialization agreements based on the same efficiencies analysis, although this section has never been used.

III. Merger Tests

77. The test applied to mergers is whether the merger 'prevents or lessens, or is likely to prevent or lessen, competition substantially'. This test is in section 92 of the Act. Generally, this test entails an analysis of the impact of the merger on the creation, maintenance or enhancement of market power. Although market shares and concentration ratios are factors to consider, they are not dispositive. For a detailed discussion of the application of the test, see Part II: Chapter 3 'Concentrations'.

144. *Canada (Commissioner of Competition) v. Superior Propane Inc.*, 2001 FCA 104, 199 D.L.R. (4th) 130, 11 C.P.R. (4th) at 289 [*Superior Propane* FCA 2001 cited to C.P.R.]. The Supreme Court of Canada in *Tervita* clarified, however, that all quantifiable effects must be quantified (even as estimates) and non-quantifiable effects will only be considered if necessary.

Chapter 4. Overview of Principal Concepts

§1. Undertaking (Business)

78. The terminology used in Canadian competition law differs from the language used in the European Union (EU). In Canada, the Act uses the term 'business' to describe a unit of commercial activities under common control,[145] whereas in the EU the same concept is expressed as an 'undertaking'.[146]

79. The Act broadly defines 'business' as including '(*a*) manufacturing, producing, transporting, acquiring, supplying, storing and otherwise dealing in articles, and (*b*) acquiring, supplying and otherwise dealing in services [... and] the raising of funds for charitable or other non-profit purposes'.[147] For a transaction to be subject to notification requirements, the transaction must fall within the definition of a business undertaking.[148] In an interpretation guideline, the Bureau has explained that business is 'broadly interpreted to capture all arrangements through which business may be carried on, including non-profit or charitable undertakings'.[149] In the context of merger oversight, notifiable transactions include only those involving an 'operating business in Canada'. An operating business in Canada is 'a business undertaking in Canada to which employees employed in connection with the undertaking ordinarily report for work'.[150] Of note, the employees in question need not be employees of the business itself, so long as they occupy themselves 'in connection' with the undertaking.

§2. Relevant Market

80. A 'market' is not explicitly defined in the legislation, yet the concept is often central to the economic theory behind the law. With regard to merger analysis, the Bureau has increasingly made use of econometric analysis of anti-competitive effects that do not rely on definition of a 'relevant market'. The Tribunal has said that the relevant market is the one in which the merging firms could exercise market power, either alone or in concert with other firms.[151] The Tribunal analyses the potential exercise of market power by identifying both the product market and the geographic market. The product market consists of each product that the firm sells

---

145. *Competition Act*, *supra* n. 26 at s. 2(1).
146. European Commission – Competition, 'Antitrust rules applying to undertakings', http://ec.europa.eu/competition/antitrust/legislation/articles.html, 16 Apr. 2012.
147. *Competition Act*, *supra* n. 26 at s. 2(1).
148. All notifiable transactions listed in s. 110 of the Act include references to an operating business.
149. *Notifiable Transactions under Part IX of the Competition Act – Interpretation Guidelines* (Competition Bureau 2000) at Interpretation Guideline No. 1 [Notifiable Transactions Interpretation Guidelines].
150. *Competition Act*, *supra* n. 26 at s. 108(1).
151. *Commissioner of Competition v. Superior Propane Inc.* (2000), 7 C.P.R. (4th) 385 (Comp. Trib.) at 404, rev'd (2001), 11 C.P.R. (4th) 289, [2001] F.C.J. No. 455 (F.C.A.), leave to appeal to S.C.C. refused 14 C.P.R. (4th) vii, 202 D.L.R. (4th) vi, 278 N.R. 196n, reconsidered (2002), 18 C.P.R. (4th) 417 (Comp. Trib.), aff'd 2003 FCA 53 [*Superior Propane* cited to C.P.R.].

and all sufficiently close substitutes. Whether a product is a sufficiently close substitute depends on whether it would draw customers away from the original product if the original product's price increased.[152] The geographic market is determined in a similar way. It consists of all supply points that are economically able to supply the merging parties.[153]

81. The Bureau's *Merger Enforcement Guidelines* (MEGs) contain the most thorough explanation of how to identify the relevant market.[154] While these guidelines deal specifically with mergers, their analytic framework is broadly applicable to other provisions of the Act dealing with market power.[155] The MEGs adopt a hypothetical monopolist approach:

> Conceptually, the relevant market is defined as the smallest group of products, including at least one product of the merging parties, and the smallest geographic area, in which a sole profit-maximizing seller (a 'hypothetical monopolist') would impose and sustain a small but significant and non-transitory increase in price ('SSNIP') above levels that would likely exist in absence of the merger.[156]

The Bureau usually considers a 5% price increase to be significant and a one-year period to be non-transitory.[157] These rough guidelines, however, are contextual.

82. The Tribunal prefers data that directly demonstrate switching behaviour. However, such data are rare. Yet there are indirect factors that the Tribunal can consider to identify the range of relevant products and suppliers from which customers can choose. Functional indicators of potential product substitution include a product's end-use, physical and technical characteristics, and price relationships and relative price levels. Another functional indicator is the cost to buyers of switching.[158] The Tribunal has also said it can consider functional interchangeability of the products, inter-industry competition, and views of industry participants.[159] However, the Tribunal has warned that these factors do not determine the competition markets. Rather, these factors help the Tribunal to identify business markets. Business markets may only be loosely comparable to competition markets.[160] Inter-industry competition may also suggest a relevant competition market, but it is non-determinative.[161]

---

152. M.J. Trebilcock et al., *The Law and Economics of Canadian Competition Policy* (University of Toronto Press Incorporated, 2002), 73 [Trebilcock].
153. *Merger Enforcement Guidelines* (MEGs) 4.19–4.21 (Competition Bureau 2011).
154. *Ibid.*, at 4.1–4.28.
155. S. Bhattacharjee and D. Rothschild, *Fundamentals of Canadian Competition Law 2015* 38 (J. Musgrove, J. Macneil & M. Osborne ed., Thomson Carswell 2015).
156. MEGs, *supra* n. 153 at 4.3.
157. *Ibid.*
158. *Ibid.*, at 4.15.
159. *Superior Propane*, *supra* n. 151 at 409.
160. *Ibid.*
161. *Canada (Director of Investigation and Research) v. Southam Inc.*, [1997] 1 S.C.R. 748, 71 C.P.R. (3d) 417 at 441–442 [*Southam* cited to C.P.R.].

83. The Supreme Court has said that functional interchangeability is insufficient to find that two products are in the same market. The Court reasoned that a functional approach would ignore the subjective attitudes of consumers towards a particular product.[162] Where buyers place a high value on actual or perceived unique physical or technical characteristics – such as product warranties, post-sales service, and order-turn-around time – it may be necessary to use these characteristics to define the relevant scope of competition.[163]

84. If the cost of switching between products is too high, seemingly interchangeable products may not fall within the same relevant market.[164] Relevant cost considerations include the costs for buyers to retool, re-package, undertake product testing, adapt marketing, breach a supply contract, learn new procedures, or convert essential equipment.[165]

85. It is also possible that a product market can exist for a grouping of diverse products. With a grouped product market, a sole seller could sustain a price increase in the group of products because a sufficient number of buyers would not respond by purchasing the components from separate sellers. The transaction costs would be too high. In such situations, the Bureau examines buyers' propensity to purchase from a single seller and the extent to which buyers would break up purchases of the group of products in response to the price change.[166]

86. The hypothetical monopolist analysis applies to the geographic market in much the same way as it does to the product market. First, a geographic candidate market is proposed for each location where the merging parties produce or sell their products. If a 5% increase to the product's price in that market could be sustained, then the candidate market is the correct market. Alternatively, if the price increase would cause buyers to purchase from further afield – rendering the increase unprofitable – then the candidate market is expanded to include the next-closest substitute supply point. This process repeats until the finder of fact has identified the smallest geographic area within which the price increase can be sustained by the hypothetical monopolist.

87. Again, only rarely is there sufficient data to directly apply the hypothetical monopolist test. The finder of fact usually identifies the geographic market through indirect evidence of substitutability from market participants or through functional indicators.[167] Evidence from market participants may relate to the views, strategies and behaviours of buyers in a given geographic area. The Bureau may look at what buyers have done in the past and try to predict how they will adapt to changes. The Bureau may also look at how sellers in another geographic area have previously

162. *Ibid.*, at 443.

163. MEGs, *supra* n. 153 at 4.14.

164. See *Superior Propane*, *supra* n. 151 (propane and natural gas were held not to be in the same market partly due to the high costs of switching from one to the other).

165. MEGs, *supra* n. 153 at 4.15.

166. *Ibid.*, at 4.16.

167. *Ibid.*, at 4.20.

responded to changes in price, packaging or servicing of the relevant product. Finally, the Bureau may consider the business and marketing strategies of other parties to determine the extent to which they can feasibly compete in the market at issue.[168]

88. Functional indicators of a relevant geographic market include particular characteristics of the product (e.g., if it is perishable). Other indicators include convenience, frequency of delivery, and reliability of service or delivery. Transportation costs play a central role. If the cost of the product in the local market – even with the 5% increase – is less than the cost of the product plus transportation from a distant market, then suppliers in the distant location will not usually be included in the relevant market.[169] A high cost of switching may also be a relevant factor.[170]

89. Service or trade areas may be helpful in delineating relevant geographic markets, but they are not decisive in determining areas where market power may be exercised.[171] The same is true of historical evidence showing that the prices have traditionally been higher or lower in a particular area.[172] It is necessary to take the analysis further and to consider whether historical pricing or trade and shipping patterns would change based on the hypothetical price increase.

90. The Act provides that, in determining whether a merger is likely to prevent or lessen competition, the Tribunal may look at the extent to which foreign products or foreign competitors are likely to provide competition.[173] Thus, relevant markets can and often do extend beyond Canada if foreign suppliers can effectively compete in some or all of Canada. The Bureau will look at buyer tastes and preferences as well as border-related issues to predict buyers' willingness or ability to turn to foreign producers.[174]

91. Where there is evidence of price discrimination, it may be appropriate to define the product market or geographic market more narrowly and with reference to a particular class of buyers or a specific location.[175] To show price discrimination, the evidence must demonstrate that the consumers systemically pay different prices based on end-use or location and that price differences are not justified by cost differences.[176]

---

168. *Ibid.*, at 4.21
169. *Ibid.*, at 4.24.
170. *Ibid.*
171. *Superior Propane, supra* n. 151 at 414.
172. MEGs, *supra* n. 153 at 4.25.
173. *Competition Act, supra* n. 26 at s. 93(a).
174. MEGs, *supra* n. 153 at 4.25.
175. See *Canada (Commissioner of Competition) v. Canadian Waste Services Holdings Inc. (2001)*, 11 C.P.R. (4th) 425 (Comp. Trib.) at 449 [*Canadian Waste*]; and *Superior Propane, supra* n. 150 at 410; and MEGs, *supra* n. 153 at 10.
176. *Superior Propane, ibid.*, at 410; and *Canadian Waste, ibid.*, at 450.

92. The base price used to calculate the price increase is the prevailing market price of the product, assuming the prevailing price is a competitive price.[177] However, if there is reason to believe that one or more persons already exert market power, prevailing prices may already be higher than the competitive base level. In such a situation, the base price may need to be adjusted in order to avoid committing the so-called 'Cellophane Fallacy'.[178] Consider that using the artificially high price for cellophane as a base price would have resulted in an artificially broad product market definition. Ultimately, there is a limit to what customers will pay for most products. To avoid the Cellophane Fallacy in abuse of dominance situations, the Bureau will estimate the hypothetical prevailing market price absent the alleged anti-competitive acts. The Bureau will then use this estimate to define the relevant market.[179] The same theory should also apply in merger cases involving pre-existing market power.

93. Market participants include persons currently selling the product. Market participants also include persons who would begin to sell the product if the product's market price increased by a small but significant amount (known as a supply response). A firm is a participant in the latter category if it would not require significant sunk investments to enter or exit the market and if it could do so rapidly.[180] In determining whether a firm meets this test the Bureau will consider: (i) whether the supplier would be able to profitably divert sales from its existing buyers to those in the relevant market in the event of a small price increase (5%); or (ii) whether the seller could profitably utilize excess capacity to begin supplying products in the relevant market.[181] The MEGs list a number of factors that the Bureau may consider, including the ability of foreign suppliers to enter the market.[182] Ultimately, if the Bureau finds that a seller is likely to encounter significant difficulty selling or distributing the relevant product, it will not deem the seller to be a participant in the market. Similarly, if the Bureau finds that the seller would need to incur significant sunk investments in production or distribution facilities to supply the relevant market, it will not deem the seller to be a participant in the market.[183] Independence from competitive market forces also turns on the particular conditions for entry and exit into the sector and the behaviour of other firms in the market.

94. Once the Bureau identifies all participants in the relevant market, the analysis proceeds to a determination of each seller's market share. While market shares and concentration are not determinative of market power, they can inform the analysis of competitive effects by describing the market role of the implicated party and

177. MEGs, *supra* n. 153 at 4.6.

178. See *United States v. E.I. du Pont de Nemours & Co.*, 351 U.S. 377 (1956), from which the 'Cellophane Fallacy' originated.

179. Enforcement Guidelines The Abuse of Dominance Provisions (ss 78 and 79 of the Competition Act) (Gatineau, Quebec: Competition Bureau, 2012) [Abuse of Dominance Guidelines].

180. MEGs, *supra* n. 153 at 5.1.

181. *Ibid.*, at 5.1.

182. *Ibid.*, at 4.25.

183. See *ibid.*, at 5.1. The possibility of such a seller entering the market may still be relevant when considering the likelihood of entry or expansion later during the merger analysis.

its rivals.[184] A number of calculation methods can indicate market share, including dollar sales, unit sales, capacities or reserves. Where the products are undifferentiated or homogeneous, and the firms are operating at full capacity, these methods should all produce similar results. If the firms are selling homogenous products but are operating below capacity, then a capacity analysis may best reflect competitive influence on the market. Where there is greater product-differentiation, the Bureau will likely calculate market share through dollar sales, but may also look at unit sales.[185]

§3. Market Power and Dominant Position

95. The Supreme Court of Canada has defined market power as the ability to behave relatively independently of the market.[186] The Tribunal defines market power as the ability of a firm or group of firms to maintain prices above the competitive level. However, market power may also be exercised in less concrete or obvious ways, including by offering poor service or quality or by restricting choice. Thus, the Tribunal has explained that 'price' is used as shorthand for all aspects of firms' actions that bear on the interest of buyers.[187] With the development of econometric methods for directly estimating anti-competitive effects, the definition of a relevant market – while still often useful – is no longer seen as a necessary precondition to merger analysis.

96. Market power exists when a firm can raise prices above competitive market rates for a considerable period of time and profitably maintain them for a substantial amount of time. The Bureau may consider direct evidence of market power, such as profitability and supra-competitive pricing, assuming it is available.[188] This evidence, though, is often difficult to obtain. Taken alone, it is also insufficient to establish market power.[189] Consequently, indirect factors such as market share and barriers to entry are usually the most important factors in assessing whether a firm has substantial or complete control of a market.

97. In *Laidlaw* the Tribunal stated:

> A *prima facie* determination as to whether a firm is likely to have market power can be made by considering the share of the relevant market held by that firm.

184. *Ibid.*, at 5.8.
185. *Ibid.*, at 5.2–5.5.
186. *R. v. Nova Scotia Pharmaceutical Society*, [1992] 2 S.C.R. 606.
187. *Superior Propane*, *supra* n. 151 at 404.
188. *Tele-Direct (Publications) Inc. v. American Business Information Inc.* [1998] 1 S.C.R. xv [*Tele-Direct*] (High revenues of at least 40% over direct costs, the ability to price discriminate against higher-spending customers and the ability to price consistently across markets with no consideration of local competition were evidence of market power. However, customer dissatisfaction was rejected as evidence of market power.)
189. Abuse of Dominance Guidelines, *supra* n. 179 at 2. See also *Canada (Director of Investigation & Research) v. NutraSweet Co.*, [1990] C.C.T.D. No. 17, at 28–29 [*Nutrasweet*].

If that share is very large the firm will very likely have market power. But other considerations must also be taken into account including: how many competitors there are in the market and their respective market shares; how much excess capacity the firms in the market have; how easily a new firm can establish itself as a competitor.[190]

98. In *Laidlaw* the Tribunal said that it would not find prima facie market power if a firm's market share is below 50%.[191] In contrast, the Bureau has indicated that a market share between 35% and 50% will not give rise to a presumption of dominance, but may lead to further examination depending on the circumstances.[192] To date, all cases under the abuse of dominance provisions have involved firms with at least an 80% market share. Coordinated effects are unlikely to be alleged where the post-merger market share accounted for by the four largest firms in the market (i.e., the four-firm concentration ratio or CR4) would be less than 65%, or when the market share of the merged entity would be less than 10%.[193]

99. In addition to market share, the Tribunal considers barriers to entry.[194] The lower the barriers to entry, the more likely it is that a firm's high market share will not translate into a finding of market power. If a firm has a high market share, a prima facie finding of control is difficult to overcome without clear evidence of low barriers to entry.[195] Barriers to entry include sunk costs, regulatory barriers, economies of scale and scope, market maturity, network effects, access to scarce or non-duplicable inputs, and existing long-term contracts.[196] The Bureau has also indicated that it considers countervailing power, technological change and innovation when assessing a firm's control of the market.[197]

§4. Agreements and Concerted Practices

100. Historically, conspiracy provisions have always been an integral part of Canada's competition law. Prior to March, 2010, agreements between competitors were subject only to criminal prosecution under section 45 of the Act.[198] Bill C-10 significantly changed the statutory structure dealing with illegal agreements between competitors. It created a dual-track system. Section 45 allows for the criminal prosecution of 'hardcore cartels'. Section 90.1 allows for the civil review of

190. *Canada (Director of Investigation & Research) v. Laidlaw Waste Systems Ltd.*, [1992] C.C.T.D. No. 1, at 98 [*Laidlaw*].
191. *Ibid.*, at 317.
192. Abuse of Dominance Guidelines, *supra* n. 179 at 9.
193. MEGs, *supra* n. 153 at 5.9.
194. *NutraSweet*, *supra* n. 189 at 28.
195. See *Tele-Direct*, *supra* n. 188 at 83 ('[L]arge market share can support an initial determination that a firm likely has market power, *absent other extenuating circumstances, in general, ease of entry*' [emphasis added]).
196. Abuse of Dominance Guidelines, *supra* n. 179 at 9.
197. *Ibid.*, at 14.
198. There are also separate provisions related to conspiracies involving professional sports (s. 48) or federal financial institutions (s. 49), and for bid rigging (s. 47).

non-criminal agreements between competitors that nonetheless are likely to, or do, substantially lessen or prevent competition. In addition, the Bureau has published the Competitor Collaboration Guidelines (CCGs).[199] The CCGs describe an analytical framework that the Bureau will apply to competitor agreements in light of the new provisions.

101. The criminal provisions apply where a person conspires, agrees or arranges with a competitor or likely competitor:

(a) to fix, maintain, increase or control the price for the supply of the product;
(b) to allocate sales, territories, customers or markets for the production or supply of the product; or
(c) to fix, maintain, control, prevent, lessen or eliminate the production or supply of the product.[200]

102. The language of the civil review provision is broader. The Tribunal can invoke the provision where it 'finds that an agreement or arrangement — whether existing or proposed — between persons two or more of whom are competitors prevents or lessens, or is likely to prevent or lessen, competition substantially in a market'.[201] There are other reviewable practice sections that may catch agreements between competitors, such as section 92 (mergers) or section 79 (collective abuse of dominant position). Where one of the narrower criminal or civil sections applies, the CCGs indicate that the Bureau will typically proceed under the specific rather than the general section. For example, the Bureau will assess an agreement within a merger – such as a non-competition provision applicable to the seller – under section 92 rather than section 90.1.[202] Sections 45.1 and 90.1(10) prevent criminal prosecution and civil review from both arising out of substantially the same facts. Hence, a person's behaviour cannot lead to a double sanction.

103. The criminal provisions apply to the most egregious competitor agreements. They apply to conduct that is 'so likely to harm competition and to have no pro-competitive benefits that they are deserving of prosecution without a detailed inquiry into their actual competitive effects'.[203] However, the civil provision has a broad scope and can also catch these agreements. Where the Bureau finds that conduct could be reviewed under the criminal track, it will first ask whether any of the criminal defences provided in section 45(4)-(6) apply (see below). If any of them apply, the Bureau will not refer the case to the Director of Public Prosecutions. However, the Bureau may still proceed under the civil track or pursue an alternative method of resolution.

---

199. *Competitor Collaboration Guidelines* (Competition Bureau 2009) [CCGs].
200. *Competition Act*, *supra* n. 26 at s. 45(1).
201. *Ibid.*, at s. 90.1(1). Again, the term 'competitors' includes likely competitors.
202. CCGs, *supra* n. 199 at 1.
203. *Ibid.*, at 6.

104. Section 45 applies to agreements or arrangements 'between competitors'. The statute defines 'competitor' broadly to include 'a person who it is reasonable to believe would be likely to compete with respect to a product in the absence of a conspiracy, agreement or arrangement to do anything referred to in paragraphs (1)(*a*) to (*c*)'. The Bureau determines whether parties are competitors or potential competitors by looking at whether they have offered or are likely to offer competing products in the same regions. This determination relies on business and strategic plans, marketing and communications with potential customers, and evidence of competition with respect to similar customers or products.[204] The provisions do not apply to agreements between affiliated companies, as defined by the Act.[205] The Bureau has said that if not all the parties to an agreement are competitors, the Bureau can still prosecute the non-competitors for aiding and abetting an offence (e.g., in the case of 'hub and spoke' conspiracies among retailers, where their supplier is the 'hub').[206]

105. Prior to the 2009 amendments (which took effect in 2010 in the case of changes to section 45 and the new 90.1), it was necessary under section 45 to show that agreements prevented or lessened competition 'unduly'. The Bureau claimed this was a very difficult threshold to meet, requiring a complex factual, legal and economic analysis to demonstrate beyond a reasonable doubt that economic harm had resulted. Consequently, Parliament eliminated this requirement with Bill C-10, but narrowed the provision to apply only to 'hardcore cartels'.[207]

106. As with the old provision, section 45 requires that the defendant conspire, agree or arrange (the old provision also included the word 'combine'). Implicit in all of these concepts is the need for an 'agreement'.[208] Consequently, there must be some meeting of the minds, and the Bureau cannot invoke the provision based on unilateral action.[209] However, section 45(3) provides that the court may infer the existence of an agreement from circumstantial evidence, and it may consider whether an agreement is the only way to explain the conduct.[210] It is not necessary for the conspiracy to have been carried out, as entering into a prohibited agreement constitutes the *actus reus* of the offence.

---

204. *Ibid.*, at 9.
205. *Competition Act*, *supra* n. 26 at s. 56(6)(a). The Act defines 'affiliate' in s. 2(2) to include corporations where one is a subsidiary of the other; corporations where both are subsidiaries of the same corporation; corporations affiliated with the same corporation; and partnerships or sole proprietorships both controlled by the same person.
206. CCGs, *supra* n. 199 at 8. As per s. 21 of the *Criminal Code*, someone who aids or abets an offence is a party to that offence and is treated in the same way as if they had committed the offence.
207. Bill C-10, *supra* n. 34 at s. 410.
208. *R v. Gage (No. 2)*, [1908] M.J. No. 2, 13 C.C.C. 428 at 449 (C.A.) (These words, taken either collectively or individually, or any one of them, express the act of agreeing to do the unlawful thing, the doing of which constitutes the conspiracy.)
209. See *R v. Armco Canada Ltd.* (1976), 70 D.L.R. (3d) 287, 13 O.R. (2d) 32 at 41 (C.A.), rev'g in part (1974) 21 C.C.C. (2d) 129, 176 (H.C.J.), leave to appeal to S.C.C. refused, 13 O.R. (2d) 32 (there must be 'a mutual arriving at an understanding or agreement') [*Armco*].
210. *R v. Canadian General Electric Co.* (1976), 15 O.R. (2d) 360, 29 C.P.R. (2d) (H.C.J.) [*Canadian General Electric*].

107. Prior to the enactment of section 45(3) (previously section 45(2.1)), in *Atlantic Sugar Refineries Co. v. Canada (Attorney General)*,[211] the Supreme Court held that conscious parallelism was not sufficient grounds to find a conspiracy. The subsequent legislative addition of section 45(3) has clarified that a finder of fact can find a conspiracy based on circumstantial evidence. Yet the more difficult issue remains distinguishing between a tacit agreement, which is illegal, and conscious parallelism, which is legal. Conscious parallelism exists where competitors arrive at very similar decisions regarding competitive strategy without a conscious agreement between them. For example, conscious parallelism may result in near-simultaneous and identical price changes among competitors. It usually occurs in oligopolistic markets.

108. There is no bright line test to determine when behaviour crosses from conscious parallelism to a tacit agreement. Generally, a finding that parallel behaviour amounts to an agreement requires evidence of communication between the parties.[212] In *Canadian General Electric* (the so-called Large Lamps case), the court found that identical pricing – in conjunction with evidence of communication between the competitors regarding prices of tenders – was evidence of an agreement between the competitors. On the facts, the communication was not otherwise normal business behaviour.[213] In another case, the Ontario Court of Appeal found that the advance publication of price lists through an industry trade association constituted a conscious effort to bring about parallel pricing in the industry. The practice was therefore illegal.[214] However, it has also been held that adopting prices based on the price list of the industry leader does not amount to conspiracy, but rather is simply an example of typical market surveillance.[215]

109. Section 45 contains a limited number of defences available to those charged under the section. Most importantly, section 45(4) creates the ancillary restraints defence. The defence can be invoked where the accused establishes on a balance of probabilities that the impugned agreement is ancillary to a broader or other arrangement including the same parties; and is directly related to, and reasonably necessary for effecting the objective of that broader or other arrangement. The broader or other arrangement must not itself violate the prohibition against cartels. Based on this defence, the Bureau has said in the CCGs that it will generally not review the following types of agreements under the criminal track:[216]

(a) A non-compete clause found in an employment agreement, or an agreement for the sale of assets or shares between parties.
(b) An agreement among competitors to charge a common price in a blanket license agreement for artistic works.

211. *Atlantic Sugar*, *supra* n. 22.
212. *Canadian General Electric*, *supra* n. 210.
213. *Ibid.*
214. *Armco*, *supra* n. 209.
215. *R v. Aluminum Co. of Canada Ltd.*, [1976] C.S. 1695, 29 C.P.R. (2d) 183 (Que. S.C.).
216. CCGs, *supra* n. 199 at 12.

(c) An agreement to abstain from making material changes to a business pending the consummation of a merger.
(d) A non-compete obligation between the parent undertakings and a joint venture where such obligations correspond only to the products, services and territories covered by the joint venture agreement.

110. Section 45(5) provides a defence for arrangements that deal with exporting products from Canada. Section 45(6)(a) exempts agreements between companies that are affiliates. Section 45(6)(b) exempts agreements between federal financial institutions, which are dealt with separately in section 49. Section 45(7) confirms that the common law Regulated Conduct Defence can be invoked by persons charged with criminal conspiracy, despite the 2009 amendments.[217] Section 90 of the Act also exempts specialization agreements[218] from prosecution under section 45.

111. In the CCGs, the Bureau provides a detailed approach as to how it will apply section 90.1, the civil track for competitor agreements. The CCGs deal specifically with six common types of competitor agreements: commercialization agreements, information sharing agreements, research and development agreements, joint production agreements, joint purchasing agreements, and non-compete agreements.[219] Generally, the Bureau's approach to what constitutes an agreement appears to mirror the approach of the criminal courts. Parallel behaviour alone is insufficient to establish an agreement, but an agreement can be found regardless of the degree of formality.

112. In determining whether an agreement 'prevents or lessens, or is likely to prevent or lessen, competition substantially in a market' the Bureau will adopt an approach consistent with the MEGs.[220] Generally, the Commissioner will not challenge an agreement if the concern relates to the unilateral exercise of market power and if the parties hold a combined market share of less than 35%. The Commissioner will also typically not challenge an agreement if the concern relates to the coordinated exercise of market power and the four largest firms in the market have a market share of less than 65%, and the share of the parties to the agreement is less than 10%. While high market share is not determinative as to a possible challenge, it is 'highly relevant'.[221] Barriers to entry are also an important consideration. The lower the barriers to entry in the market, the less likely it is that the arrangement will allow the firms to substantially prevent or lessen competition. Section 90.1(2) provides an additional list of factors that the Tribunal must consider in deciding whether to make a finding under subsection (1). Generally, these factors deal with

217. See 'Part 1: Chapter 2: §2. Special Sectors' for discussion of the regulated conduct defence.
218. See 'Part II: Chapter 1: §1 Horizontal Agreements: III. Cooperation agreements: B. Specialization' for discussion of specialization agreements.
219. CCGs, *supra* n. 199 at 19.
220. See '§2. Relevant Market', '§3. 'Market Power/Dominant Position', and '§6. Monopolization and abuse of dominance' in this chapter.
221. CCGs, *supra* n. 199 at 21.

barriers to entry, the availability of substitutable products, the elimination of competitors, and the technological state of the market.

113. Section 90.1 provides for several defences. Many of the exemptions mirror the criminal provisions.[222] Section 90 of the Act exempts specialization agreements[223] from prosecution under section 90.1. Section 90.1(4) prevents the Tribunal from making an order under 90.1 when the gains in efficiency from a particular agreement are likely to be greater than, and offset, the negative effects of the arrangement, and when the gains in efficiency would likely not actualize if the order was made. The Bureau has indicated that its approach to assessing efficiencies under this section will be the same as its approach to efficiencies in the context of mergers.[224] Efficiencies refer to savings in input costs by way of a reduction in the inputs required to produce a given output. The following cost-savings do not constitute efficiencies: savings resulting from a reduction in output, service, quality or product choice; gains that could be attained through alternative means notwithstanding a Tribunal order; and gains that are merely redistributive (e.g., by forcing suppliers to accept lower prices).[225]

§5. Restriction of Competition

114. The threshold for determining whether a particular practice restricts competition varies based on the wording of specific provisions. In most cases, the phrase used is along the lines of 'substantially prevent or lessen competition'. There is no single, broadly-applicable definition for what constitutes a substantial lessening or prevention of competition. However, in the context of abuse of dominance the Federal Court of Appeal described the requirement as a comparative analysis between the state of the market with the impugned conduct and without it.[226] Yet the court did not say what would constitute a 'substantial' change in competition, leaving the assessment to the Tribunal's discretion. In some cases, the Act provides guidance as to the relevant factors for determining whether there is a substantial lessening of competition.[227] Generally, these factors deal with barriers to entry, the availability of substitutable products, the elimination of competitors, and the technological state of the market. Competition is substantially lessened or prevented when the impugned behaviour creates, reinforces, or enhances market power.[228]

---

222. See s. 90.1(9) dealing with federal financial institutions; s. 90.1(8) dealing with export agreements; and s. 90.1(7) exempting agreements between affiliates.
223. See 'Part II: Ch. 1: §1 Horizontal Agreements: III. Cooperation agreements: B. Specialization' for discussion of specialization agreements.
224. CCGs, *supra* n. 199 at 22.
225. *Ibid.*, at 23.
226. *Commissioner of Competition v. Canada Pipe Company Ltd./Tuyauteries Canada Ltée*, 2006 FCA 233, 49 C.P.R. (4th) 241 at 260 [*Canada Pipe*].
227. See s. 93 (factors to be considered regarding prevention or lessening of competition related to mergers); and s. 90.1(2) (dealing with agreements between competitors).
228. *Nutrasweet*, *supra* n. 189.

115. The guidelines published by the Bureau provide additional insight into when the Bureau will consider challenging a particular practice as substantially lessening or prevention of competition.[229] In the MEGs, the Bureau describes the prevention and lessening of competition as occurring when a firm is able to sustain higher prices than it could have prior to the merger.[230] The Bureau considers the lessening of competition substantial if two conditions obtain: first, if the price of the product is likely to be materially greater in a substantial part of the market; second, if likely and sufficient entry by new competitors is not likely to nullify the price increase in a timely manner. The phrase 'materially greater' does not denote a specific numerical value; instead, the Bureau assesses the increase with regard to the factors listed in section 93 of the Act.[231] The Bureau's approach in other contexts is very similar.

§6. Monopolization and Abuse of Dominance

116. Abuse of dominance occurs in a market when a dominant firm or group of firms engages in a practice of anti-competitive acts with the result that competition is thereby substantially lessened or prevented.[232] Prior to 1986, the only criminal enforcement against abuse of dominance fell under the *Combines Investigation Act* as a criminal matter. The Crown needed to prove beyond a reasonable doubt that the impugned behaviour had been detrimental to the public. This was a difficult threshold to meet.[233] As a result, the criminal provisions gave the impression of being wholly ineffective.[234] In 1986, section 79 of the Act replaced these provisions. Abuse of dominance became civilly reviewable by the Tribunal. The new legislation also provided the Tribunal with the authority to issue prohibition orders and mandatory orders. In 2009, the addition of AMPs expanded the scope of the enforcement provisions.[235] Also, the legislature repealed criminal provisions for predatory pricing, price discrimination and promotional allowances. Section 79's newly expanded scope would address the conduct previously covered by the repealed provisions.[236]

117. Sections 78 and 79 deal with abuse of dominance. Section 78 provides a non-exhaustive list of behaviours that will be considered 'anti-competitive acts'. Section 79 makes abuse of dominance a reviewable practice and provides the Tribunal with the authority to issue orders and AMPs. It also establishes the elements

229. See MEGs, *supra* n. 153 at 5.9; Abuse of Dominance Guidelines, *supra* n. 179 at 19–20; CCGs, *supra* n. 199 at 20–21; and Competition Bureau, *Predatory Pricing Enforcement Guidelines* 18–19 (Competition Bureau 2008) [PPEGs].
230. MEGs, *ibid.*, at 2.6.
231. *Ibid.*, at 2.14 n. 14.
232. Abuse of Dominance Guidelines, *supra* n. 179 at 1.
233. There was only one conviction, occurring in *R v. Eddy Match Co. Ltd.*, [1953] Q.J. No. 8, 20 C.P.R. 107 (C.A.).
234. M. Kilby & A. Piotrowski, *2015 Competition Act and Commentary* 119 (D.J. Brown ed., Lexis Nexis Canada Inc. 2014).
235. Bill C-10, *supra* n. 34 at s. 428.
236. *Ibid.*, s. 413.

that the Commissioner must prove for the Tribunal to find that an abuse of dominance has occurred:

(a) one or more persons substantially or completely control, throughout Canada or any area thereof, a class or species of business,
(b) that person or those persons have engaged in or are engaging in a practice of anti-competitive acts, and
(c) the practice has had, is having or is likely to have the effect of preventing or lessening competition substantially in a market[.][237]

The first element deals with the ability to influence a relevant market, typically through the exercise of market power (see above under 'Market Power and Dominant Position'), and the Tribunal and Bureau generally consider 'control' to mean 'market power'.[238] The Bureau considers a 'class or species of business' as synonymous with 'relevant product market'.[239] The phrase 'throughout Canada or any area thereof' is synonymous with 'geographic market'.[240]

118. The second element of section 79 requires the Commissioner to show that the firm – or group of firms, in the case of joint dominance – '[has] engaged in or [is] engaging in a practice of anti-competitive acts'. This element focuses on the purpose of the action. The Federal Court of Appeal has defined anti-competitive acts as those 'whose purpose is an intended negative effect on a competitor that is predatory, exclusionary or disciplinary'.[241] Proof of the intended negative effect can 'be established directly through evidence of subjective intent, or indirectly by reference to the reasonably foreseeable consequences of the acts themselves and the circumstances surrounding their commission, or both'.[242]

119. The reasonably foreseeable consequences of a firm's actions may support an inference that the firm intended to negatively affect its competitors. A firm can overcome this inference by showing that it had a valid business justification for engaging in the conduct. A valid business justification exists if there is a 'credible efficiency or pro-competitive rationale for the conduct in question, attributable to the [the firm], which relates to and counterbalances the anti-competitive effects and/or subjective intent of the acts'.[243] The Bureau has said that 'credible efficiency or pro-competitive rationale[s]' often include activities intended to minimize the cost

237. *Competition Act*, *supra* n. 26 at s. 79(1).
238. It should be noted that in a 2014 case, the Federal Court of Appeal held that as a matter of statutory interpretation, paragraph 79(1)(a) of the *Act* does not require that the person alleged to exercise 'control' be a competitor in the allegedly restrained market. The Court noted that a non-competitor might exercise 'control' of the market by controlling a significant input to competitors in the market or by making rules that effectively control the business conduct of those competitors. *Commissioner Of Competition v. Toronto Real Estate Board* 2014 FCA 29, leave to appeal to SCC denied, 2014 CanLii 40570 (SCC) [TREB].
239. Abuse of Dominance Guidelines, *supra* n. 179 at 3.
240. *Ibid.*, at 9.
241. *Canada Pipe*, *supra* n. 226 at 276.
242. *Ibid.*, at 274.
243. *Ibid.*, at 274.

of production or operation, independent of the elimination or discipline of a rival. The Bureau has also said that valid business justifications include activities that improve a firm's product, service or some other aspect of the firm's business. The Bureau must also consider any other factors that are relevant to intention.[244]

120. Section 78 provides a non-exhaustive list of types of anti-competitive behaviour. Detailed discussions appear throughout this monograph of specific behaviours listed in the Act or held by the Tribunal or courts to be anti-competitive.

121. The final element of section 79 requires that 'the practice has had, is having or is likely to have the effect of preventing or lessening competition substantially in a market'. This element focuses on the impact of the action on competition, as opposed to its impact on competitors. In *Canada Pipe* the Federal Court of Appeal phrased the appropriate test as follows: '[W]ould the relevant markets—in the past, present or future—be substantially more competitive but for the impugned practice of anti-competitive acts?'[245] The Court did not create any clear criteria for applying this test, but said the test may be applied by constructing hypothetical comparisons between markets that are identical except for the impugned behaviour. The test's application may also involve a temporal analysis comparing the market prior to and subsequent to the commencement of the anti-competitive behaviour.[246]

122. In examining whether there has been a substantial prevention of competition, the Bureau considers whether the anti-competitive behaviour has created, preserved or enhanced barriers to entry. If it has done so, the Bureau then asks if, but for the anti-competitive behaviour, an effective competitor or group of competitors would have emerged within a reasonable period of time. If new competition would have emerged 'but for' the impugned behaviour, the Bureau will conclude that there has been a substantial lessening or prevention of competition.[247] Other factors that the Bureau considers include 'whether or not consumer prices might be substantially lower; product quality, innovation or choice might be substantially greater; or consumer switching between products or suppliers might be substantially more frequent in the absence of the practice'.[248]

§7. CONCENTRATIONS (MERGERS)

123. Mergers involve the acquisition and combination of companies and other similar entities. Mergers raise competition issues because they can enhance dominant positions and eliminate competitors. Recall that section 91 of the Act defines a 'merger' as:

244. *Canada Pipe*, *supra* n. 226 at 276.
245. *Ibid.*, at 260.
246. *Ibid.*, at 264.
247. Abuse of Dominance Guidelines, *supra* n. 179 at 13.
248. *Ibid.*, at 20.

> [T]he acquisition or establishment, direct or indirect, by one or more persons, whether by purchase or lease of shares or assets, by amalgamation or by combination or otherwise, of control over or significant interest in the whole or part of a business or a part of a business of a competitor, supplier, buyer or other person.[249]

The key legal concepts in this definition are 'control' and 'significant interest'. Also important, mergers may involve firms that supply competing products (horizontal mergers) or firms that do not compete (non-horizontal mergers).[250]

124. Section 2(4) of the Act defines control of a corporation as de jure (legal) control, meaning direct or indirect holding of over 50% of the votes that may be cast to elect the corporation's directors.[251] The votes must be sufficient to elect a majority of the directors. In addition, the section defines control of a partnership as belonging to the person who holds an interest entitling them to receive over 50% of the profits or over 50% of the assets upon dissolution. Section 2(4) also defines control in the context of Crown corporations.[252]

125. The Act is silent on the meaning of 'significant interest'. However, the MEGs provide guidance as to the Bureau's interpretation of the term:

> [A] 'significant interest' in the whole or a part of a business is held qualitatively when the person acquiring or establishing the interest … obtains the ability to materially influence the economic behaviour of the target business, including but not limited to decisions relating to pricing, purchasing, distribution, marketing, investment, financing and the licensing of intellectual property rights.[253]

The MEGs also list numerous factors that are potentially relevant to their analysis of whether a minority shareholding, interest in a combination, or other relationship confers 'material influence':[254]

- the voting rights attached to the interest;
- the acquirer's status in a partnership (general or limited) and the nature of the acquirer's rights;
- the distribution of the remaining shares or interests (widely held or closely held);
- board composition and historical voting patterns;
- the existence of special voting rights;
- the terms of shareholder or voting agreements;
- the dividend or profit share of the minority interest as compared to the acquirer's equity share;

249. *Competition Act, supra* n. 26 at s. 91.
250. MEGs, *supra* n. 153 at 11.1.
251. *Ibid.,* at 1.3.
252. *Competition Act, supra* n. 26 at 2.4.
253. MEGs, *supra* n. 153 at 1.5.
254. *Ibid.,* at 1.6.

- the status and expertise of the acquirer;
- the extent of the acquirer's influence over management and committee selection;
- the services provided by the acquirer to the business;
- the acquirer's liquidity rights;
- the acquirer's access to confidential information;
- and the acquirer's practical ability to impose pressure on the business' decision-making processes.

Also significant, the Bureau presumes that notifiable transactions constitute the acquisition or establishment of a significant interest in a business.[255] Generally, a transaction is notifiable if it exceeds specified transaction-size and party-size thresholds. Part III: Chapter 2 of this monograph discusses notification requirements. For a discussion of thresholds, also see the above 'Market Power and Dominant Position'.

126. The Bureau assesses whether a minority share acquisition confers a significant interest on a case-by-case basis.[256] It should be clear that a party may acquire a significant interest in many ways. The Bureau specifically mentions that it is possible to acquire a significant interest through share acquisitions, asset acquisitions, enhancement of an existing interest, contractual arrangements, or the establishment of a relationship that confers material influence.[257]

§8. Joint Ventures

127. When a joint venture constitutes a merger, the Bureau generally treats it no differently than other mergers, except if it is a non-corporate joint venture that fits within the narrow exception articulated in section 95. Section 95 precludes the Tribunal from making an order under section 92 pertaining to joint ventures formed through a non-corporate means. This exception obtains provided, first, that the joint venture's purpose is to undertake a specific project or a programme of research and development; second, that the agreement provides for the termination of the joint venture at the end of the project; third, that the project would not otherwise have been likely absent the joint venture; and, fourth, that the joint venture prevents or lessens competition only to a reasonably necessary extent for completion of the project.

128. Prior to 2010, there was no section of the Act to address situations involving joint ventures that were not mergers unless the agreement amounted to a criminal conspiracy under section 45. Bill C-10 created section 90.1, which makes agreements between competitors civilly reviewable.[258] The Bureau has indicated that, going forward, it will review joint ventures under the civil track instead of the

255. *Ibid.*, at 1.7.
256. *Ibid.*, at 1.8.
257. *Ibid.*, at 1.6, 1.18.
258. Bill C-10, *supra* n. 34 at s. 429.

criminal track.[259] Section 90.1 precludes any agreement between competitors that 'prevents or lessens, or is likely to prevent or lessen, competition substantially in a market'. However, section 90.1(4) is likely to be particularly relevant in the context of certain joint ventures. Recall that section 90.1(4) prevents the Tribunal from making an order where the gains in efficiency from a particular agreement are likely to be greater than, or offset, the negative effects of the arrangement, and the gains in efficiency would not likely be attained if the order was made.

259. CCGs, *supra* n. 199 at 1.

Chapter 5. Consequences of Violations and Enforcement Institutions

§1. Administrative Enforcement

129. Administrative enforcement is the primary means of applying Canadian competition law. The Bureau has the ability to investigate anti-competitive conduct, make orders related to the conduct and to enter into consent agreements in respect of civilly reviewable conduct which, when registered with the Competition Tribunal, become enforceable as Tribunal orders.

I. Antitrust Authorities

130. There are four principal institutions involved in competition law enforcement in Canada: the Commissioner of Competition, the Competition Tribunal, the Director of Public Prosecutions (formerly the Attorney General) and the courts. The Act allows the Commissioner to launch both civil and criminal inquiries and to challenge civil matters (including mergers) before the Competition Tribunal. The Act also enables the Commissioner to make recommendations on the prosecution of criminal matters to the Director of Public Prosecutions of Canada (the DPP) and to intervene as a competition advocate before federal and provincial bodies. The Tribunal is a quasi-judicial body responsible for presiding over and deciding civilly reviewable matters under the Act.

A. *Formation and Composition*

131. The Governor in Council (the federal cabinet) appoints the Commissioner of Competition.[260] The Commissioner has the primary authority to enforce both the civil and criminal provisions of the Act, as well as the *Consumer Packaging and Labelling Act*, the *Precious Metals Marking Act*, and the *Textile Labelling Act*. The Commissioner heads the Competition Bureau, which is part of the federal department of Industry Canada. That said, the Commissioner is statutorily independent from the Minister of Industry (the Minister) and reports directly to Parliament. This independence means that the Minister cannot restrain the Commissioner from acting, although the Minister can require the Commissioner to make inquiries under the Act. The Commissioner's length of tenure is at the discretion of the Governor in Council at the time of appointment. Appointments under the Act are generally made for five-year terms.[261]

132. Below the Commissioner, the senior level of the Bureau consists of several Deputy Commissioners. The Commissioner may delegate authority over certain

260. *Competition Act, supra* n. 26 at s. 7.
261. See http://www.appointments-nominations.gc.ca/prsnt.asp?page=Process&lang=eng.

matters to a Deputy Commissioner.[262] In practice, each Deputy Commissioner is responsible for a particular branch. The Bureau contains four branches, including a Mergers and Monopolistic Practices branch (the civil side), a Cartels and Deceptive Marketing Practices branch (the criminal side), a Competition Promotion branch, and a Corporate Services branch – the first two comprising the primary enforcement arms of the Bureau.[263]

133. Up to six judges of the Federal Court and up to eight lay members compose the Tribunal.[264] All members receive seven-year terms.[265] Between three and five members of the Tribunal hear each contentious proceeding. At least one member hearing a proceeding must be a judge and at least one must be a lay member.[266] Only judicial members may make findings on issues of pure law.[267] Applications made pursuant to certain sections of the Act are heard by one judicial member sitting alone.[268]

B. Investigative Powers

134. The Commissioner's main purpose, and by extension that of the Bureau, is to investigate conduct that may violate or require a remedy under the Act. Investigations are either informal or formal. The Bureau sometimes commences informal investigations based on complaints from members of the public, or may do so on its own initiative based on public information. When the Bureau begins an informal investigation it may send the implicated parties a 'request for information' (RFI). The Bureau then decides how to proceed based on the information provided. The Bureau is less likely to resort to formal investigations if the parties cooperate during the informal process.[269]

135. The authority to conduct formal investigations is granted by section 10 of the Act. The Act provides that the Commissioner must investigate if there is reason to believe that there are grounds to issue an order under the Act. The Commissioner must also launch a formal investigation if a group of at least six resident Canadians make a complaint, or if the Minister issues a directive to investigate.[270] If a formal

262. *Competition Act, supra* n. 26 at s. 8.
263. For a complete list and description of the branches see Competition Bureau, *Our Branches*, http://www.competitionbureau.gc.ca/eic/site/cb-bc.nsf/eng/h_00018.html (1 Apr. 2015).
264. *Competition Tribunal Act, supra* n. 27 at s. 3.
265. *Ibid.*, at s. 5.
266. *Ibid.*, at s. 10.
267. *Ibid.*, at s. 12.
268. *Ibid.*, at s. 11.
269. See D. Royal and M. Walli, *2015 Competition Act and Commentary* 26 (D.J. Brown ed., Lexis Nexis Canada Inc. 2014) [Royal].
270. The rules governing the making of such an inquiry are in s. 9(1) of the Act. Case law has held that the Commissioner is not obliged to complete such an inquiry: (*Ashley v. Canada (Commissioner of Competition)* (2006), 47 C.P.R. (4th) 379 (F.C.T.D.). [*Ashley*]).

investigation is discontinued, the Commissioner must report it to the Minister, who may order further inquiries.[271]

136. Once a formal investigation begins, the Commissioner wields a number of investigatory powers. Section 11 of the Act allows the Commissioner to apply on an ex parte basis to a judge for an order compelling the attendance of a person to give oral evidence (section 11(1)(a); an order compelling the production of documents (section 11(1)(b)); or an order compelling the delivery of written information under oath (section 11(1)(c)). To obtain an order, the Commissioner must establish that a formal inquiry has begun under section 10 and that the target of the order has, or is likely to have, information relevant to the inquiry. The target of the order does not need to be the party under investigation. If the target is a corporation, an order can force non-Canadian affiliates to disclose documents. Because a judge can grant the order without notice to the target and on an ex parte basis – with one party absent from the proceedings – the Commissioner must fully disclose all of the relevant factual and legal principles at stake. Material non-disclosure by the Commissioner can result in the order being overturned.[272] Once granted, an order is inalterable without a further court order.

137. Section 15 of the Act allows a judge to grant the Commissioner a search warrant, again on an ex parte basis. A search warrant permits the Commissioner or someone else named in the warrant to enter and search a premises and seize or copy any record or thing (subject to any conditions stipulated in the warrant). Generally, the Commissioner uses search warrants when investigating criminal offences under the Act although they have also been used in civil investigations. To obtain a warrant the Commissioner must first, through sworn evidence, demonstrate the fulfilment of one of three conditions: (i) a person has violated an order made under the Act; (ii) grounds exist for making an order under Part VII.1 (deceptive marketing) or Part VIII (reviewable matters); or (iii) a criminal offence has been, or is about to be committed, under Parts VI or VII of the Act. Second, the Commissioner must satisfy the judge that there are reasonable grounds to believe that there is, on the premises in question, a record or thing that will afford relevant evidence. The definition of 'record' is broad, including any 'correspondence, memorandum, book, plan, map, drawing, diagram, pictorial or graphic work, photograph, film, microform, sound recording, videotape, machine readable record, and any other documentary material, regardless of physical form or characteristics, and any copy or portion thereof'.[273] Section 16 provides that, during the search, persons conducting the search may access computer systems on the premises to search for records anywhere on the computer system to which it connects. Warrants are typically very detailed and must identify the specific record or class of records sought in the search.

---

271. *Competition Act*, *supra* n. 26 at s. 22.
272. See *Canada (Commissioner) v. Labatt Brewing Co.*, [2008] F.C.J. No. 127, 2008 FC 59 (F.C.) [*Labatt Breweries*].
273. *Competition Act*, *supra* n. 26 at s. 2.

138. In addition to these investigatory powers, the Commissioner may rely on the *Criminal Code* to employ a judicially authorized wiretap in criminal investigations under the Act. Recall that criminal investigations under the Act may relate to agreements or arrangements between competitors (section 45), bid rigging (section 47), criminal misleading advertising (section 52), deceptive telemarketing (section 52.1(3)), deceptive prize notices (section 53), multi-level marketing plans (section 55) or pyramid schemes (section 55.1).[274] A judge may authorize a wiretap if, first, it would be in the best interests of justice to do so; and second, other investigatory techniques have failed, would be unlikely to succeed, or urgency renders other techniques impractical.[275] The Bureau only uses wiretaps in exceptional circumstances.[276]

139. To facilitate certain investigations, the Bureau has in place immunity[277] and leniency[278] programmes whereby individuals can potentially avoid criminal prosecution or receive a lesser penalty by coming forward early and cooperating with the Bureau's investigation. Although the Commissioner does not ultimately decide what charges are laid, the Bureau can recommend that the DPP grant immunity or leniency.[279]

140. In addition to the immunity and leniency programmes, the Act grants whistleblower protection to persons who disclose to the Commissioner information about offences that have been committed, or will be committed, under the Act. Section 66.1(2) provides that, if the Commissioner promises to keep an informant's identity confidential, the Commissioner must keep that promise. Section 66.2 prohibits employers from taking retaliatory action against employees who provide information to the Commissioner in respect of their employer's wrongdoings. For more information, see paragraphs 194–196 below.

C. Adjudicating Powers: Ascertaining and Sanctioning

141. The Commissioner does not have formal adjudicative power. On paper, the Commissioner is responsible only for investigating and prosecuting civil matters. However, the Commissioner can work with the implicated parties to reach a

---

274. *Criminal Code*, *supra* n. 19 at s. 183(c). The Code defines the term 'offence' to include these violations of the *Competition Act*.
275. *Ibid.*, at s. 186(1).
276. See *Information Bulletin: Interception of Private Communications and the Competition Act* 1 (Competition Bureau 1999).
277. *Immunity Program Under the Competition Act* (Competition Bureau 2010) [Immunity Program Bulletin].
278. Leniency Program (Competition Bureau 2010) [Leniency Program Bulletin].
279. For an overview of both programmes see 'Part I: Chapter 5: §3 Criminal Enforcement: I. Criminal sanctions for antitrust violations'.

consent agreement. Following an investigation, if the Commissioner believes that formal enforcement is necessary, the Commissioner either refers the case to the DPP for criminal prosecution, or makes an application to the Competition Tribunal for civil enforcement.

142. According to the Conformity Continuum Information Bulletin, the Bureau divides its responses to non-conformity into three categories: suasion, consent, and adversarial response.[280] Where the Bureau believes it can achieve a resolution by providing guidance on the law, the Bureau relies on suasion to achieve conformity. The Bureau may contact the relevant party and explain the legislation to him or her. The Bureau may also send an information letter or a more formal cautionary letter. In some circumstances, the Bureau may hold a compliance meeting and require senior officials of a company to attend and discuss the history of inspections, record of compliance, and corrective measures that the party will undertake. Depending on the company's corrective undertakings, the Bureau may continue investigating, may continue to monitor the conduct at issue, or may close the file.[281]

143. Where formal resolution is called for, the Bureau commences consent proceedings or adversarial proceedings. In the criminal context, the Commissioner refers the case to the DPP, so any plea agreement is then at the DPP's discretion. However, upon the Bureau's recommendation, the DPP may offer leniency to a cooperating party in the form of full immunity, partial immunity or a negotiated plea and settlement.[282] Although the decision is that of the DPP, the Commissioner works closely with the DPP throughout the process.

144. In the case of a civil issue, less serious contraventions of the law may lead to consent proceedings. Generally, infrequent and inadvertent offences lead to consent agreements, provided that the parties are cooperative and willing to offset the damage to the marketplace.[283] Consent proceedings are essentially negotiations in which the Bureau tries to reach a legally binding agreement with the implicated party or parties. Generally, the party will undertake to correct the problem in a specific way. For example, the Bureau may require a party to cease or amend a particular activity; to divest assets or shares; to establish a corporate compliance programme; to voluntarily recall a product; to amend labelling, packaging or advertising material; to pay restitution to damaged parties; or to publish corrective

280. *Conformity Continuum Information Bulletin* (Competition Bureau 2000) [Conformity Continuum]. On 20 May 2015, the Bureau published a draft version of the *Competition and Compliance Framework* bulletin for public comment. The Competition and Compliance Framework bulletin updates and replaces the Conformity Continuum Information Bulletin. The public consultation period ended 20 Jul. 2015. At the time of writing, the final version of the Competition and Compliance Framework bulletin had not been released.

281. *Ibid.*, at 9.

282. *Ibid.*, at 10.

283. *Ibid.*, at 11. See also *ibid.*, at 12–13 for a discussion of the factors the Bureau considers when deciding how to proceed.

notices.[284] The undertakings must be actions that the Tribunal could have ordered had it heard the case.[285]

145. Once an agreement is reached it is filed with the Tribunal and becomes binding as if it were an order of the Tribunal. The Tribunal no longer has any power to review consent agreements. Varying or rescinding a consent agreement requires application to the Tribunal on the grounds that the terms could not have been an order of the Tribunal;[286] that circumstances have changed such that the order would not have been made or would have been ineffective under the new circumstances; or that the Commissioner and the consenting party to the agreement have consented to an alternative order.[287]

146. For more serious civil matters or if parties cannot reach a consent agreement, the Commissioner commences adversarial proceedings by referring the case to the Tribunal for adjudication. The Commissioner then adopts the role of prosecutor. The Tribunal has all the powers of a superior court, including the authority to compel the attendance of witnesses, compel the production of documents, and enforce its orders.[288] The Tribunal has discretion to issue orders, injunctions and, in some cases, AMPs (fines). It also has jurisdiction to hear references posed by the Commissioner or individuals who are under investigation by the Commissioner. References may be questions of law, mixed law and fact, jurisdiction, practice or procedure.[289]

D. Other Institutional Tasks: Consulting the Government

147. By law, the Commissioner must report annually to Parliament.[290] In addition, the Bureau sometimes makes submissions to other administrative boards or government panels and may do so as of right before federal bodies where

284. *Ibid.*, at 11–12. See for example, Competition Bureau, *Competition Bureau takes steps to ensure Parrish and Heimbecker complies with pre-merger notification obligations*, (29 May 2015), http://www.competitionbureau.gc.ca/eic/site/cb-bc.nsf/eng/03948.html, where agri-food business company Parrish and Heimbecker, Limited (P&H), recently agreed to adopt a compliance program following its failure to notify the Bureau of two proposed acquisitions.
285. See *Competition Act, supra* n. 26 at s. 105(2).
286. The Tribunal has recently held its jurisdiction in applications to vary or rescind consent agreements brought by third parties under subsection 106(2) of the *Act* is limited to determining whether the terms of the agreement are outside the scope of the types of order(s) the Tribunal is permitted to issue in respect of the reviewable trade practice in question. It is not open to the applicant to attempt to establish that one of the substantive elements of the trade practice has not been met or that a defence or exception under the *Act* is applicable. See *Kobo Inc. v. Commissioner of Competition*, 2014 CACT 14 (CanLii), leave to appeal to FCA granted [*Kobo*].
287. *Competition Act, supra* n. 26 at s. 106. See *Rona Inc. v. Canada (Commissioner of Competition)* (2005), 42 C.P.R. (4th) 53 (the Tribunal allowed the rescission of a consent order that had required the applicant to divest one of its stores when the applicant's main competitor opened a store in the same geographic market with the result that there would no longer be a substantial lessening of competition if the applicant was allowed to maintain ownership of its store).
288. *Competition Tribunal Act, supra* n. 27 at s. 8(2).
289. *Competition Act, supra* n. 26 at s. 124.2.
290. *Ibid.*, at s. 127. See Competition Bureau, *Annual Reports*, http://www.competitionbureau.gc.ca/eic/site/cb-bc.nsf/eng/h_00169.html (18 Oct. 2013).

competition is relevant, and with leave before provincial bodies.[291] The Bureau also considers education as fundamental to implementing effective competition policy.[292] Consequently, it makes available, through its website, a number of documents including guidelines, reports and information pamphlets.[293] The Bureau directs this information at both businesses and consumers. In addition, the Bureau often holds public consultations before implementing major policy changes.[294]

II. The Government's Direct Enforcement Activities

148. The executive branch of the government does not have any direct role in enforcing the Act. By statute, the four main enforcement bodies (the Commissioner, the Tribunal, the DPP and the courts) operate independently of the government. The Act limits the Minister of Industry's authority to requesting that the Commissioner investigate a matter.[295]

III. Other Administrative Agencies Applying Antitrust Rules

149. There are no other agencies who directly apply antitrust rules. Sometimes competition concerns are relevant to matters dealt with by other specialized bodies. In these cases, as noted, the Commissioner may make representations to other boards and tribunals.[296] For example, the Commissioner has made submissions to the Canadian Radio-television and Telecommunications Commission and the Canadian International Trade Tribunal, as well as various provincial bodies.[297]

IV. Administrative Fines

150. AMPs are available exclusively for an abuse of dominance, or in respect of the civil deceptive marketing provisions. The Tribunal may impose AMPs following civil proceedings (courts award criminal fines, but pursuant to more stringent criminal procedures and standards of proof).

---

291. For an example of a submission made to a government panel see Commissioner of Competition, *Submission to the Policy Review Panel*, 11 Jan. 2008 http://www.competitionbureau.gc.ca/eic/site/cb-bc.nsf/eng/02555.html (27 Jun. 2014).
292. See Conformity Continuum, *supra* n. 280 at 5–6.
293. See Competition Bureau, *Pamphlets*, http://www.competitionbureau.gc.ca/eic/site/cb-bc.nsf/eng/h_00140.html (14 Feb. 2012); and Competition Bureau, *Publications*, http://www.competitionbureau.gc.ca/eic/site/cb-bc.nsf/eng/h_00139.html (18 Feb. 2013).
294. See Competition Bureau, *Public Consultations*, http://www.competitionbureau.gc.ca/eic/site/cb-bc.nsf/eng/h_00142.html (21 Sept. 2012).
295. *Competition Act*, *supra* n. 26 at s. 10(1)(c).
296. See *Ibid.* at ss 125 (dealing with federal boards) and 126 (dealing with provincial boards).
297. To access the Bureau's previous submissions see Competition Bureau, *Submissions and Studies*, http://www.competitionbureau.gc.ca/eic/site/cb-bc.nsf/eng/h_02800.html (27 Jun. 2014).

151. Violations of section 79 can result in AMPs of up to CAD 10 million for a first order and CAD 15 million for each subsequent order against the same party.[298] In determining whether to issue an AMP, the Tribunal must consider evidence related to all relevant factors. These factors include the effect of the impugned activity on competition in the relevant market; the gross revenue from sales affected by the practice; any actual or anticipated profits affected by the practice; the financial position of the person bearing the AMP; and the history of that person's compliance with the Act.

152. Recall that Part VII.1 of the Act deals with civil deceptive marketing practices. For this part of the Act, a court[299] can impose penalties of up to CAD 750,000 for a first violation committed by an individual and up to CAD 1 million for a subsequent violation. For corporations, a court can impose a CAD 10 million penalty for a first violation and CAD 15 million for subsequent violations.[300] The Act provides a number of aggravating and mitigating factors to consider in any decision to impose an AMP. Factors include the frequency and duration of the conduct, the materiality of the misleading representation, the likelihood of self-correction in the relevant geographic market, and the financial position of the person subject to the order.[301] AMPs for deceptive marketing existed prior to 2009; however, the 2009 amendments significantly increased the potential size of the AMPs.[302]

153. The Bureau's recent enforcement record under the Act has underscored its determination to seek the maximum AMPs for conduct involving false or misleading representations, particularly in the telecommunications context. For example, in June 2011, Bell Canada entered into a consent agreement with the Commissioner that required it to pay a CAD 10 million administrative monetary penalty for making false or misleading representations in its advertising regarding the prices consumers are required to pay for its home, internet, television, and wireless services.

154. The inclusion of AMPs in the Act is controversial, particularly in light of the 2009 amendments increasing their size and availability. The Act describes the purpose of AMPs as to promote conformity with the Act, rather than to punish offenders.[303] However, critics argue that such sizable fines, by their very size, are inherently punitive. Consequently, say critics, persons potentially subject to AMPs should enjoy the protection of the *Charter*. If the *Charter* does apply, AMPs may violate it in at least three ways. First, AMPs may violate the presumption of innocence because the Tribunal decides cases on a balance of probabilities, rather than by the criminal standard of proof beyond a reasonable doubt. Second, in criminal

298. *Competition Act*, *supra* n. 26 at s. 79(3.2).
299. The Act defines 'court' to include the Tribunal, the Federal Court or the superior court of a province (*Ibid*, at s. 74.09).
300. *Ibid*, at s. 74.1(1)(c).
301. See *ibid.*, at s. 74.1(5) for a complete list of mitigating and aggravating factors to be considered.
302. Bill C-10, *supra* n. 34 at s. 424. Prior to 2009, the amounts were CAD 50,000 for individuals (CAD 100,000 for a subsequent offence), and CAD 100,000 for corporations (CAD 200,000 for a subsequent offence).
303. *Competition Act*, *supra* n. 26 at ss 74.1(4) & 79(3.1).

proceedings the defendant has a right to silence and a right to full disclosure. The right to disclosure in cases before the Tribunal is more limited than in the criminal context, and there is no right to silence. Finally, some say that reviewable practices are overly vague in the sense that there is no clear standard on which companies can rely.[304]

155. In *Canada (Commissioner of Competition) v. Gestion Lebski Inc.* (*Gestion Lebski*),[305] the Tribunal addressed the constitutionality of AMPs in the context of misleading advertising. The Tribunal held that section 11 of the *Charter* did not apply because AMPs of that size – then a maximum of CAD 100,000 for an individual and CAD 200,000 for a corporation – were not criminal sanctions and did not lead to true penal consequences. Furthermore, the legislature solely intended AMPs to encourage compliance with the Act. However, the Tribunal rendered this decision before the significant increase to the size of the AMPs.[306] That said, the Federal Court of Appeal considered the issue in the context of proceedings against U.S. Steel alleging a violation of its undertakings under the *ICA* and seeking AMPs of CAD 10,000 per day under that statute. The Court agreed with the Tribunal on the legality of AMPs in that context.[307]

156. More recently, the Ontario Superior Court of Justice rejected a constitutional challenge to the AMPs available under Part VII.1 of the Act in respect of misleading advertising.[308] In November 2010, following a two-month investigation, the Bureau instituted legal proceedings against Rogers based on what it alleged was misleading advertising on the part of Rogers' Chatr discount cell phone and text service. The Commissioner sought an order against Rogers for the maximum AMP of CAD 10 million for an alleged contravention of subsection 74.01(1)(b) of the Act. Rogers argued that a CAD 10 million AMP was unconstitutional because penalties of that magnitude are essentially criminal fines, but under section 74.1 of the Act, they are awarded after a civil trial. In effect, this means that the various aspects of criminal procedure that protect defendants, such as requiring the Crown to prove its case beyond a reasonable doubt, are lacking under section 74.1 proceedings.[309] The Superior Court of Justice disagreed, finding that the AMPs provided for in section 74.1(1)(c) 'are not "true penal consequences"' and therefore do 'not engage s.11 of the Charter'.[310] Ultimately, the Court dismissed the Commissioner's claims of false advertising under paragraph 74.01(1)(a) of the Act against Rogers, but found that

304. These arguments were made by Peter Hogg in an appearance before the House of Commons regarding previous proposed amendments to the Act. See Parliament, Standing Committee on Industry, Natural Resources, Science and Technology, *Evidence*, No. 058 (25 Oct. 2005) (Peter Hogg).
305. 2006 Comp. Trib. 32 CT-2005-07.
306. Moreover, the Supreme Court has held that that only courts of competent jurisdiction can rule definitively on constitutional questions. Consequently, the decisions of administrative tribunals on constitutional issues only have effect with respect to the individual case being decided and do not establish a legally binding precedent.
307. *Canada (Attorney General) v. United States Steel Corp.*, 2011 FCA 176 [*U.S. Steel*].
308. *Canada (Competition Bureau) v. Chatr Wireless Inc.*, 2013 ONSC 5315 [*Chatr Wireless*].
309. See *Nova Scotia (Workers' Compensation Board) v. Martin; Nova Scotia (Workers' Compensation Board) v. Laseur* 2003 SCC 54, [2003] 2 SCR 504.
310. *Chatr Wireless*, *supra* n. 308 at paras. 556-58.

Rogers had violated paragraph 74.01(1)(b) by failing to conduct adequate and proper testing prior to making a performance claim to the public. The Court imposed an AMP of USD 500,000 against Rogers.[311]

V. Administrative Injunctions and Other Restrictive Orders

157. The ability of the Tribunal to issue prohibition or other restrictive orders varies based on the particular conduct being addressed. In all cases of reviewable conduct, the Tribunal can issue an order prohibiting particular acts or conduct. In some situations, the Tribunal enjoys broader authority to make other orders.

158. For instance, in the context of abuse of dominance, the Tribunal can order the divestiture of assets, or issue any other reasonable order that is necessary to overcome the effects of the conduct on the market. However, any order must minimally interfere with the rights of the person that it targets.[312] This limitation would prohibit the issuance of punitive orders.

159. In the context of mergers, the Tribunal also has some leeway to issue a broader range of orders. In the case of a completed merger, the Tribunal may order dissolution of the merger or the disposition of assets or shares. It may also grant any other order agreed upon by the Commissioner and the merging parties.[313] In the case of a proposed merger, the Tribunal may stop the merger in whole or in part or allow it to proceed subject to conditions. It may also grant any other order agreed upon by the Commissioner and implicated parties.[314]

160. For civil deceptive marketing, the Tribunal can order a party to publish a notice describing its reviewable conduct, the area affected by the conduct, and the steps taken to remedy the conduct.[315] Where the order pertains to a false and misleading representation, the Tribunal may order a party to compensate purchasers of the product in an amount not exceeding what they paid for the product.[316]

VI. Interim Measures

161. The Tribunal can grant injunctive relief under section 100, which deals with interim orders to prevent proposed mergers from closing when the Commissioner needs more time to complete his review; under section 103.3, which deals with interim orders to prohibit reviewable conduct where proceedings have not yet commenced; and under section 104, which deals with interim measures to prohibit reviewable conduct while proceedings are ongoing.

311. *Canada (Commissioner of Competition) v. Chatr Wireless Inc.*, 2014 ONSC 1146 at paras. 50-77.
312. *Competition Act*, *supra* n. 26 at s. 79(2)-(3).
313. *Ibid.*, at s. 92(1)(e).
314. *Ibid.*, at s. 92(1)(f).
315. *Ibid.*, at s. 74.1(b).
316. *Ibid.*, at s. 74.1(d).

162. Section 104 applies in the context of a formal application made under any provision in Part VIII of the Act (Matters Reviewable by Tribunal), other than an application for interim relief under either section 100 or 103.3. Under section 104, the Tribunal can make any order that it considers appropriate, 'having regard to the principles ordinarily considered by superior courts when granting interlocutory or injunctive relief'. The Supreme Court articulated the test for granting injunctive relief in *RJR-Macdonald Inc. v. Canada (Attorney General).*[317] To obtain an injunction, the applicant must show, first, that there is a serious issue to be tried; second, that the applicant would suffer irreparable harm if the injunction is not granted; and, third, that the balance of convenience favours granting the order.[318]

163. Both the Supreme Court and the Tribunal have said there is a low threshold for the first requirement – that there be a serious issue to be tried.[319] Generally, the applicant meets the requirement by satisfying the Tribunal that the issue is neither frivolous nor vexatious. The second element deals with the nature of the harm the applicant may suffer, rather than the magnitude of the harm. The harm is irreparable where it cannot be quantified or it cannot be remedied through monetary compensation. For example, if a failure to grant the injunction would put the applicant out of business, the applicant satisfies the second requirement.[320] If the injunction seeks to prevent threatened conduct (e.g., a potential merger), the harm can be inferred. However, the inference must follow from clear evidence that the harm will occur.[321] The final element deals with the issue of which of the parties would suffer the greater harm from the granting or refusal of the injunction.[322] If the Tribunal finds that applicant's situation satisfies the test, then the Tribunal has discretion to grant any order that it considers appropriate. Thus, there is quite a broad range of interim relief potentially available under section 104, once proceedings are commenced.

164. Section 100 applies if the Commissioner is investigating a proposed merger, but has not yet decided whether to challenge it under section 92 (consequently, section 104 cannot be invoked). The threshold for granting an injunctive order under section 100 is lower than that under section 104, however the order is limited to forbidding 'any person named in the application from doing any act or thing it appears to the Tribunal may constitute or be directed toward the completion or implementation of a proposed merger'. A section 100 injunctive order may be issued if the Commissioner certifies an inquiry is ongoing, more time is required to complete the inquiry, and if the Tribunal finds that, absent the order, an action would be taken that would substantially impair the ability of the Tribunal to remedy the

317. [1994] 1 S.C.R. 311 [*RJR Macdonald*].
318. *Ibid.*, at 340.
319. *Ibid.*, at 347–348; and *Nadeau Poultry Farm Ltd. v. Groupe Westco Inc.*, 2008 Comp. Trib. 16 CT-2008-004 at para. 17 [*Nadeau Poultry Farm* 2008].
320. *Nadeau Poultry Farm* 2008, *ibid.*, at 25.
321. *Ibid.*, at 26.
322. *RJR Macdonald, supra* n. 317 at 342.

effect of the proposed merger;[323] or if a party has failed to notify the Commissioner of a proposed transaction in accordance with the requirements of section 114. In *Canada (Commissioner of Competition) v. Labatt Breweries Co.*,[324] the Commissioner argued that an order should be granted on the basis of the first criterion that is to prevent a step that the Tribunal would not be able to remedy. The Commissioner argued that the proposed merger of two beer companies would be difficult to reverse once the transaction had closed. Notwithstanding this argument, the Tribunal held that the circumstances did not meet the requirement because even if the transaction closed the Tribunal would have sufficient remedies available to it under section 92 with respect to any potential lessening of competition.

165. When the Tribunal issues a section 100 injunctive order to provide the Commissioner with more time to complete her inquiry, the injunction lasts for up to thirty days.[325] When the Tribunal issues an injunctive order due to a failure to comply with section 114, the order lasts for up to thirty days from the time when compliance with section 114 begins, unless the Tribunal granted the order on an ex parte basis, in which case it will last for up to ten days from the time when compliance with section 114 begins.[326] In either case, the Tribunal may extend the duration of the order to a day not more than sixty days after it takes effect.[327]

166. In non-merger cases, section 103.3 permits the issuance of certain interim orders on an ex parte basis and without the requirement for formal proceedings to have commenced under the Act. Such interim orders can prevent the continuation of certain reviewable conduct including refusal to deal, price maintenance, exclusive dealing, tied selling, market restriction, abuse of dominance, delivered pricing and refusal to supply by a foreign supplier. Such orders can also prevent the implementation of foreign judgments, laws or directives in Canada. The Commissioner must swear that a formal inquiry has begun under section 10(b). The Tribunal must be satisfied as to the existence of one of several factors: first, injury to competition is likely to occur that cannot adequately be remedied by the Tribunal; second, a competitor faces likely elimination; or third, a person likely faces a significant loss of market share, a significant loss of revenue, or other harm that cannot be adequately remedied by the Tribunal.[328] Parliament added this section to the Act in 2002[329] and the courts have yet to interpret the changes. Orders issued under section 103.3 have an initial duration (on ex parte application) of up to ten days, but

---

323. In this case, the Commissioner must swear that a formal inquiry under s. 10(b) is underway, and that the Commissioner is of the opinion that more time is required to investigate.
324. 2007 Comp. Trib. 9 CT-2007-03, affirmed 2008 FCA 22, 64 C.P.R. (4th) 181.
325. *Competition Act*, *supra* n. 26 at s. 100(5).
326. *Ibid.*, at s. 100(6). Generally, s. 100 applications cannot be brought on an ex parte basis, as s. 100(2) requires that the commissioner provide forty-eight hours notice to each party against whom the order is sought. Section 100(3) provides an exception where the order is sought because of a failure to comply with s. 114, or when s. 100(2) either cannot be reasonably complied with, or the situation is urgent such that complying with it would not be in the public interest.
327. *Ibid.*, at s. 100(7).
328. *Ibid.*, at s. 103.3(2).
329. Bill C-23, *supra* n. 33 at s. 12.

may be extended (on notice to the parties) once or twice for additional periods of thirty-five days each.

§2. Civil Enforcement

167. There are several ways for individuals to enforce competition law through private actions. First, section 36 of the Act creates a private right of action for damages for parties who have been harmed by certain criminal conduct under Part VI of the Act (including conspiracy and bid rigging provisions), or by a defendant who has failed to comply with an order of the Tribunal or a court. Any such parties have standing to bring a claim pursuant to this section subject to a two-year limitation period.[330] However, an exception to the limitation period exists for situations where a defendant concealed the alleged conduct from the plaintiff, such that the plaintiff could only recently have discovered it.[331] The Act also seems to allow for the possibility that a limitation period might expire, but that criminal proceedings could subsequently commence and effectively restart the limitation period.

168. For a private civil action for damages to succeed, the wrongful conduct need not have resulted in a criminal conviction. However, proof of a conviction constitutes prima facie evidence that the defendant engaged in the conduct.[332] The plaintiff can access information from any public court proceedings, though it may not be possible to access information stemming from the Commissioner's inquiry. The Bureau has said that it is 'committed to treating confidential information responsibly and in accordance with the law' and that 'the general policy of the Bureau is one of minimizing the extent to which confidential information is communicated to other parties'.[333] The Bureau maintains the right to secrecy of the information based on section 29 of the Act. Section 29 precludes the disclosure of most information obtained during an inquiry except for 'the purposes of the administration or enforcement of this Act'. In at least one instance, the Commissioner allowed the disclosure of evidence for the purpose of section 36 proceedings. The Commissioner allowed disclosure on the basis that the civil proceedings served the purpose of administering and enforcing the Act and therefore the disclosure fell within the section 29 exception.[334]

169. In recent years, class action proceedings have become increasingly common under section 36. Provincial governments set the specific requirements for

330. *Competition Act, supra* n. 26 at s. 36(4). The two years begins to run either when the conduct was engaged in, or when the relevant court has disposed of the issue, whichever is later.
331. *Chadha v. Bayer Inc.*, [1998] O.J. No. 6419, 82 C.P.R. (3d) 202 (Gen. Div.), aff'd [2003] O.J. No. 27, 63 O.R. (3d) 22 (C.A.).
332. *Competition Act, supra* n. 26 at s. 36(2).
333. Competition Bureau, *Information Bulletin on the Communication of Confidential Information under the Competition Act,* 1 (Competition Bureau 2013).
334. See *Forest Protection Ltd. v. Bayer A.G.*, [1996] N.B.J. No. 238, 68 C.P.R. (3d) 59, 178 N.B.R. (2d) 129 (Q.B.).

class proceedings before provincial courts, but certification of a class action generally requires the plaintiff to demonstrate that class proceedings are the preferable procedure. A key issue has been developing a workable method for establishing factual harm on a class-wide basis.[335] The Supreme Court has made clear that individualized personal injury is necessary for compensation to be awarded.[336] Thus, while indirect purchasers can recover under section 36, it is practically difficult to demonstrate which purchasers along the distribution chain sustained damages. In some instances, this problem has led to courts refusing to certify class proceedings under section 36.[337]

170. In a recent landmark trilogy of cases,[338] the Supreme Court of Canada addressed the requirements for class certification of damages claims brought under section 36 of the *Act*. While holding that indirect purchasers can assert a cause of action based upon alleged price-fixing,[339] the Supreme Court noted that, in bringing their claims, indirect purchasers 'willingly assume the burden of establishing that they have suffered loss' from the impugned conduct, a task which is likely to require 'expert testimony and complex economic evidence'.[340]

171. The Supreme Court of Canada held that, at the certification stage, the plaintiffs' burden is to establish the commonality of loss-related issues for the class by demonstrating that sufficient proof is available, for use at trial, 'to prove antitrust impact common to all members of the class', which in an indirect purchaser action means an evidence in the form of a methodology capable of showing that 'overcharges have been passed on to the indirect-purchaser level in the distribution chain'.[341] To support class certification, the proposed methodology must 'offer a realistic prospect of establishing loss on a class-wide basis'; it must be 'grounded in the facts of the particular case in question' and there 'must be some evidence of the availability of the data to which the methodology is to be applied'.[342] In *Microsoft*,

335. K. Kay & E. Kolers, *2015 Competition Act and Commentary* 38 (D.J. Brown ed., Lexis Nexis Canada Inc. 2014).
336. *Bou Malhab v. Diffusion Metromedia CMR Inc.*, [2011] 1 S.C.R. 214.
337. See e.g., *Chadha v. Bayer Inc.*, [2003] O.J. No. 27, O.R. (3d) 22 (C.A.), additional reasons [2003] O.J. No. 1162, leave to appeal to S.C.C. denied [2003] S.C.C.A. No. 106, 65 O.R. (2d) xvii (S.C.C.).
338. *Pro-Sys Consultants Ltd. v. Microsoft Corporation*, 2013 SCC 57 [*Microsoft*], *Sun-Rype Products Ltd. v. Archer Daniels Midland Company*, 2013 SCC 58, and *Infineon Technologies AG v. Option Consommateurs*, 2013 SCC 59.
339. The Supreme Court also rejected the defendants' ability to raise a 'pass-on' defence against the claims of direct purchasers (*i.e.*, a defence that the direct purchasers suffered no loss because any overcharge they paid was passed on to their indirect purchaser customers). The Supreme Court recognized the potential for multiple recovery created by its decision (*i.e.*, that a defendant might be found liable to pay damages for the same overcharge several times (to both direct and indirect purchasers), the Court held that this could be avoided through sound judicial management, such that judges could deny indirect purchaser claims or modify damages awards based on evidence of damages awards made in parallel proceedings against the defendants, whether in the same court or in other jurisdictions. See *Microsoft*, *ibid*, at paras. 33-41.
340. *Ibid.*, at para. 45.
341. *Ibid.*, at para 115.
342. *Ibid.*, at paras 103 and 118.

the Supreme Court of Canada upheld the certification motion judge's determination that the plaintiffs had met the requirements for certification of the claims brought by indirect purchasers of Microsoft's software products on the facts of that case.

172. In recent years, there has been a notable upsurge in class action activity under section 36 of the Act, often following upon proceedings against the defendants brought by the Commissioner or in foreign jurisdictions. For example, in March 2011 a class action was brought against VISA and MasterCard, as well as the major Canadian banks by a representative plaintiff in British Columbia. The suit, which follows on the heels of the Commissioner's related application against VISA and MasterCard for the reviewable practice of price maintenance, alleges, among other things, that the defendants fixed, maintained, and controlled the Merchant Discount Fees charged to businesses who accept credit cards as payment.[343]

173. Aside from class action proceedings, private parties may seek relief on the basis of a common law tort action, an option often pursued in conjunction with an action under section 36. Potentially relevant torts include civil conspiracy; the unlawful means tort; and misrepresentation. Common law tort actions may also proceed as class actions.

174. Civil conspiracy actions can target persons who used unlawful means to reach a lawful end (conspiracy by unlawful means). Alternatively, civil conspiracy actions can target persons who used lawful or unlawful means to achieve an unlawful end (conspiracy to injure).[344] In a conspiracy by unlawful means action, the plaintiff must prove four elements on a balance of probabilities: first, that there was an agreement between two or more persons; second, that the defendant enacted the agreement by unlawful means that were directed, at least in part, at the plaintiff; third, that the defendants had actual or constructive knowledge that injury to the plaintiff would ensue;[345] and fourth, that the plaintiff suffered damage as a result.[346] In a conspiracy to injure action, the plaintiff must demonstrate three elements on a balance of probabilities: first, that there was an agreement between two or more persons; second, that the agreement's purpose was predominantly to injure the

343. In July 2013, the Tribunal dismissed the Commissioner's application against Visa and MasterCard, finding that the respondents had not violated section 76 of the Act. The Tribunal found that section 76 only prohibits price maintenance of products provided for resale, whereas Visa and MasterCard provided products ('Credit Card Network Services') to Acquirers (such as banks and financial payments processing companies) that were not resold by the Acquirers. See *Commissioner of Competition v. Visa Canada Corporation and MasterCard International Incorporated*, 2013 CACT 10 (CanLii) [*Visa*]. The class action proceeding continues at the time of writing.

344. See *Canada Cement LaFarge Ltd. v. British Columbia Lightweight Aggregate Ltd.*, [1983] 1 S.C.R. 452 at 454 [*Canada Cement*].

345. The British Columbia Court of Appeal has said that 'a constructive intent must constitute more than a greater than 50% chance that injury to the plaintiff will occur; it must amount to a clear expectation' (*Golden Capital Securities Ltd. v. Holmes* (2004), [2005] 1 W.W.R. 631 (B.C.C.A.) at 644, additional reasons at [2005] 8 W.W.R. 412 (B.C.C.A.)).

346. *Canada Cement*, *supra* n. 344 at 471.

plaintiff;[347] and third, that the plaintiff suffered damage as a result.[348] An agreement does not need to be a formal contract in either case. However, there 'must be intentional participation with a view to the furtherance of the common design and purpose'.[349]

175. In the case of *A.I. Enterprises Ltd. v. Bram Enterprises Ltd.*,[350] the Supreme Court of Canada provided some needed clarification on the scope of the unlawful means tort – which previously did not even have a settled nomenclature in Canada.[351] The Supreme Court established that the unlawful means tort has three elements: (1) the defendant must use unlawful means against a third party; (2) in so doing, the defendant must intend to cause harm to the plaintiff; and (3) the defendant must actually cause harm (economic loss) to the plaintiff. The Supreme Court of Canada held that, to constitute 'unlawful means', the defendants' conduct must be actionable (under statute or the common law) by the third party. The courts have held that a breach of the criminal provisions of the *Competition Act* (which can support a private right of action under section 36) constitutes 'unlawful means' for purposes of this tort.[352]

176. Finally, section 103.1 of the Act provides private parties with a limited right of access to the Tribunal if impugned conduct affects a person under section 75 (refusal to deal); under section 76 (resale price maintenance); or under section 77 (exclusive dealing, tied selling or market restriction). With leave from the Tribunal, the person can apply under one or more of these sections (but not in respect of abuse of dominance). For the Tribunal to grant leave in the case of section 75 or 77, applicants must show that their business is directly and substantially affected by the impugned practice. In the case of section 76, applicants must show that they are directly affected by the conduct.[353] In either context, it must be demonstrably clear that the alleged anti-competitive conduct could be subject to an order under the relevant section.[354] This requirement entails that on a leave application the Tribunal must consider all the elements applicable to the particular reviewable practice. However, the Court of Appeal has clarified that the applicant 'need only provide

347. Where there are a variety of potential ends to a particular course of action, if the defendant's predominant purpose was legitimate, there will not be a finding of conspiracy. See *Daishowa Inc. v. Friends of Lubicon* (1998), 158 D.L.R. (4th) 699 (Ont. Gen. Div.). See also Adam Fanaki and Erika Douglas, *Fundamentals of Canadian Competition Law 2015* 356 (J. Musgrove, J. Macneil & M. Osborne eds., Thomson Carswell 2015).
348. *Canada Cement*, *supra* n. 344 at 471.
349. *Culzean Inventions Ltd. v. Midwestern Broom Co.*, [1984] 3 W.W.R. 11 (Sask. Q.B.) at 40.
350. *A.I. Enterprises Ltd. v. Bram Enterprises Ltd.* 2014 SCC 12, [2014] 1 S.C.R. 177.
351. The tort had been variously referred to as 'unlawful interference with economic relations', 'interference with a trade or business by unlawful means', 'intentional interference with economic relations', or simply 'causing loss by unlawful means'.
352. See *Westfair Foods Ltd. v. Lippens Inc.*, [1989] M.J. No. 572, 64 D.L.R. (4th) 335 at 341, leave to appeal to S.C.C. refused, [1990] S.C.C.A. No. 17.
353. *Competition Act*, *supra* n. 26 at s. 103.1(7)-(7.1).
354. *National Capital News Canada v. Canada (House of Commons)*, [2002] C.C.T.D. No. 38, 23 C.P.R. (4th) 77 (Comp. Trib.), aff'd [2004] F.C.J. No. 38 (F.C.A.).

sufficient credible evidence of what is alleged to give rise to a bona fide belief by the Tribunal. This is a lower standard of proof than proof on a balance of probabilities, the standard applicable to the decision on the merits'.[355] If the Commissioner has already begun an inquiry or has settled the matter, the Tribunal will not grant leave.[356] The parties in a private action before the Tribunal are free to reach a consent agreement, which like consent agreements reached with the Commissioner are enforceable as orders of the Tribunal upon registration with the Tribunal.[357]

177. In a decision released on 4 March 2011, the Tribunal considered the test that parties must satisfy under section 103.1 before they will be permitted to bring applications before the Tribunal alleging refusal to deal. In *Brandon Gray Internet Services Inc. v. Canadian Internet Registration Authority*, the applicant, Brandon Gray, argued that the Canadian Internet Registration Authority (CIRA) had refused to re-certify its domain name and as a result of this non-certification, it was unable to register a '.ca' name for its clients.[358] The Tribunal, however, relying on the Federal Court of Appeal's test for leave under section 103.1[359] dismissed Brandon Gray's application for leave under section 75 on the basis that 'it has provided no evidence dealing with whether the alleged refusal to deal is likely to have an adverse effect on competition in a market pursuant to paragraph 75(1) of the Act'.[360]

178. In *Used Car Dealer's Association of Ontario v. Insurance Board of Canada*, however, the Tribunal granted the Used Car Dealer's Association (UCDA) leave to bring an application under section 75 of the Act, notwithstanding the argument by the Insurance Board of Canada (IBC) that UCDA had failed to provide sufficient evidence that it was 'substantially affected' in its business by the alleged refusal to deal.[361] In this case, the Tribunal concluded that the service which UCDA claimed was being negatively affected by IBC's refusal to deal represented more than 50% of its net income. This was sufficient to show a direct and substantial effect.[362]

179. In addition to the right to make an application under section 103.1, private parties can apply for leave to intervene in a proceeding before the Tribunal involving any reviewable practice except for deceptive marketing under Part VII.1 of the Act.[363] To be granted leave to intervene, an applicant must satisfy four conditions:

355. *Symbol Technologies Canada ULC v. Barcode Systems Inc.*, [2004] F.C.J. No. 1657, 2004 FCA 339 (F.C.A.) at para. 17. [*Symbol Technologies*].
356. *Competition Act, supra* n. 26 at s. 103.1(4).
357. *Ibid.*, at s. 106.1(1).
358. *Brandon Gray Internet Services Inc. v. Canadian Internet Registration Authority* (4 Mar. 2011) CT-2011-001. [*Brandon Gray*].
359. *Symbol Technologies, supra* n. 355.
360. *Brandon Gray, supra* n. 358 at para. 13.
361. *Used Car Dealers Association of Ontario v. Insurance Bureau of Canada* (9 Sep. 2011) CT-2011-06.
362. *Ibid.*, at para. 31.
363. *Competition Tribunal Act, supra* n. 27 at s. 9(3).

first, the matter allegedly affecting the applicant must be within the Tribunal's jurisdiction; second, the applicant must be directly affected by the conduct; third, representations by the applicant must be relevant to an issue raised by the Commissioner; and fourth, the applicant must bring a unique or distinct perspective that will assist the Tribunal in determining the issues before it.[364]

I. Competent Civil Courts

180. For an action under section 36, competent courts include any superior provincial court or the Federal Court of Canada.[365] Private tort actions can proceed in any competent provincial court. The Tribunal is the only body competent to hear private applications under the reviewable conduct provisions of the Act; however, the Federal Court of Appeal hears appeals from decisions of the Tribunal.[366]

II. Sanctions

A. *Nullity*

181. There are no nullity provisions in the Act. However, the doctrine of restraint of trade may render certain contractual provisions that restrain a person's ability to carry on business or trade unenforceable. A restraint on trade is contrary to public policy and prima facie unenforceable, unless it is reasonable as between the parties and with regard to the public interest.[367] The onus is on the party seeking to enforce the covenant to demonstrate the agreement's validity. There are two considerations under the restraint of trade doctrine. First, any restriction in an agreement cannot be overly broad, meaning it cannot restrain trade further than is necessary to protect the interests of the parties.[368] Second, the restriction must not be unreasonable 'in reference to the interests of the public as expressed in one or more propositions of law, rather than in reference to the interests of the public at large'.[369] A restriction that violates the *Competition Act* would thus be unreasonable with regard to the public interest and would therefore fulfil the second branch of the restraint of trade doctrine.

364. *Canada (Commissioner of Competition) v. United Grain Growers*, [2002] C.C.T.D. No. 18, 19 C.P.R. (4th) 157 (Comp. Trib.) [*United Grain Growers*].
365. *Competition Act*, *supra* n. 26 at s. 36(1) and (3).
366. *Competition Tribunal Act*, *supra* n. 27 at s. 13(1).
367. *Doerner v. Bliss & Laughlin Industries Inc.*, [1980] 2 S.C.R. 865, 54 C.P.R. (2d) 1, 117 D.L.R. (3d) 547, 34 N.R. 168.
368. *Tank Lining Corp. v. Dunlop Industries Ltd.* (1982), 40 O.R. (2d) 219 (Ont. CA), 225. See also Fanaki, *supra* n. 347 at 241.
369. *Stephens v. Gulf Oil Canada Ltd.* (1976), 11 O.R. (2d) 129 (Ont. C.A.) at para. 54, leave to appeal refused [1976] 1 S.C.R. xi.

B. Damages

182. Compensatory damages are the only remedy available to a plaintiff under section 36. The award may only consist of damages actually suffered. This class of damages includes any damage sustained by the plaintiff due to the defendant's conduct, and any additional costs the plaintiff incurred in investigating the misconduct or bringing the proceeding. A plaintiff cannot receive punitive damages under section 36.[370] However, if the plaintiff brings a tort action – either alone or in conjunction with the section 36 claim – then punitive damages are available if warranted.[371] Damages are not available in private actions brought before the Tribunal, but the Tribunal may award costs.[372]

C. Interim Measures

183. Interim measures are not available in private actions under section 36.[373] In private tort actions, though, the court may issue interim orders if the plaintiff satisfies three conditions: first, that there is a serious issue to be tried; second, that the applicant would suffer irreparable harm if the injunction is not granted; and third, that the balance of convenience favours granting the order.[374] The Tribunal may issue interim orders in accordance with section 104 of the Act in private applications before the Tribunal under section 75, section 76 or section 77 of the Act.[375]

§3. CRIMINAL ENFORCEMENT

184. Only relatively egregious violations of the Act invite criminal enforcement. Parts VI and VII of the Act contain all of the statute's criminal offences. The scope of these offences was wider prior to 2009, but Bill C-10 repealed the provisions criminalizing predatory pricing, price discrimination, and promotional allowances. Bill C-10 also converted resale price maintenance from a per se criminal offence to a civilly reviewable practice.[376] There is no limitation period for the prosecution of indictable offences under the Act, but for summary prosecutions there is a two-year limitation period.[377]

370. *Wong v. Sony of Canada Ltd.*, [2001] O.J. No. 1707, 9 C.P.C. (5th) 122 (S.C.J.).
371. The Supreme Court has said that punitive damages are an exceptional remedy, only available where compensatory damages are insufficient to achieve the objectives of retribution, deterrence or denunciation (see *Whiten v. Pilot*, [2002] 1 S.C.R. 595 at para. 94).
372. *Competition Tribunal Act*, *supra* n. 27 at s. 8.1.
373. *947101 Ontario Ltd. v. Barrhaven Town Centre Inc.*, [1995] O.J. No. 15, 121 D.L.R. (4th) 748, 17 B.L.R. (2d) 186 (Gen. Div.).
374. *RJR Macdonald*, *supra* n. 317 at 340. For a detailed discussion of these elements see 'Part 1: Chapter 5: §1. Administrative Enforcement: VI. Interim Measures.'
375. For a discussion of s. 104 see 'Part 1: Chapter 5: §1. Administrative Enforcement: VI. Interim Measures.'
376. Bill C-10, *supra* n. 34 at ss 413 and 417.
377. *Competition Act*, *supra* n. 26 at s. 67(6).

185. The Bureau usually undertakes the initial investigation of criminal conduct, as discussed previously. If the Commissioner has reason to believe that an offence has been committed or is about to be committed, the Commissioner refers the case to the DPP. A Memorandum of Understanding (MOU) outlines the responsibilities of both the Bureau and the DPP, which jointly publish the document.[378] Ultimate authority over the prosecution lies with the DPP, but in practice the Bureau remains heavily involved. The Bureau is responsible for referring evidence to the DPP and making recommendations concerning appropriate charges, sanctions, and grants of immunity or leniency.[379]

I. Criminal Sanctions for Antitrust Violations

186. Maximum punishments vary by offence. Criminal conspiracy under section 45 carries a maximum sentence of fourteen years imprisonment or a maximum fine of CAD 25 million, or both. Bid rigging under section 47 also carries a maximum sentence of fourteen years or a fine at the court's discretion, or both. Most other offences also provide for imprisonment, fines, or both; but for most offences the maximum fine does not exceed CAD 200,000. In many cases, offences are punishable by summary conviction or indictable conviction. If the DPP chooses to proceed by summary conviction, the maximum fines and prison sentences are lower.[380] Further, if convicted of 'integrity' offences, including criminal violations of the Act, an individual or company seeking to do business with the Canadian government, together with its affiliates, is subject to a 10-year debarment period under the federal government's procurement policies, whereby the individual or company is ineligible to do business with the federal government following a conviction or guilty plea with a conditional or absolute discharge.[381]

187. Besides imprisonment and fines, a court may grant an interim injunction or issue a prohibition order to prevent someone from doing anything constituting or directed toward the commission of a criminal offence under the Act. The Attorney General of Canada or the attorney general of a province can apply for an interim order under section 33 of the Act. A court may grant an injunction if it appears that competition will be injured in a way that cannot adequately be remedied under any other provision of the Act. For an offence under section 52.1 (telemarketing) or section 53 (deceptive notice of winning a prize), it is not necessary to show that the

378. Competition Bureau & Pub. Prosecution Serv. Can., *Memorandum of Understanding with Respect to the Conduct of Criminal Investigations and Prosecutions of Offences under the Competition Act, the Consumer Packaging and Labelling Act, the Textile Labelling Act and the Precious Metals Marking Act* (Competition Bureau & Pub. Prosecution Serv. Can. 2010) [MOU].

379. *Ibid.*, at para. 2.2.

380. Part VI offences punishable by indictable or summary conviction include s. 52 (false and misleading representations), s. 52.1 (deceptive telemarketing), s. 53 (deceptive notice of winning a prize), s. 55 (multi-level marketing schemes) and s. 55.1 (pyramid selling). Section 54 (double ticketing) is punishable by summary conviction only.

381. Government of Canada, Public Works and Government Services Canada, 'PWGSC's Integrity Framework' (25 Mar. 2015), online: http://www.tpsgc-pwgsc.gc.ca/ci-if/ci-if-eng.html.

injury cannot be remedied by another provision of the Act. A court can also grant an injunction upon finding that a person will suffer substantial damage that cannot be remedied by the Act (again this requirement does not apply for an offence under section 52.1 or 53). An injunction may also be granted to prevent damage that would be greater than the potential damage from the injunction if no subsequent offence were found. When a court grants an injunction, the Attorney General must 'proceed as expeditiously as possible to institute and conclude any prosecution or proceedings arising out of the actions on the basis of which the injunction was issued'.[382]

188. Prohibition orders can also be issued pursuant to section 34 of the Act to remedy criminal conduct either upon conviction or without an actual prosecution. Section 34(1) applies if a person has been convicted of an offence under Part VI of the Act. The prohibition order prevents such a person from repeating the offence or doing any other act or thing directed toward the continuation or repetition of the offence. The prohibition order can also include prescriptive terms requiring a person to take steps to prevent the commission or continuation of an offence. All prohibition orders last for ten years, unless the court specifies a shorter period.[383] A court can also vary or rescind an order either on consent, or if a court finds that circumstances have changed such that the order would not have been made or would be ineffective for its intended purpose.[384]

189. A court can issue a prohibition order under section 34(2) without a finding of guilt, if it 'appears' to the court that a person has done, is about to do, or is likely to do any act or thing constituting or directed toward the commission of an offence under Part VI of the Act. Once an order has been sought under section 34(2), however, criminal proceedings cannot commence against the person for substantially the same facts.[385] Invocation of the section is possible on a contested or uncontested basis (i.e., following negotiations between the DPP and the implicated party).

190. Under section 35, a court can order a person convicted under Part VI of the Act to disclose to the court any business transactions, operations or activities for up to three years.

191. Although the Bureau does not ultimately decide what remedies to apply, the DPP generally follows the Bureau's recommendations. In the Leniency Bulletin,[386] the Bureau describes its Leniency Program for cartel cases.[387,388]

382. *Competition Act*, *supra* n. 26 at s. 33(6).
383. *Ibid.*, at s. 34(2.2).
384. *Ibid.*, at s. 34(2.3).
385. *Ibid.*, at s. 34(2.4).
386. Leniency Bulletin (Competition Bureau 2010).
387. *Ibid.*, at 9.
388. *Ibid.*, at 9. See also *Criminal Code* (sections 718, 718.1, 718.2 and 718.21) and sentencing case law with respect to section 45 matters under the Act.

192. In determining the fine, the Bureau normally assesses the fine at 20% of the volume of commerce affected by the defendant's participation in the cartel.[389]

193. In the 2005 case of *R. v. Mitsubishi Corp.*, the court noted that fines imposed for major international cartel cases prosecuted under section 45 and related sections of the Act have ranged from CAD 70,000 to CAD 48 million.[390]

194. The Bureau has immunity and leniency programmes that may affect its recommendations regarding charges and sanctions.[391] Under certain conditions, the programmes allow individuals who come forward early in the process to receive more lenient sentencing recommendations or escape criminal prosecution in some cases.

195. Under the immunity programme, the Commissioner recommends immunity in two circumstances: first, where the Bureau is unaware of an offence and a party is the first to disclose it; second, where the Bureau is aware of an offence, and the party comes forward before there is enough evidence to warrant a referral of the matter to the DPP.[392] To receive immunity, the party must fully cooperate with the Bureau, must terminate its illegal activity, and must not have coerced other parties to participate in illegal activity. Furthermore, the party is under an ongoing obligation to cooperate with the Bureau throughout the investigation and at the party's own expense. This obligation implicitly requires the party to provide full, complete, frank and truthful disclosure of all non-privileged information, evidence and records in the party's possession, under its control or available to it. The party must also reveal any and all conduct of which it is aware, or becomes aware, that may constitute an offence under the Act.[393]

196. The leniency programme applies to cartel offences (i.e., conspiracy under section 45 and bid rigging under section 47). The programme allows for lenient treatment of parties who come forward subsequent to involvement with a cartel. To qualify for leniency the party must have terminated its involvement with the cartel, must cooperate with the Bureau in a timely manner and at the party's own expense, and must agree to plead guilty.[394] The first leniency applicant accepted to the programme typically receives a fine reduction of 50%.[395] If the applicant is a corporation, the Bureau usually recommends against separate charges for the applicant's current directors, officers or employees, provided these individuals cooperate with the investigation in a timely manner. If the applicant is an individual, the Bureau typically recommends against laying criminal charges if the individual is fully cooperative, provided that the individual is not a repeat offender, has not impeded the investigation, and has not coerced other participants into the cartel. Second leniency

389. *Ibid.*, at 9.
390. *R. v. Mitsubishi Corp.*, [2005] O.J. No. 2394 at para. 20.
391. See Immunity Program Bulletin, *supra* n. 277; and *ibid.*
392. Immunity Program Bulletin, supra n. 277, at 3.
393. *Ibid.*, at 4.
394. Leniency Program Bulletin, *supra* n. 278 at 8.
395. *Ibid.*

applicants can receive up to 30% reductions of their fines. Subsequent leniency applicants may receive reductions to their fines, but as a rule later leniency applicants will not receive greater reductions than earlier applicants.[396] If a party provides information disclosing further cartel activity, the party may qualify for 'Immunity Plus' status and a larger discount on its fine.[397]

II. Other Applications of Criminal Law to Relevant Conduct

197. The *Interpretation Act*[398] provides:

> All the provisions of the *Criminal Code* relating to indictable offences apply to indictable offences created by an enactment, and all the provisions of that Code relating to summary conviction offences apply to all other offences created by an enactment, except to the extent that the enactment otherwise provides.[399]

Consequently, the *Criminal Code* applies to offences under the Act provided there is no indication otherwise.

198. In Canada, the prosecution must prove criminal offences beyond a reasonable doubt. In addition, the *Charter* protects all persons charged with a criminal offence. The sentencing principles in Part XXIII of the *Criminal Code* apply to all sentencing decisions made by Canadian judges, including those made under the *Competition Act*. Also of note, as a law enforcement agency the Bureau can make use of the investigatory tools provided in sections 183–197 and section 487 of the *Criminal Code*.

199. The sections of the *Criminal Code* dealing with parties to an offence are particularly important. First, section 22.2 establishes that corporations are criminally liable where a senior official, acting with the intent to benefit the corporation: (i) is a party to an offence, while acting within the scope of his or her duties; (ii) has the mental state to commit the offence and, acting within the scope of his or her duties, directs others to do the act or make the omission specified in the offence; or (iii) know that a representative of the corporation is about to commit an offence, and does not take reasonable measures to stop the person from being a party to the offence. Section 21 of the *Criminal Code* establishes who is a party to an offence. Parties include anyone who commits the offence, aids or abets the commission of the offence, or forms a common intention to carry out an unlawful purpose and ought to have known the offence would be a probable consequence of carrying out the unlawful purpose. Section 22 of the *Criminal Code* provides that parties who counsel an offence are parties to the offence, even if the offence was carried out in a different way from what was counselled.

396. *Ibid.*, at 9.
397. *Ibid.*, at 10.
398. R.S.C. 1985, c. I-21.
399. *Ibid.*, at s. 34(2).

III. Role of Prosecutors

200. The DPP conducts all criminal enforcement of the *Competition Act*. The DPP heads the Public Prosecution Service of Canada, which is an independent federal organization that discharges the criminal law mandate of the Attorney General of Canada. The Commissioner may refer any situation to the DPP, or the Attorney General may independently commence a prosecution under the Act.[400] Although the ultimate authority to lay charges lies with the DPP, the Bureau works closely with the DPP during the investigation and prosecution process and makes recommendations regarding charges to the DPP.[401] The DPP has a reciprocal obligation to provide general and specific prosecutorial advice to the Commissioner during the investigatory process.[402]

201. In addition to laying charges and prosecuting the case, the DPP may negotiate with the accused to reach a plea settlement or to invoke a prohibition order under section 34(2). In practice, the DPP usually accepts the Commissioner's sentencing recommendations. A judge must approve any settlement, and the DPP's recommended sentence does not bind judges. However, it is well established that judges should not reject joint submissions except if they believe that the sentence is contrary to the public interest, or that it will bring the administration of justice into disrepute.[403]

IV. Competent Criminal Courts

202. Criminal offences under the Act can proceed to trial in any provincial superior court of criminal jurisdiction, or in the Federal Court if the proceedings are under Part VI or section 66 of the Act and by indictment.[404]

400. *Competition Act*, *supra* n. 26 at s. 23.
401. Conformity Continuum, *supra* n. 280 at 10.
402. MOU, *supra* n. 378 at para. 2.18.
403. *R. v. Cerasuolo* (2001), 151 C.C.C. (3d) 445, 140 O.A.C. 114, (Ont C.A.); *R. v. Steeves*, 2010 NBCA 57 (CanLii).
404. *Competition Act*, *supra* n. 26 at s. 73. Offences under ss 45–49 must be tried by indictment, whereas most other offences are hybrid offences, meaning they can be tried by summary or indictment.

Part II. Application of the Prohibitions

Chapter 1. Restrictive Agreements

203. Agreements between competitors can lead to enforcement proceedings on either the criminal track (sections 45–49) or the civil track (section 90.1). This dual-track option was introduced by Bill C-10 and came into effect in 2010. Before this measure, competitor agreements only garnered punishment if they were egregious enough to warrant criminal charges under section 45, or could be characterized as a joint abuse of dominance. It was difficult to secure convictions under section 45, however, because the charges required proof beyond a reasonable doubt that the agreement limited competition 'unduly'. The legislature eliminated this requirement in 2010, and the types of prohibited agreement narrowed. Today several types of agreements between competitors are per se illegal: price-fixing agreements, customer allocation agreements, and agreements to restrict the output of a product. All other agreements between competitors are subject to civil review under section 90.1 of the Act, and are only prohibited if they are 'likely to prevent or lessen, competition substantially in a market'.

204. The first sentence handed down under the amended section 45 occurred on 5 January 2012 when Domfoam International Inc. and Valle Foam Industries (1995) Inc. pled guilty to conspiracy under the Act for their participation in a polyurethane foam price-fixing cartel. The companies were fined a total of CAD 12.5 million.

205. With respect to section 90.1, the first case under this provision was brought in June 2011 against a joint venture between Air Canada and the United Continental Airlines.[405] It is unclear how the courts will assess specific practices under these sections. For criminal conduct, cases decided under the old section 45 may provide some guidance, particularly with regard to what constitutes an agreement.[406] The Bureau's CCGs[407] provide insight into the Bureau's intended approach to certain agreements with respect to the dual-track framework.[408]

---

405. The application was resolved without judicial determination by consent agreement dated 24 Oct. 2012.
406. For a discussion of how courts have interpreted 'agreement' see 'Part I: Chapter 4: §4. Agreements and Concerted Practices'.
407. CCGs, *supra* n. 199.
408. For an overview of agreements generally see 'Part I: Chapter 4: §4. Agreements and Concerted Practices'.

§1. HORIZONTAL AGREEMENTS

I. Cartels

206. Sections 45–49 create criminal offences related to cartel activity. The most important and widely-applicable of these provisions is section 45, which criminalizes all price-fixing agreements, customer allocation agreements and agreements to restrict the output of a product. Senior members of the Bureau have stated that these per se criminal provisions will apply only to the most egregious forms of cartel activity.[409] The other criminal sections of the Act deal with foreign directives (section 46), bid rigging (section 47), professional sports (section 48) and federal financial institutions (section 49).

A. *Price-Fixing*

207. Section 45(a) of the Act criminalizes any agreement between competitors 'to fix, maintain, increase or control the price for the supply of the product'. The Act defines 'price' broadly as including 'any discount, rebate, allowance, price concession or other advantage in relation to the supply of a product'.[410] The Bureau interprets this section to mean that any agreement by competitors to control any component of price violates the Act.[411] In the CCGs, the Bureau provides several examples of agreements that would violate section 45(a). These examples include:

- agreements to fix prices at a predetermined level;
- agreements to eliminate or reduce discounts;
- agreements to increase prices;
- agreements to reduce the rate or amount by which prices are lowered;
- agreements to eliminate or reduce promotional allowances and to eliminate or reduce price concessions or other price related advantages provided to customers;
- agreements to use a common price list in their negotiations with customers;
- agreements to apply specific price differentials between grades of products;
- agreements to apply a pricing formula or scale; and
- agreements to not sell products below cost.[412]

---

409. See e.g., Competition Bureau, *Remarks by Melanie L. Aitken, Commissioner of Competition: Remarks to the Economic Club of Canada*, http://www.competitionbureau.gc.ca/eic/site/cb-bc.nsf/eng/03246.html (14 May 2010) (… if an agreement among competitors does not constitute a naked agreement to fix prices, allocate markets, or restrict output, that agreement will be subject to – at most, and only – a separate, civil review requiring proof of economic harm.)
410. *Competition Act*, *supra* n. 26 at s. 45(8). Of note, this language appeared in the now-repealed prohibition against price discrimination under the old s. 50(1)(a) of the Act (repealed in 2009), and the cases under that section may be relevant.
411. CCGs, *supra* n. 199 at 10.
412. *Ibid.*, at 10.

As this list demonstrates, an illegal agreement need not actually establish a particular price for a product. To violate section 45(a), it is sufficient that an agreement between competitors establishes a method for setting a particular price.

208. While price-fixing is a per se offence, the Bureau has indicated that it will not find an agreement illegal on the sole basis that it would effectively raise prices. For example, agreements to implement new industry standards or new environmental protection measures will not be illegal, even if they result in increased product prices (so long as the increase is not agreed upon). Alternatively, if such agreements violate section 45(a) then the ancillary restraints defence would apply.[413] Consequently, the Bureau would not pursue a criminal investigation and at most would review the agreement under the civil track.

B. Market and Client Allocation

209. Section 45(b) of the Act criminalizes agreements between competitors to 'allocate sales, territories, customers or markets for the production or supply of the product'. In the CCGs, the Bureau explains that this section applies to any kind of market allocation agreement between competitors or potential competitors. Conduct that violates section 45(b) includes:

- an agreement between competitors to not compete with respect to specific customers, groups or types of customer, in certain regions or market segments, or in respect of certain types of transactions or products;
- an agreement to not compete with respect to direct sales to distributors, resellers or customers; or
- an agreement entered into by suppliers to not compete in respect of indirect sales that are made through distributors or resellers.

Dual-distribution arrangements between customers and suppliers are not subject to review under section 45. Rather, they are subject to review under section 90.1. This is because the Bureau does not consider a customer and a supplier to be competitors within the meaning of section 45, even if the supplier also competes with the customer with regard to the particular product.[414]

C. Limitation of Production and Innovation

210. Section 45(c) criminalizes agreements that 'fix, maintain, control, prevent, lessen or eliminate the production or supply of the product'. This section prohibits

---

413. *Ibid.*, at 12. The ancillary restraints defence is in s. 45(5) of the Act, and generally applies if the agreement is part a broader legal agreement, and is directly related to and reasonably necessary to give effect to the objective of the broader agreement.

414. *Ibid.*

any output agreements between competitors. Again, the Bureau provides examples of conduct that violates the section, including agreements between competitors:

- to limit the quantity or quality of products supplied;
- to reduce the quantity or quality of products supplied to specific customers or groups of customers;
- to limit increases in the quantity of products supplied by a set amount; or
- to discontinue supplying products to specific customers or groups of customers.[415]

Agreements related to the production and manufacturing of products may also violate the section. These could include agreements between competitors:

- to impose production quotas;
- to permanently or temporarily close manufacturing facilities;
- to reduce the quality of components used in a product; or
- to reduce the quantity or quality of products that are produced.[416]

Of note, section 45 does not prohibit agreements in respect of purchasing, which are actionable only if they substantially lessen or prevent competition under section 90.1.

D. Group Boycott

211. There are no criminal provisions that expressly address agreements to engage in group boycotts. Thus, group boycotts would not receive criminal punishment unless they fit within section 45. Boycotts are also civilly reviewable pursuant to section 90.1 if they substantially lessen or prevent competition.

E. Collusion on Other Objects

212. Section 47(2) of the Act makes bid rigging a per se criminal offence. Big rigging occurs in situations where there has been a 'call or request for bids or tenders'. Bid rigging involves an agreement whereby at least one party undertakes to not submit a bid or to withdraw a bid, or whereby two or more parties arrive at their bids by arrangement or agreement.[417] In each case, the practice is bid rigging unless the person who made the call for bids or tenders has been made aware of the agreement at or before the time when the tender was submitted or withdrawn. Because

415. *Ibid.*, at 12.
416. *Ibid.*
417. *Competition Act, supra* n. 26 at s. 47(1).

bid rigging is a per se offence it is unnecessary to prove any lessening of competition, and the effect of the agreement on competition is irrelevant.[418] A conviction requires an express agreement or arrangement between the implicated parties; it is insufficient for the parties to have a pre-existing business relationship that enables them to estimate each other's bids.[419]

213. Section 48 of the Act applies to conspiracies related to professional sports. It is an offence for any person to conspire, combine, agree or arrange with any other person, first, to limit unreasonably the ability of a person to participate in a professional sport, or to impose unreasonable terms or conditions on participants; or, second, to limit unreasonably the opportunity for a person to negotiate with, and if an agreement is reached, play for the team of his choice in a professional league.[420] When assessing an agreement under this section, courts must consider the desirability of maintaining a reasonable balance among teams in the same league, and whether limitations are legitimate in Canada because the sport is organized internationally.[421] This section has received very little judicial interpretation. In *Yashin v. National Hockey League*,[422] the court addressed the section in the context of an arbitration decision forcing a professional hockey player to fulfil his contract in order to attain free-agent status pursuant to a collective bargaining agreement. The judge found no violation of section 48(1), noting that section 4(1) exempts collective bargaining activities from review under the Act, and that collective bargaining agreements entered into by trade unions do not constitute illegal restraints on trade.

214. Section 49 establishes a per se prohibition against arrangements between federal financial institutions. Section 49 also establishes personal liability for institutions' directors, officers or employees for their role in any prohibited agreement made on behalf of their institution. Illegal agreements include agreements regarding interest rates on deposits, interest and charge rates on loans, charges on services, the

418. See *R v. Charterways Transportation Ltd.* (1981), 32 O.R. (2d) 719 (Ont. H.C.); and *R v. Coastal Glass & Aluminum Ltd.* (1986), 27 C.C.C. (3d) 289 (B.C.C.A.).

419. See *R v. McLellan Supply Ltd.* (1986), 69 A.R. 132 (sub nom. *R v. 215626 Alta. Ltd.*) 12 C.P.R. 53 (Q.B.) (the accused consulted with its supplier regarding pricing and appropriate mark-up on fencing and both parties went on to bid on the same tender, but they were acquitted for lack of an agreement). More recently, a jury in the Ontario Superior Court of Justice found nine defendants not guilty on 60 charges of bid-rigging and conspiracy to rig bids. Another individual was also acquitted in a directed verdict. The Bureau had commenced a criminal inquiry in 2006 into bid-rigging allegations against 14 individuals and seven companies, regarding allegations that the accused had coordinated their bids for certain information technology (IT) services contracts with the Canadian federal government (throughout the course of the proceedings, several individuals chose trial by judge alone, two individuals pled guilty, and the charges were dropped against one individual). Since the jury did not have to provide reasons, it is not clear what prompted their decision to acquit the nine defendants, however the reasons in the directed verdict are instructive, and provided that there was no evidence upon which a reasonable jury could return a verdict of guilty. The evidence demonstrated that the companies were working together to submit one large joint venture bid; however, due to changes to the request for proposal process during the relevant time period, such activities were entirely legal (see: *R v. Durward,* 2015 O.N.S.C. 1562).

420. *Competition Act*, *supra* n. 26 at s. 48(1).

421. *Ibid.*, at s. 48(2).

422. (2000), 192 D.L.R. (4th) 747 (Ont. S.C.J.).

amount or kind of loan made to customers or the person, or the class of persons eligible for services or loans. Section 49(2) provides several specific exceptions from the prohibition. To date, there have been no reported cases under this section.

215. Finally, section 46 of the Act deals with international cartels whose agreements may affect the Canadian marketplace. Section 46 prohibits corporations that do business in Canada from implementing any foreign directive that would effectuate an agreement or arrangement which would – had it been agreed to in Canada – have constituted a violation of section 45.[423]

II. Information Exchange Practices

216. In the context of criminal cartels, evidence of sharing competitively sensitive information may evince an agreement to commit one of the criminal practices under section 45. This has been the case in situations of conscious parallelism, where evidence of information sharing provides the additional factor necessary to find the existence of a tacit agreement.[424] Prior to 2010, this was the only context in which a finder of fact would consider information sharing between competitors. However, agreements to share information may now themselves be subject to civil review under section 90.1.

217. The Bureau does not subject an information sharing agreement to civil review unless the parties to the agreement have or are likely to have market power, or unless the relevant market is sufficiently concentrated to allow for the exercise of coordinated market power.[425] Problematic information includes information related to pricing, costs, trading terms, strategic plans or marketing strategies. The Bureau does not generally consider publicly available information to be sensitive. However, the Bureau would have concerns about an agreement between parties to publicly disclose competitively sensitive information, assuming the disclosure does not further a legitimate objective.[426] The Bureau is less concerned with information provided to a third party, especially if the information only appears publically in an aggregate form, such that the data do not identify with a particular business.[427]

---

423. See *R v. Mitsubishi* (2005), 40 C.P.R. (4th) 333 (Ont. S.C.J.) (the accused plead guilty to aiding and abetting a conspiracy contrary to s. 46 and was fined CAD 1 million on a joint submission after its representative was seconded to a subsidiary that implemented a conspiracy agreement); and *R v. UCAR Inc.* (1999) (sub. nom. *Canada v. UCAR Inc.)* 164 F.T.R. 85 (Fed. T.D.) (the accused pleaded guilty and was fined CAD 11 million on a joint submission following a five year conspiracy carried out on the directives of its international parent company).
424. See e.g., *Canadian General Electric, supra* n. 210.
425. CCGs, *supra* n. 199 at 28.
426. *Ibid.*, at 27.
427. *Ibid.*, at 28.

III. Cooperation Agreements

218. The Bureau assesses cooperation agreements under the new section 90.1. The section allows the Tribunal to issue prohibition orders if 'an agreement or arrangement – whether existing or proposed – between persons two or more of whom are competitors prevents or lessens, or is likely to prevent or lessen, competition substantially in a market'. The CCGs provide guidance on the Bureau's approach to specific types of arrangements.[428]

219. Non-compete clauses arise in various contexts (most often the sale of a business). The Bureau considers non-compete clauses to determine if they substantially lessen or prevent competition in a particular market. This analysis entails asking whether the agreement is reasonably necessary to the agreement as a whole, with regard to the scope of the clause, its duration, and the parties and products affected.[429]

A. Research and Development

220. Like any agreement under section 90.1, research and development agreements are problematic if they substantially prevent or lessen competition in a market. In determining whether an agreement lessens competition, the Bureau first considers whether the parties are competitors with regard to the product that is the subject of the agreement. This point turns on whether the parties could have independently developed the product. If the parties could not have developed the product independently, the Bureau does not view the parties as competitors and will not challenge the agreement. Where the parties could have developed the products independently, the Bureau views the parties as competitors and the analysis proceeds to other factors.[430]

221. Next, the Bureau considers whether the agreement involves joint exploitation. The Bureau is less likely to challenge agreements dealing exclusively with research and development and not involving any element of joint exploitation. These agreements are only likely to lessen competition in situations where there is an unnecessary disclosure of competitively sensitive information; or if the agreement imposes unnecessary restrictions on innovation that would not otherwise exist; or if the parties would likely develop competing products absent the agreement.[431]

222. Where the agreement involves joint exploitation of the product, the Bureau next considers two main factors: the market power of the parties; and whether the restrictions in the agreement are reasonably necessary. If the parties do not hold

---

428. For a general discussion of the Bureau's approach to s. 90.1 see 'Part I: Chapter 4: §4. Agreements and Concerted Practices'.
429. CCGs, *supra* n. 199 at 36.
430. *Ibid.*, at 28–29.
431. *Ibid.*, at 29–30.

market power and are unlikely to hold market power in the future, the agreement will not substantially lessen competition. In situations where the agreement relates to improving an existing product, the product typically has a defined market. Yet in situations where the agreement involves a completely new product, the Bureau attempts to identify competitive substitutes to define the market. Next, the Bureau considers whether restrictions in the agreement are reasonably necessary with regard to time and scope. Generally, the Bureau deems restrictions unreasonable if they limit output levels, or limit research and development on products or fields outside the agreement.[432]

B. Specialization

223. Sections 85–90 of the Act address specialization agreements. These provisions establish a regime whereby parties can register specialization agreements with the Tribunal. Registration exempts parties from prosecution or review under sections 45 and 77 (as it applies to exclusive dealing) and 90.1 with regard to the contents of the agreement.[433] Although these sections of the Act are not new, there has never actually been a specialization agreement registered under the Act.

224. As defined in section 85 of the Act, a specialization agreement exists if, first, each party agrees to discontinue producing an article or service on the condition that the other parties discontinue selling or producing an article or service; and, second, the parties agree to exclusively buy from each other the articles and services named in the agreement. Prior to registering such an agreement, the Tribunal applies a balancing test. To pass, the agreement must be likely to lead to gains in efficiency that would be improbable absent the agreement. These gains must exceed – and thereby offset – the effects of any lessening of competition that results or is likely to result from the agreement.[434] As well, it must not be the case that any party attempted to coerce any other person to become a party to the agreement.

225. It is unclear how the Tribunal would apply this test in practice, but the Act indicates that the Tribunal must consider the impact of the agreement on imports and exports. Specifically, section 86(2)(a) seems to indicate that the Tribunal must consider whether the monetary value of Canadian exports will increase as a result of the agreement. Section 86(2)(b) seems to refer to the ability of Canadian suppliers to better compete against foreign imports.[435] With respect to balancing efficiencies, the mere distribution of income from one party to another party does not constitute a gain in efficiency.[436]

432. *Ibid.*, at 30.
433. Section 86 of the Act provides for the registration of agreements, while s. 90 creates the exemption.
434. *Competition Act*, *supra* n. 26 at s. 86(1).
435. See O. Wakil, *The 2015 Annotated Competition Act* 234-5 (Thomson Reuters 2009).
436. *Competition Act*, *supra* n. 26 at s. 86(3).

226. If the Tribunal finds that an agreement meets all the requirements for registration but will result in a lack of substantial competition in the relevant market, the Tribunal may register the order on a conditional basis. Conditional registration means that the order will not take effect unless a certain event occurs. To effectuate the agreement, the parties may have to divest specific assets or to engage in wider licensing of patents or registered integrated circuit topographies. Conditions could also require the occurrence of an event outside of the parties' control, including a reduction in tariffs or the removal of import quotas or licensing requirements.[437]

C. Standardization

227. The Act does not specifically address standardization agreements, and the CCGs do not discuss them in any detail. The CCGs only mention standardization agreements in the context of price-fixing agreements under section 45(a). The CCGs clarify that the Bureau will not subject arrangements made to implement new industry standards to criminal investigation, even if the arrangements entail price increases. This policy is justified because standardization agreements are not price-fixing agreements or, in the alternative, the ancillary restraints defence applies.[438] However, like any other agreement between competitors, standardization agreements can give rise to civil review under section 90.1 and can invite prohibition orders if they cause a substantial lessening or prevention of competition.

D. Joint Production

228. When assessing a joint production agreement the Bureau focuses on whether the agreement effectively eliminates or reduces competition between suppliers. The Bureau considers the effects on both the downstream market (i.e., the market for the products produced by the parties to the agreement) and the upstream market (i.e., the market for the purchase of inputs to the parties' production process). An agreement can lessen competition if the parties are competitors in either the upstream or the downstream market. If the parties are competitors, the Bureau first focuses on whether the agreement reduces the parties' ability or incentive to compete independently in the downstream market. Problematic agreements may include agreements that restrain production quantities, set prices, allocate customers, or align other competitively significant aspects of the parties' operations. Agreements may also reduce the parties' ability to compete effectively if the joint production agreement reflects a substantial percentage of the cost of production,

437. *Ibid.*, at s. 86(4). A third potential condition outside the parties' control is 'the making of an order in council under s. 23 of the *Financial Administration Act* effecting a remission or remissions specified in the order of the Tribunal of any customs duties on an article that is a subject of the agreement' (*ibid.*, s. 86(4)(d)).

438. CCGs, *supra* n. 199 at 9–10.

such that the parties will lose the ability to effectively compete on price. This inability to compete on prices could also arise if the parties agree to share key production facilities and consequently lose their control over assets that influence prices.[439]

229. Finally, the Bureau considers market power. Without collective market power, the parties cannot substantially lessen competition. The Bureau assesses market power both in relation to the upstream and downstream markets. If the agreement relates to an intermediate good – that is, one part of the final product – the Bureau considers whether competition will diminish with regard to the final product. The Bureau is unlikely to challenge the agreement if the intermediate product does not represent a significant proportion of the costs of the final product, and if the parties do not hold collective market power in the downstream market.[440]

E. Joint Purchasing

230. The Bureau recognizes that joint purchasing agreements can increase competition by allowing smaller companies to cooperate to achieve input costs comparable to those available to larger companies. Joint purchasing agreements cannot be subject to conspiracy provisions under section 45,[441] but they may be subject to civil orders under section 90.1 if they substantially lessen or prevent competition. In assessing the competitive effects of joint purchasing agreements, the Bureau primarily considers the impact on the upstream market (i.e., the market for the purchase of inputs to the production process).

231. A joint purchasing agreement lessens competition if it increases the monopsony or oligopsony power of the firms in the relevant purchasing market. The Bureau defines monopsony as existing where a single buyer:

> holds market power in the relevant purchasing market such that it has the ability to decrease the price of a relevant product below competitive levels with a corresponding reduction in the overall quantity of the input produced or supplied in a relevant market, or a corresponding diminishment in any other dimension of competition.[442]

Oligopsony exists if a coordinated group of buyers exercise market power, rather than a single buyer.

232. When assessing a joint purchasing agreement, the Bureau first considers whether a monopsony or oligopsony exists in the relevant purchasing market. The

439. *Ibid.*, at 31.
440. *Ibid.*, at 32.
441. *Ibid.*, at 11.
442. *Ibid.*, at 33.

Bureau conducts this analysis using a modified version of the hypothetical monopolist approach. In the context of a monopsony, the Bureau considers the substitutability of products from the perspective of the supplier, rather than from the perspective of the buyer. Generally, the Bureau does not challenge an agreement as monopsonistic if the upstream market share held by the parties is less than 35%. If the concern relates to oligopsony power, the Bureau usually does not challenge an agreement if, first, the market share of the four largest purchasing firms in the relevant upstream market is less than 65%; and if, second, the parties to the agreement each have less than a 10% market share. If the parties meet the thresholds and there are significant barriers to entry, the Bureau typically finds that the parties hold monopsony or oligopsony power.[443]

233. The fact that the firms hold monopsony or oligopsony power does not mean that a joint purchasing agreement will necessarily lessen or prevent competition. Relevant considerations include:

> i) whether supply is highly elastic; ii) whether the upstream supply of the input is characterized by a large number of sellers and low barriers to entry such that the normal selling price of a supplier is likely competitive; and iii) whether it seems likely that certain suppliers will exit the market in response to the anticipated price decrease or will scale back production.[444]

The Bureau also considers whether the exercise of market power will jeopardize a long-run source of supply; and whether costs will increase for parties in the downstream market following decreased input purchases.[445]

F. Joint-Selling

234. A joint-selling agreement is subject to criminal review under section 45 if, in substance, it is an agreement to restrain competition between the parties. Otherwise, joint-selling agreements are only reviewable under section 90.1. The Bureau assesses joint-selling and commercialization agreements in the same way.[446]

235. The Bureau considers several factors in determining whether a joint-selling or commercialization arrangement substantially prevents or lessens competition in a market. An agreement is most vulnerable to a finding of illegality where it 'restricts competition on key aspects of competitive rivalry between the participants'.[447] Restrictions on competition that relate to price are most likely to be

443. *Ibid.*, at 35.
444. *Ibid.*, at 35.
445. *Ibid.*
446. *Ibid.*, at 24–26.
447. *Ibid.*, at 25.

problematic (and criminal under section 45). If the rivalry between the parties centres on another component – like level of service or delivery terms – then restrictions related to these components could also be problematic under section 90.1.[448] Consequently, an assessment of an arrangement's validity necessitates identifying the key aspects of competitive rivalry between the parties. The Bureau can then determine the impact of the agreement on these aspects of the competitive relationship.

236. The Bureau also considers parties' ability to exercise independent discretion over key elements of the competitive rivalry, such as setting prices or other trade terms. In the case of a joint-selling agreement, this means considering whether the agreement allows the parties to sell outside of the agreement.[449] Furthermore, if the collaboration is independent from its participants it is less likely to be problematic. Factors that bear on independence include separate incorporation; participants' power to appoint the board of directors; managerial independence of the collaboration; members' power to obstruct competitively significant decisions; and the degree of competitors' control over the collaboration's actions. Finally, the Bureau considers whether sensitive business information passes between the parties, either directly or indirectly.[450]

§2. Vertical Agreements

237. No single section of the Act deals with vertical agreements in a general way. Rather, certain agreements are reviewable under section 77, which addresses exclusive dealing, market restriction and tied selling. Also, section 76 makes resale price maintenance civilly reviewable (until 2009 it was a per se criminal offence), but only if it has an adverse impact on competition (it is therefore covered in Chapter 2: Dominant Undertakings' Prohibited Practices). Some vertical agreements could also invite review under section 79, which deals with abuse of dominance.

238. Vertical agreements are unlikely to ever face prosecution under the criminal provisions of the Act. While it is possible for manufacturers and their distributors to compete in the same market (many manufacturers utilize 'dual distribution' channels, whereby they both sell directly to customers and sell through distributors), the Bureau does not generally consider them competitors within the meaning of section 45. Consequently, distribution agreements, as such, are unlikely to attract criminal prosecution.[451]

448. *Ibid.*, at 26.
449. *Ibid.*
450. *Ibid.*
451. *Ibid.*, at 11.

I. Distribution

A. *Exclusive Distributorship*

239. The Act does not explicitly prohibit or mark for review exclusive distributorship agreements even by dominant firms. Such arrangements are reviewable under each of sections 77 and 79, and may be prohibited if they lead (or are likely to lead) to a substantial lessening of competition.

B. *Exclusive Dealing*

240. Section 77 defines 'exclusive dealing' as:

(a) any practice whereby a supplier of a product, as a condition of supplying the product to a customer, requires that customer to
  (i) deal only or primarily in products supplied by or designated by the supplier or the supplier's nominee, or
  (ii) refrain from dealing in a specified class or kind of product except as supplied by the supplier or the nominee, and

(b) any practice whereby a supplier of a product induces a customer to meet a condition set out in subparagraph *(a)*(i) or (ii) by offering to supply the product to the customer on more favourable terms or conditions if the customer agrees to meet the condition set out in either of those subparagraphs[.][452]

For the Tribunal to issue an order prohibiting the agreement, it must find that:

> because [exclusive dealing] is engaged in by a major supplier of a product in a market or because it is widespread in a market, is likely to
>
> *(a)* impede entry into or expansion of a firm in a market,
> *(b)* impede introduction of a product into or expansion of sales of a product in a market, or
> *(c)* have any other exclusionary effect in a market,
>
> with the result that competition is or is likely to be lessened substantially[.][453]

The Tribunal can make an order prohibiting the agreement or 'containing any other requirement that, in its opinion, is necessary to restore or stimulate competition in relation to the product'.[454] Exclusive distributorship agreements are also reviewable under section 79 (abuse of dominance). For example, section 78(1)(h) defines an anti-competitive act, for the purposes of section 79, as 'requiring or inducing a supplier to sell only or primarily to certain customers, or to refrain from

452. *Competition Act*, *supra* n. 26 at s. 77(1).
453. *Ibid.*, at s. 77(2).
454. *Ibid.*, at s. 77(3).

selling to a competitor, with the object of preventing a competitor's entry into, or expansion in, a market'.[455] The issuance of a prohibition order or an AMP would require evidence that the agreement had or was likely to have or was having the 'effect of preventing or lessening competition substantially in a market'.[456]

241. To date, only two cases have proceeded to litigation before the Tribunal under section 77. The Tribunal also heard both cases under section 79 (abuse of dominance). In *NutraSweet*, the Tribunal addressed exclusive dealing in the context of an aspartame (an artificial sweetener) company, which allegedly practiced exclusive dealing pursuant to both (a) and (b).[457] The Nutra Sweet Company's (NSC) supply contracts featured clauses precluding customers from purchasing aspartame from other suppliers long after the expiry of the Canadian patents. The Director of Investigation and Research (who occupied the role now held by the Commissioner) argued that the mere existence of such a clause constituted exclusive dealing as per subsection (a). However, the Tribunal rejected this argument, holding that it would be necessary to show the NSC had required its customers to accept the clause as a condition of purchasing the aspartame. No evidence suggested that this had been the case, but contrary evidence suggested that at least some customers had requested an exclusive contract. Consequently, there was no exclusive dealing arrangement as per subsection (a) of the definition.

242. The NSC's contracts provided that customers would pay substantially less for aspartame if the customer placed the NSC's logo on its product's packaging. The practical result of the contracts was that any customer who did not accept the NSC as its exclusive supplier would pay substantially more for aspartame because the customer would be unable to feature the logo on its products. Consequently, the Tribunal found that this provision created more favourable terms that constituted exclusive dealing under subsection (b) of the Act.

243. More recently, the Tribunal and the Federal Court of Appeal addressed the meaning of 'exclusive dealing' (section 77) in *Canada Pipe*. The case involved a stocking distribution programme (SDP) whereby customers received significant rebates and discounts in return for stocking only cast iron products produced by Canada Pipe's Bibby Ste-Croix division (Bibby).[458] As in *NutraSweet*, the Tribunal found that the SDP constituted an exclusive dealing arrangement as per subsection (b).

244. The Act does not prohibit exclusive dealing arrangements on a per se basis. Instead, the Act enables the Tribunal to prohibit exclusive dealing arrangements in certain circumstances involving a major supplier or a widespread product. Specifically, exclusive dealing is problematic in a given market if it impedes new market

455. *Ibid.*, at s. 78(1)(h).
456. *Ibid.*, at s. 79(1)(c). For an overview of the elements of abuse of dominance see 'Part 1: Chapter 4: §6 Monopolization and Abuse of Dominance'.
457. *NutraSweet*, *supra* n. 189.
458. *Canada Pipe*, *supra* n. 226.

entrants or prevents a firm's expansion; if it impedes the introduction of new products or the expansion of sales; or if it has any other exclusionary effect whereby competition is or is likely to be lessened substantially.[459]

245. In *NutraSweet* and *Canada Pipe*, the Tribunal respectively concluded that the NSC and Bibby were major suppliers of the relevant product. In *NutraSweet*, the Tribunal explained that a company is a major supplier if its actions would 'have an appreciable or significant impact on the markets where it sells'.[460] This determination relies on the company's market share, financial strength, record of innovation, and other industry-relevant factors. The Tribunal easily concluded that the NSC was a major supplier on the basis that its market and production shares both exceeded 90%.[461] In *Canada Pipe*, the Tribunal found that Bibby was a major supplier because it had more than an 80% market share; it was the only supplier of the full line of all three relevant products; and it supplied all but one Canadian distributor.[462] Having found that the parties in each case were major suppliers, the Tribunal did not have to consider whether the practice was 'widespread in a market'. Such an analysis would be necessary if the company was not a major supplier.

246. Once the Tribunal either finds that the supplier in an exclusive dealing contract is a major supplier or that the practice is widespread, the analysis proceeds to the next phase. The next issue is whether 'competition is or is likely to be lessened substantially' because of the agreement. In *NutraSweet*, the Tribunal recognized the likelihood of a substantial lessening of competition; however, it did not engage in any analysis under section 77.[463] Rather, the Tribunal adopted the conclusions of its section 79 analysis. Recall that a section 79 analysis requires a determination of whether the anti-competitive conduct 'is having or is likely to have the effect of preventing or lessening competition substantially in a market'.[464]

247. The Tribunal adopted the same method in *Canada Pipe*. In this case, the Tribunal found it unlikely that competition would be lessened substantially based on its previous conclusions under section 79. However, the Federal Court of Appeal subsequently found that the Tribunal had erred in its section 79 analysis. Consequently, the court remitted the decision back to the Tribunal for reconsideration under both sections.[465] In its decision, the Federal Court of Appeal implied that,

459. *Competition Act*, *supra* n. 26 at s. 77(2). Of note, a 'prevention' of competition is not caught by s. 77, only by s. 79 (abuse of dominance).
460. *NutraSweet*, *supra* n. 189 at 55. The Tribunal adopted the definition from *Director of Investigation and Research v. Bombardier Ltd.* (1980), 53 C.P.R. (2d), 47 (R.T.P.C.).
461. *NutraSweet*, *ibid.*, at 55.
462. *Canada (Commissioner of Competition) v. Canada Pipe* (2005), 40 C.P.R. (4th) 453 at 541 (Comp. Trib.).
463. *NutraSweet*, *supra* n. 189 at 56.
464. *Competition Act*, *supra* n. 26 at s. 79(1)(d).
465. It was later settled on consent (see *Canada (Commissioner of Competition) v. CanadaPipe Co.*, 2007 CarswellNat 5896 (Comp. Trib.)) [*Canada Pipe* Consent Order]. For a discussion of lessening of competition in the context of abuse of dominance, including the Federal Court of Appeal's decision in *Canada Pipe*, see 'Part I: Chapter 4: §6. Monopolization and Abuse of Dominance'.

despite the strong similarity in the wording of sections 77 and 79, there may be differences in the appropriate way to assess the lessening of competition element in each context.[466] Thus, in a future case the Tribunal may re-evaluate the correct method for evaluating whether competition is, or is likely to be, lessened substantially in the context of section 77.

248. If the Tribunal finds that an exclusive dealing arrangement substantially lessens competition, it can issue an order prohibiting the arrangement and containing 'any other requirement that, in its opinion, is necessary to overcome the effects thereof in the market or to restore or stimulate competition in the market'.[467] However, the Tribunal does not issue an order if it finds that the exclusive dealing agreement is a temporary measure to facilitate entry by a new seller into the market.[468]

249. Also important, private parties can, with leave, bring cases to the Tribunal with respect to allegations surrounding exclusive dealing, as well as market restriction and resale price maintenance (see 'Selective Distribution (Market Restriction)' and 'Excessive/Unfair Pricing' respectively).

C. *Selective Distribution (Market Restriction)*

250. In addition to dealing with tied selling and exclusive dealing, section 77 addresses distribution agreements that impose geographic market restrictions. The Act defines 'market restriction' as 'any practice whereby a supplier of a product, as a condition of supplying the product to a customer, requires that customer to supply any product only in a defined market, or exacts a penalty of any kind from the customer if he supplies any product outside a defined market'.[469] For the Tribunal to issue an order prohibiting the agreement, it must find that:

> because [the market restriction] is engaged in by a major supplier of a product in a market or because it is widespread in a market, is likely to
>
> *(a)* impede entry into or expansion of a firm in a market,
> *(b)* impede introduction of a product into or expansion of sales of a product in a market, or
> *(c)* have any other exclusionary effect in a market,
>
> with the result that competition is or is likely to be lessened substantially[.][470]

466. *Canada Pipe*, *supra* n. 226 at 283. ('For the purposes of this appeal, I need not consider whether the differences in wording between para. 79(1)(*c*) and subsec. 77(2) might in particular cases properly yield substantively different results with respect to the substantial lessening of competition element.')
467. *Competition Act*, *supra* n. 26 at s. 77(2)(c).
468. *Ibid.*, at s. 77(4)(a).
469. *Ibid.*, at s. 77(1).
470. *Ibid.*, at s. 77(2).

This definition of market restriction could cover an agreement that prevented a distributor from selling the product outside of a particular geographic area. This definition could also cover an agreement that included a location clause requiring a distributor to sell exclusively from a specific location. The Tribunal can make an order prohibiting the agreement or 'containing any other requirement that, in its opinion, is necessary to restore or stimulate competition in relation to the product'.[471] The Tribunal does not make an order if it finds that the market restriction is a temporary measure to allow a new seller into the market.[472]

251. There have not yet been any cases dealing with market restriction. However, the test for market restriction is the same as for exclusive dealing and tied selling, so cases dealing with those practices offer insight into how the Tribunal will apply section 77 to cases of market restriction.[473]

D. Franchising

252. The Bureau does not regard franchisors and franchisees as competitors within the meaning of the section 45 criminal cartel provisions. Consequently, the Bureau does not subject franchising agreements to criminal review, except where an agreement is 'in fact, an agreement among franchisees to restrain competition among themselves'.[474]

253. The Bureau's position with respect to franchise agreements was supported by a 2012 decision of the Ontario Superior Court of Justice involving an action by Tim Hortons' franchisees where they alleged, among other things, breaches of the price maintenance and conspiracy provisions of the Act by the franchisor, Tim Hortons, and its partner in a joint venture. This case related to Tim Hortons' 'Always Fresh' conversion in which the franchisor began baking doughnuts off-site through a partnership with another company and then delivered the doughnuts flash frozen to franchisees for in-store completion of baking. The franchisees claimed that Tim Hortons' 'Always Fresh' conversion, which they were required to abide by pursuant to their supply agreements, was the result of price maintenance and a criminal conspiracy to fix prices at the expense of franchisees. The Court rejected all of the franchisees' claims, including the allegations pertaining to breaches of the *Competition Act*. The Court found that the franchisees undertook to be bound by Tim Hortons' supply arrangement when they agreed to the terms of the franchise agreement and thereby relinquished their status as independent business people. In effect, the Court held that the lack of autonomy under the circumstances was the result of 'legitimate

471. *Ibid.*, at s. 77(3).
472. *Ibid.*, at s. 77(4)(a).
473. See 'Part II: Chapter 1: §2. Vertical Agreements: I. Distribution: B. Exclusive Dealing' and 'Part II: Chapter 2: §2 Exclusionary Practices: II. Tying'. For relevant case law see *NutraSweet*, *supra* n. 189 (dealing with exclusive dealing); *Canada Pipe*, *supra* n. 226 (dealing with exclusive dealing); and *Tele-Direct*, *supra* n. 188 (dealing with tied-selling).
474. CCGs, *supra* n. 199 at 10.

agreements entered into by the plaintiffs and Tim Hortons for legitimate purposes'.[475]

254. Although the Tim Hortons case clearly established that certain parts of the Act do not apply to the relationship between franchisors and franchisees owing to the fact that they are not competitors of one another, this does not mean that all agreements between such parties are exempt from *Competition Act* scrutiny. Indeed, the Bureau has said that where franchisors and franchisees allocate markets and customers among themselves the agreements are reviewable under Part VIII of the Act.[476] This position entails the possibility of civil review under section 90.1 if the franchisor and franchisee are competitors or potential competitors, and if the agreement creates a substantial lessening of competition in the market.

255. The Bureau may also review certain practices within the context of franchise agreements as anti-competitive acts constituting abuses of dominance. Section 78 of the act lists a number of anti-competitive practices that, if they lead to a substantial lessening or prevention of competition, may be prohibited under section 79. Among these is the 'adoption of product specifications that are incompatible with products produced by any other person and are designed to prevent his entry into, or to eliminate him from, a market'.[477] An example of this practice would be a 'franchise agreement in which the product specifications given to the franchisee are delineated in such a way that only the franchisor or the franchisor's designate could possibly meet them'.[478]

II. Technology Licensing

256. Recent years have seen the development of a general consensus that competition law and intellectual property (IP) law do not serve antithetical purposes. Rather, both regimes share the core objective of promoting an efficient economy, innovation and consumer welfare.[479] The Bureau adopted this position in 2000 when it first published the Intellectual Property Enforcement Guidelines (IPEGs), and reconfirmed it in 2014 with the release of partially updated IPEGs.[480] Nonetheless, there is some opportunity for practical conflict between the two legal regimes. Competition law seeks to promote the efficient allocation of market resources,

475. *Fairview Donut Inc. v. The TDL Group Corp.*, 2012 ONSC 1252 (CanLii), at para 603, affirmed, 2012 ONCA 867 (CanLii).
476. CCGs, *supra* n. 199, at 10.
477. *Competition Act*, *supra* n. 26 at s. 78(1)(g).
478. Wakil, *supra* n. 439 at 214.
479. See S. Hutton & A. Stockwell, *North American Developments in the Interface Between Intellectual Property and Competition Law*, http://www.stikeman.com/en/pdf/IP_Competition_Interface_Paper.pdf (Oct. 2008).
480. Competition Bureau, *Intellectual Property Enforcement Guidelines* (Competition Bureau 2014). The updated IPEGs were released in September 2014 following the first phase of a two-phase consultation process, the second phase of which was ongoing as of Fall 2015: see *Competition Bureau Releases Updated Intellectual Property Enforcement Guidelines*, http://www.competitionbureau.gc.ca/eic/site/cb-bc.nsf/eng/03814.html (Sept. 2014).

whereas intellectual property rights (IPRs) allow firms to enforce the exclusive use of IPRs in an effort to encourage long-term development and investment in new technologies and intellectual products. In light of this tension, a report published by Industry Canada recognized the danger that:

> the traditional competition law emphasis on shorter-term allocative efficiency may result in enforcement activities that adversely impact the incentives to innovate and the long-term benefits to society that flow from the research and development activities which are fostered by the protection of IPRs.[481]

The IPEGs and the limited jurisprudence on the interaction between the two regimes indicate that the Bureau and the courts will take a conservative approach to limiting IPRs.

257. Canadian competition law can apply to intellectual property licensing through one of two routes. First, the general provisions of the Act can apply to licensing agreements if there is anti-competitive conduct that extends beyond the 'mere exercise' of IPRs. This conduct could include a criminal conspiracy or a reviewable practice such as exclusive dealing or abuse of dominance. Of note is the changed definition of the 'mere exercise' of an IPR in the Bureau's updated IPEGs by removing the reference to 'non-use' of IP from the type of conduct that constitutes the 'mere exercise' of an IPR. By removing 'non-use' from the definition, the Bureau has effectively opened the door to challenging practices involving non-use of an IPR under the general provisions of the Act. Second, section 32 is a unique feature of the Act that exists to deal specifically with IPRs where the mere exercise of the right unduly limits some aspect of competition. This section allows the Federal Court to make a broad range of orders, including an order voiding a licensing agreement, granting a license to a particular person, or even revoking a patent. However, in the more than seventy years that this provision has existed in Canada's competition legislation, the courts have never used it to grant an order. This is not surprising, given that licensing is considered to be 'something more' than the 'mere exercise' of the IPR holder's right to exclude; the licensing terms are therefore examined under the general provisions of the Act. In practice, there is little scope for the application of section 32. In the IPEGs, the Bureau establishes its analytical framework for dealing with agreements involving the exercise of IPRs.

258. In *Tele-Direct*, the Tribunal held that the mere exercise of an IPR to refuse to grant a license could not be an anti-competitive act for the purposes of section 79, but the terms associated with the grant of license could be.[482] The Bureau regards its typical analytical framework for assessing anti-competitive conduct as

481. R. Corley, N. Joneja & P. Narayanan, *The Interface Between Competition Law And Intellectual Property Law: Present Concerns And Future Challenges Facing Industry Canada* (Industry Canada 2007).

482. *Tele-Direct, supra* n. 188 at 32.

flexible enough to deal with IPRs.[483] Thus, the guidelines and jurisprudence that apply depend on the specific anti-competitive conduct.

259. Even absent identifiable anti-competitive conduct, the mere exercise of IPRs can raise a competition issue. In such a situation, the Bureau would refer the case to the Attorney General for an application under section 32. However, the IPEGs acknowledge that such a recommendation would only occur under very rare circumstances (e.g., refusal to license a patented technology or product).[484] To determine whether the 'mere exercise' of IPRs has lessened competition or created an undue restraint of trade, the Bureau undertakes a two-step analysis. First, the Bureau must find that competition has been adversely affected to a substantial degree in a market that is different or significantly larger than either the IP's subject matter or the IP's resultant product or service.[485] Satisfaction of this first element requires that the IPR holder dominates the relevant market and that other firms cannot compete effectively in the relevant market because of their inability to use the IP. Second, a remedy against the IPR holder cannot adversely alter the incentives to invest in research and development. This element is satisfied if the refusal to license stifled further innovation.[486]

260. For cases involving IPRs the Bureau takes its usual evaluative approach, but the IPEGs provide additional IP-specific factors that may influence the Bureau's analysis. When defining the relevant market the Bureau is likely to use one of three possible factors: first, the intangible knowledge or know how that constitutes the IP; second, the processes based on the IPRs; or third, the final or intermediate goods resulting from or incorporating the IP.[487] The Bureau assesses market power in the typical way, but the Bureau emphasizes ease of entry as a more important consideration than market concentration. Evidence of rapid technological change often alleviates competition concerns, as firms may innovate around or 'leap-frog' over the entrenched position.[488] In addition, the assessment of efficiencies is vital in the IP context, given that the purpose of IPRs is to 'foster dynamic efficiency and competition by facilitating the creation of valuable works or processes that result in long-term increases in product selection, quality, output and productivity'.[489]

261. Though IP licensing agreements are vertical agreements between a monopoly-holding licensor and a licensee, these vertical agreements can function as terms of larger horizontal agreements between competitors. Like any hardcore cartel activity, competitor agreements involving IPRs can attract criminal prosecution if they violate the price-fixing, market allocation or output restriction prohibitions of section 45. In *Apotex Inc. v. Eli Lilly and Company,*[490] the Federal Court of

483. IPEGs, *supra* n. 484 at 2.
484. *Ibid.*, at 13.
485. *Ibid.*
486. *Ibid.*
487. *Ibid.*, at 15.
488. *Ibid.*, at 16.
489. *Ibid.*, at 18.
490. 2005 FCA 361, 260 D.L.R. (4th) 202, 44 C.P.R. (4th) 1.

Appeal confirmed that 'when the effect of an assignment is to increase the assignee's market power by more than that inherent in the rights assigned, section 50 [of the *Patent Act*] does not preclude the possibility, as a matter of law, that the assignment unduly lessened competition'.[491] Although this judgment pertained to the old criminal cartel provision, presumably the principle endures that assignments and licenses of IPRs are subject to the Act generally.

262. Section 45 potentially catches agreements between competitors or between licensors and licensees. For example, the section may prohibit cross-licensing agreements that include a concurrent agreement not to compete in a particular territory. The section may also prohibit patent pooling agreements that include a concurrent agreement to fix prices for patent licensing. However, if these agreements are facially pro-competitive they should not attract review under section 45. In support of this point, the CCGs state that section 45 applies to 'naked restraints' only, meaning 'restraints that are not implemented in furtherance of a legitimate collaboration, strategic alliance or joint venture'.[492] Furthermore, the ancillary restraints defence applies if the agreement is part of a broader legal agreement and is directly related to and reasonably necessary to give effect to the objective of the broader agreement.[493] In the CCGs, the Bureau lists a number of agreements protected by the ancillary restraints defence, including '[a]n agreement among competitors to charge a common price in a blanket licence agreement for artistic works'.[494] However, until a court considers the ancillary restraints defence, it will remain unclear when the defence might excuse otherwise criminal conduct.

263. Several reviewable practice sections have already been litigated in the context of anti-competitive behaviour involving IPRs. Additional sections may eventually give rise to litigation. In *Director of Investigation and Research v. Warner Music Canada Ltd.*,[495] the Tribunal held that a refusal to license copyrights in sound recordings to a fledgling mail-order record club did not constitute a refusal to deal within the meaning of section 75 of the Act. The Director of Investigations and Research (as the Commissioner was then called) argued that the licenses of master recordings were the relevant product. Although these masters could constitute a product under other parts of the Act, the Tribunal held that they were not a product under section 75. For a refusal to deal to draw prohibition there must be 'ample supply' of the product. Given that IPRs are exclusive by their very nature, there cannot be 'ample supply' of them, and they cannot constitute products within the meaning of section 75.[496] Thus, *Warner Music* stands for the proposition that the mere refusal to grant IP licenses does not constitute a refusal to deal (but note that if such refusal to license were anti-competitive in other respects, it could be the subject of scrutiny under section 32 of the Act). It is unclear whether this proposition will be challenged by the Bureau in the future in light of the fact that according to the revised

491. *Ibid.*, at para. 4.
492. CCGs, *supra* n. 199 at 3.
493. *Competition Act*, *supra* n. 26 at s. 45(4).
494. CCGs, *supra* n. 199 at 12.
495. [1997] C.C.T.D. No. 53, 78 C.P.R. (3d) 321 (Comp. Trib.) [*Warner Music* cited to C.P.R.].
496. *Ibid.*, at 333.

IPEGs issued in 2014, non-use of an IPR no longer constitutes a 'mere exercise' of an IPR.

264. Section 76 of the Act applies to price maintenance. Price maintenance involves a supplier driving up a resale price, refusing to supply, or discriminating against a purchaser because of their resale price.[497] The Act prohibits price maintenance if it has or is likely to have an adverse effect on competition in a market. The Act explicitly provides that section 76 can apply in the context of IPRs.[498] Thus, a licensor of IPRs could invite review under this section like a distributor of any other product.[499]

265. Agreements involving IPRs could also give rise to review under section 77 of the Act, which addresses exclusive dealing, market restriction and tied selling. The practice of exclusive dealing requires or induces a customer to buy exclusively from one distributor. The practice of tied selling requires a customer to purchase another product or refrain from selling a particular brand of product in conjunction with the first product. In the context of IPRs, both these practices would represent examples of manufacturers trying to leverage their rights beyond the limits of the IPR regime.[500] Thus, prohibiting such anti-competitive agreements is wholly compatible with IP law. However, enforcement of the market restriction section could prove problematic since IPR holders may license or assign their rights, or any partial interest therein.[501]

266. Vertical IP licensing agreements can also create the opportunity for abuse of dominance. For a dominant firm, any conduct that is predatory, exclusionary or disciplinary could potentially attract review under section 79 (abuse of dominance). However, section 79(5) precludes a finding of abuse of dominance for:

> an act engaged in pursuant only to the exercise of any right or enjoyment of any interest derived under the *Copyright Act*, *Industrial Design Act*, *Integrated Circuit Topography Act*, *Patent Act*, *Trade-marks Act* or any other Act of Parliament pertaining to intellectual or industrial property is not an anti-competitive act.[502]

Hence, abuse of dominance does not interfere with the mere exercise of IPRs, which agrees with the Bureau's approach as articulated in the IPEGs.

497. *Competition Act*, *supra* n. 26 at s. 76(1).
498. *Ibid.*, at s. 76(3)(c).
499. For a discussion of price maintenance generally see 'Part II: Chapter 2: §1 Exploitive Practices: I. Excessive/Unfair Pricing'.
500. D.J. Brown & A. Stockwell, *2015 Competition Act and Commentary* 169 (D.J. Brown ed., Lexis Nexis Canada Inc. 2014).
501. See e.g., *Copyright Act*, R.S.C. 1985, c. C-42, s. 13(4): 'The owner of the copyright in any work may assign the right, either wholly or partially, and either generally or *subject to limitations relating to territory*, medium or sector of the market or other limitations relating to the scope of the assignment, and either for the whole term of the copyright or for any other part thereof, and may grant any interest in the right by licence … ' [emphasis added]; see also *ibid.*, 142.
502. *Competition Act*, *supra* n. 26 at s. 79(5).

267. The Tribunal addressed abuse of dominance in *Tele-Direct.* The Tribunal applied section 79(5), holding that a company was free to selectively refuse the right to license its trademark.[503] Here again, however, the issue of non-use of an IPR under the updated IPEGs may result in a challenge to the previous understanding of what actions (involving non-use of its IP) a company may be free to take without scrutiny. In *NutraSweet*, which dealt in part with patents, the Tribunal was less forgiving. It found that the NSC had abused its dominance by inducing customers to enter long-term contracts shortly before the NSC's Canadian patent on aspartame expired. These contracts effectively prolonged the exclusivity under the Canadian patent and precluded market entry by competitors or potential competitors.

268. A third notable case is *Canada (Director of Investigation and Research) v. Bank of Montreal.*[504] The case addressed joint dominance in the Interac electronic banking network and resulted in a consent resolution. Among other conditions, the order required that Interac grant a commercially reasonable software license to members and provide free and commercially reasonable trademark licenses to members upon request.

269. In March 2014, the Commissioner discontinued his inquiry into whether a Canadian pharmaceutical company, Alcon Canada Inc. (Alcon), had engaged in anti-competitive conduct contrary to the abuse of dominance provision. The Commissioner's inquiry was initiated in November 2012 to examine whether Alcon was dominant in a relevant market and, if so, whether it had, among other things, intentionally disrupted the supply of its prescription ocular anti-allergy drug, Patanol, as part of a strategy to switch patients to a second generation formulation of the drug, which was protected by patent until 2022, and hinder meaningful competition from generic drug companies. Following commencement of the Bureau's inquiry, Alcon voluntarily resumed supply of Patanol, thus alleviating the Bureau's competition concerns.[505] Although not explicitly mentioned in the 2014 IPEGs, this inquiry by the Bureau into Alcon's conduct may have been part of the reason for removing the reference to 'non-use' from what constitutes a 'mere exercise' of an IPR.

270. Finally, IPRs may have relevance under section 92 of the Act, in the context of mergers. The Act defines 'merger' as the 'acquisition or establishment … of control over or significant interest in the whole or a part of a business of a competitor, supplier, customer or other person'.[506] In certain circumstances, the acquisition, assignment or licensing of IPRs could constitute the acquisition of a significant interest, which would give rise to merger review. If the Tribunal finds that a merger or proposed merger prevents or lessens, or is likely to prevent or

503. *Tele-Direct, supra* n. 188 at 43.

504. (1996), 68 C.P.R. (3d) 527 (Comp. Trib.).

505. Competition Bureau, *Competition Bureau Statement Regarding the Inquiry into Alleged Anti-Competitive Conduct by Alcon Canada Inc.*(19 Mar. 2014), http://www.competitionbureau.gc.ca/eic/site/cb-bc.nsf/eng/03686.html.

506. *Competition Act, supra* n. 26 at s. 91.

lessen, competition substantially, it can make various orders, including an order for the divestiture of assets. Hence, the Tribunal could issue an order to divest IPRs.[507]

A. *Patent Licensing*

271. Patent rights are entirely statutory and exist by virtue of the *Patent Act.*[508] Agreements involving patent licensing elicit the same treatment as all other agreements involving IPRs, as discussed above.

B. *Trademark Licensing*

272. Trademark rights exist at common law (or civil law in Quebec) and by virtue of the *Trade-marks Act.*[509] The IPEGs recognize the existence of both these sets of rights.[510] Again, trademark licensing elicits the same treatment as all other agreements involving IPRs, as discussed above.

C. *Know-How and Trade Secret Licensing*

273. Rights related to know-how and trade secrets exist exclusively by virtue of common law and, in Quebec, civil law. Nonetheless, the Bureau treats them like statutorily protected forms of IP.[511] However, differences may arise where the Act specifically references statutory intellectual property. For example, section 32 would not apply to the licensing of trade secrets or know-how. Further, section 79(5) of the Act would not apply to trade secrets or know-how. Recall that section 79(5) precludes a finding of abuse of dominance for 'an act engaged in pursuant only to the exercise of any right or enjoyment of any interest derived under [a federal IP statute]'. For know-how and trade secrets, the practical effect of this distinction may be insignificant given that the IPEGs adopt the same general approach as that set out in section 79(5).

507. See e.g., *Southam, supra* n. 161.
508. R.S.C. 1985, c. P-4.
509. R.S.C. 1985, c. T-13.
510. IPEGs, *supra* n. 484 at 4.
511. *Ibid.*

Chapter 2. Dominant Undertakings' Prohibited Practices

274. Sections 78–79 of the Act make abuse of dominance a civilly reviewable practice. Where the Tribunal finds that there has been an abuse of dominance it can issue an order prohibiting the conduct or requiring a remedial measure. The Tribunal can also issue an administrative monetary penalty (AMP) of up to CAD 10 million for a first violation and CAD 15 million for subsequent violations.[512] To find an abuse of dominance under section 79(1), the Tribunal must find that: (a) one or more persons substantially or completely control, throughout Canada or any area thereof, a class or species of business; (b) the controlling person or persons have engaged in or are engaging in anti-competitive conduct; and (c) the conduct has had, is having, or is likely to have the effect of preventing or lessening competition substantially in a market.[513]

275. The types of behaviour that may be anti-competitive, within the meaning of section 79(1)(b), are not exhaustively defined in the Act. Section 78 sets out a number of behaviours that constitute 'anti-competitive acts', including:

(a) squeezing, by a vertically integrated supplier, of the margin available to an unintegrated customer who competes with the supplier, for the purpose of impeding or preventing the customer's entry into, or expansion in, a market;
(b) acquisition by a supplier of a customer who would otherwise be available to a competitor of the supplier, or acquisition by a customer of a supplier who would otherwise be available to a competitor of the customer, for the purpose of impeding or preventing the competitor's entry into, or eliminating the competitor from, a market;
(c) freight equalization on the plant of a competitor for the purpose of impeding or preventing the competitor's entry into, or eliminating the competitor from, a market;
(d) use of fighting brands introduced selectively on a temporary basis to discipline or eliminate a competitor;
(e) pre-emption of scarce facilities or resources required by a competitor for the operation of a business, with the object of withholding the facilities or resources from a market;
(f) buying up of products to prevent the erosion of existing price levels;
(g) adoption of product specifications that are incompatible with products produced by any other person and are designed to prevent his entry into, or to eliminate him from, a market;
(h) requiring or inducing a supplier to sell only or primarily to certain customers, or to refrain from selling to a competitor, with the object of preventing a competitor's entry into, or expansion in, a market; and

512. *Competition Act, supra* n. 26 at s. 79(3.1).
513. *Ibid.*, at s. 79(1). For a discussion of how these elements are applied generally see 'Part 1: Chapter 4: §6 Monopolization and Abuse of Dominance'.

(i) selling articles at a price lower than the acquisition cost for the purpose of disciplining or eliminating a competitor.[514]

As this list is non-exhaustive, anti-competitive behaviour can encompass a wide range of conduct, including conduct that is reviewable under other sections of the Act.[515] The Federal Court of Appeal has said that anti-competitive acts should be assessed with regard to their purpose.[516] An act has an anti-competitive purpose if it is intended to have a negative effect on a competitor that is predatory, exclusionary, or disciplinary.[517] Whether such conduct actually has an anti-competitive effect on the market, as applied to competitors, is a separate question.

276. The Bureau recognizes two types of abusive conduct: (i) exclusionary conduct designed to artificially raise a rival's costs and reduce the rival's revenues; and (ii) predatory conduct.[518] The purpose of exclusionary conduct is to make rivals less effective competitors and to eliminate them from the market. The anti-competitive behaviours listed in section 78 are primarily examples of exclusionary conduct. Predatory conduct deals with product pricing. It occurs when a firm artificially lowers its prices below a competitive level (i.e., the firm takes a loss from the low selling price), with the goal of disciplining, eliminating, or constraining competition such that the firm can later exercise market power by raising its prices.

277. In addition, there are a few other provisions in the Act that deal specifically with certain exploitive pricing practices. Prior to 2009, the Act contained per se criminal prohibitions on predatory pricing, price maintenance and price discrimination. The legislature repealed these criminal provisions in the face of controversy over competing policy goals. Price discrimination provisions were problematic because they were implemented to protect smaller business from higher supply prices. Yet the Act did not account for the fact that, in the context of large customers, lower prices are often the result of more efficient purchasing methods, and lower prices may also result from many other benign factors. Price discrimination is now actionable only if it satisfies all the elements of section 79 (although how charging different prices can be intended to exclude, discipline or predate against a rival has yet to be explained). The per se predatory pricing provisions similarly did not effectively account for the fact that, generally speaking, lower prices are pro-competitive and should be encouraged to enhance economic efficiency.[519] That said, the

514. *Competition Act, supra* n. 26 at s. 78(1).
515. *Laidlaw, supra* n. 190 at 336–339 (in which the Tribunal held that mergers could be considered under s. 79, despite that s. 91 deals with mergers).
516. *Canada Pipe, supra* n. 226 at 272.
517. *Ibid.*, at 272. See also *NutraSweet, supra* n. 189 at 34; and Abuse of Dominance Guidelines, *supra* n. 179 at 11.
518. *Ibid.*, at 20.
519. For discussion of the policy concerns stemming from the old criminal predatory pricing provisions see S. Hutton & M. Macdonald, *2015 Competition Act and Commentary* 89-91 (D.J. Brown ed., Lexis Nexis Canada Inc. 2014).

Commissioner's predatory pricing case against Air Canada predated the amendments but already was brought under abuse of dominance and not the criminal provisions.[520]

278. In addition to the anti-competitive conduct listed in section 78, the Tribunal has recognized a number of other behaviours as being anti-competitive. In *NutraSweet*, the Tribunal found that the NSC – a corporation with a 90% share of the aspartame supply market – had engaged in an abuse of dominance on the basis of several behaviours. Specifically, the NSC had granted exclusive supply contracts including meet-or-release and most favoured-nation-clauses;[521] and the NSC had issued significant rebates to its Canadian customers, which were facilitated by the NSC's dominant position in the United States due to its unexpired American patent. In addition, the Tribunal held that pricing below the cost of a manufactured product could be anti-competitive, though there was a lack of evidence to conclude that the NSC had actually engaged in predatory pricing in this case. The Director (as the Commissioner was then called) also argued that an alleged failure to properly file and pay appropriate Canadian income taxes constituted anti-competitive behaviour, as did a non-compete agreement between the NSC and a major international supplier of aspartame. The Tribunal rejected both these arguments (the latter, because the agreement did not harm the competitor and as such was not properly scrutinized as an abuse of dominance – it could well have been challenged as a conspiracy but the Director had not so alleged).[522]

279. Exclusivity formed the basis of the anti-competitive allegations in *Nielsen*.[523] Nielsen was the sole supplier of scanner-based market tracking services in Canada. The Tribunal found the company to have engaged in anti-competitive conduct based on several behaviours. Specifically, Nielsen provided better rates to induce customers to enter into exclusive contracts, and its contracts featured most-favoured-nation clauses to prevent customers from selling to other market tracking services.[524] Nielsen also staggered the expiry of its contracts in an attempt to preclude any potential competitors from acquiring sufficient data-sources to compete with it. The Director framed these behaviours as falling under section 78(1)(e) or (h), or as non-enumerated anti-competitive behaviour. The Tribunal accepted the practices as anti-competitive on the whole.

520. *Canada (Commissioner of Competition) v. Air Canada* (2003), 26 C.P.R. (4th) 476 (Comp. Trib.), 76 [*Air Canada*].

521. The Tribunal considered the contracts as a whole, without determining whether individual clauses would have been anti-competitive on their own.

522. *NutraSweet*, *supra* n. 189.

523. CT-94/01 [*Nielsen*].

524. Most-favoured-nation clauses require that a supplier sell to all purchasers on the same terms. In this case the clause would have ensured exclusivity because no other buyer would have been able to pay as much as Nielsen could (as the incumbent in a monopoly market), and no seller would wish to lower the price at which it was selling to Nielsen (see Trebilcock, *supra* n. 152 at 541).

280. In *Laidlaw*, the Tribunal again found abuse of dominance on the basis of several anti-competitive behaviours.[525] These behaviours included acquiring any new entrants in certain markets to gain monopolistic control and eliminate all competitors; threatening spurious litigation to prevent customers from switching to competitors; requiring customers to report competitor's bids, such that *Laidlaw* could always identify competitors and know their terms; and imposing exclusive contracts with significant liquidated damage clauses. Similarly, in a Consent Agreement involving commercial waste disposal, two firms agreed not to enforce similar contractual provisions which effectively precluded customers from switching suppliers.[526] In an ongoing case brought against Direct Energy Marketing Limited, the Commissioner has challenged Direct Energy's policies with respect to the rented water heaters as exclusionary conduct designed to impede customers from soliciting to competitors, allegedly in violation of section 79(1) of the *Act*.[527] A recent ruling by the Tribunal in this case confirmed that the Bureau can proceed with its allegations against Direct Energy, despite the fact that Direct Energy has not been active in the Ontario rental water heater industry since October 2014.[528]

281. In *Tele-Direct*, the Tribunal found that Tele-Direct had engaged in a number of anti-competitive practices, including discrimination and tied selling. However, the Tribunal rejected the argument that Tele-Direct engaged in anti-competitive conduct by aggressively targeting rivals in geographic areas where there was greater threat of competition. The Tribunal explained that targeting, 'in the sense of a differentiated response to competitors, is a competitive reaction'.[529]

§1. Exploitative Practices

I. Excessive/Unfair Pricing

282. The Act's abuse of dominance provisions do not explicitly recognize excessive or unfair prices as being anti-competitive, nor does the Act explicitly deal with excessive or unfair prices elsewhere. However, the Tribunal may review these behaviours under section 79 if they serve an anti-competitive purpose. To date, there have not been any reported cases that have considered excessive or unfair pricing as an abuse of dominance.

283. While the Act does not explicitly address excessive or unfair pricing, section 76 of the Act deals with price maintenance. Price maintenance occurs when a supplier or other person upwardly influences the sale price of a product. The legislature introduced section 76 in 2009, but a largely identical criminal section had

525. *Laidlaw, supra* n. 190.
526. CT-2010-005.
527. *The Commissioner of Competition v. Direct Energy Marketing Ltd.*, CT-2012-003.
528. *The Commissioner of Competition v. Direct Energy Marketing Ltd.*, 2015 Comp Trib 2.
529. *Tele-Direct, supra* n. 188 at 194.

previously existed. Thus, cases decided under the old criminal provision (the former section 61) should be useful in interpreting the new section 76.

284. Section 76 allows the Tribunal to issue a remedial order where a producer or supplier directly or indirectly coerces the distributor to maintain high sale prices or refuses to supply or otherwise discriminates against discounters on the basis of low sale prices. In particular, the Tribunal may issue a remedial order against a party if by agreement, threat, promise or any like means, the party influences upward or discourages the reduction of the price at which the person's customer (or any other person to whom the product comes for resale) supplies, offers to supply or advertises a product within Canada. The Tribunal may also issue an order if the party refuses to supply a product to or otherwise discriminates against any person or class of persons engaged in business in Canada because of the low pricing policy of that other person or class of persons.[530] In the above cases, the Tribunal must find that the conduct has had, is having, or is likely to have an adverse effect on competition in a market. The Tribunal can also issue a remedial order if it finds that someone has induced a supplier, whether within or outside Canada, as a condition of doing business with the supplier, to refuse to supply a product to a particular person or class of persons because of the low pricing policy of that person or class of persons.[531] Again, the conduct must have, or be likely to have, an adverse effect on competition in a market.

285. The first civil price maintenance case to be brought before the Competition Tribunal was filed by the Commissioner against Visa and MasterCard on 15 December 2010. In this application, the Commissioner alleged that Visa and MasterCard restrained competition in the market for credit card network services by imposing restrictions on merchants that limit their ability to decline certain credit cards with higher acceptance fees. The Commissioner has sought an order under section 76 of the Act prohibiting the credit card companies from entering into, enforcing or continuing agreements or arrangements that influence upward or discourage the reduction of the Card Acceptance Fees. On July 2013, the Tribunal dismissed the Commissioner's application, finding that the requirement of a 'resale' in section 76(a) was not met, because Visa and Mastercard did not sell products that were resold by others.[532]

286. The requirement of an adverse effect did not exist in the criminal provisions (which prohibited price maintenance on a per se basis until 2009). However, the Tribunal has interpreted the meaning of 'likely to have an adverse effect on competition in a market' in the context of section 75 (refusal to deal). In *Nadeau*

530. *Competition Act*, *supra* n. 26 at s. 76(1). In addition to producers and suppliers, these provisions also apply to anyone who 'extends credit by way of credit cards or is otherwise engaged in a business that relates to credit cards; or has the exclusive rights and privileges conferred by a patent, trade-mark, copyright, registered industrial design or registered integrated circuit topography' (s. 76(3)).

531. *Ibid.*, at s. 76(8).

532. *Visa*, *supra* n. 343.

Poultry Farm Ltd. v. Groupe Westco Inc.,[533] the Tribunal held that the phrase required a 'relative and comparative assessment of the market in two time frames, namely with the refusal to deal and without the refusal to deal'.[534] The Tribunal also explained that 'adverse' amounted to a lower standard than 'substantial' (which is used in several other sections of the Act, including abuse of dominance), and that 'likely' meant that the adverse effects must be probable.[535] The Tribunal then analysed the market to determine whether the refusal to deal created, enhanced or preserved the market power of the remaining participants of the market.[536] In *Visa*, the Tribunal adopted this test for purposes of section 76 of the *Act*, stating that its task was to 'compare the level of competitiveness of the market in the presence of the conduct with that which would exist in its absence' and that the comparison 'must be done with reference to actual effects in the past and present, as well as likely future effects'.[537]

287. As with the old criminal provisions, a person can be found to have engaged in prohibited price maintenance under section 76 based on influence exerted through an 'agreement, threat, promise or any like means'.[538] An agreement may be found where consensual pricing behaviour results in higher prices or prevents prices from falling. Examples of prohibited agreements found under the former section 61 include: a supplier's agreement to bear part of a dealer's advertising costs in exchange for the dealer advertising the supplier's goods at a minimum price set by the supplier;[539] an agreement preventing retailers from initiating any price reductions;[540] and an agreement to confer a 5% commission to a retailer in exchange for selling on certain terms, including price.[541]

288. The old criminal cases under section 61 defined a 'threat' as 'an urged course of action which carries with it some sanction or penalty if not carried out. It is a form of intimidation, fulmination, harassment or warning which carries with it some form of penalty'.[542] A threat can exist even without any explicit communication of potential consequences. This occurred in *Shell Canada*. The case involved a supplier suggesting that a retailer should increase its prices. The suggestion occurred in a situation where the retailer was dependent on the supplier and the supply contract could be easily terminated. The Tribunal held the suggestion to constitute a threat because a reasonable customer would fear retaliation.[543] Evidence

533. [2009] C.C.T.D. No. 6, 2009 Comp. Trib. 6 CT-2009-004 [*Nadeau Farms* 2009].
534. *Ibid.*, at para. 365.
535. *Ibid.*, at para. 369.
536. *Ibid.*, at para. 379.
537. *Visa, supra* n. 343 at para. 353.
538. *Competition Act, supra* n. 26 at s. 76(1)(a)(i).
539. *R v. Moffats Ltd.*, [1957] O.R. 93 (C.A.).
540. *R v. Sunoco Inc.*, [1986] O.J. No. 3043, 11 C.P.R. (3d) 557 (Dist. Ct.), var'd [1988] O.J. No. 2170, 28 C.P.R. (3d) 287 (Ont. C.A.).
541. *R v. Campbell*, [1964] O.J. No. 790, [1964] 2 O.R. 487 (C.A.).
542. *R v. Shell Canada Products Ltd.*, [1989] M.J. No. 305, 24 C.P.R. (3d) 501 at 507 (Q.B.) [*Shell Canada*].
543. *Ibid.*

that a retailer has sold below the supplier's price in the past, without retaliation, can constitute evidence that the retailer did not perceive itself as bound by the suggestion.[544] The meaning of 'any like means' is not completely clear, but it has been held to include a promise or offer.[545] Presumably, the phrase could encompass any attempt to upwardly influence resale prices through complicity, duress, inducement or some similar behaviour.[546]

289. If a supplier has provided a 'suggested selling price' or advertised a resale price, the Act establishes a presumption that the supplier has influenced price.[547] However, the Act provides that the presumption is rebuttable if the supplier has made it clear that there is no obligation on the retailer to sell at the suggested price.[548] In *Sony*, it was held that a list of suggested prices did not need to explicitly state that the pricing was not mandatory. The fact that retailers had been pricing below the suggested retail price for many years was sufficient to rebut the presumption of influence, as it showed that the retailers did not believe themselves to be bound by the price list.[549]

290. The Act provides a number of defences for someone who comes under review for price maintenance. A supplier may refuse to supply in certain limited circumstances including: (i) when the supplier uses a product as a 'loss leader', meaning the supplier uses the product for advertising purposes rather than making a profit;[550] (ii) when the supplier uses a product not to make a profit, but to attract customers in order to sell other products; (iii) when the distributor makes a practice of engaging in misleading advertising; or (iv) when the distributor makes a practice of not providing the level of service purchasers of the product might otherwise expect.[551] Furthermore, the section does not apply if the supplier (or other person subject to the order) and customer are principal and agent; mandator and mandatory; affiliated corporations; or directors, agents, mandatories, officers or employees of the same corporation, partnership or sole proprietorship, or an affiliated corporation partnership or sole proprietorship.[552]

291. Finally, sections 80–81 of the Act address delivered pricing. The Act defines 'delivered pricing' as a:

544. See *R v. Sony of Canada Ltd.* (1987), 16 C.P.R. (3d) 50 (Ont. Dist. Ct.) [*Sony*].
545. *R v. Royal Lepage Real Estate Services Ltd.* (1993), 12 Alta. L.R. (3d) 282, [1994] 1 W.W.R. 228, 50 C.P.R. (3d) 161, 105 D.L.R. (4th) 556, 143 A.R. 241 (Q.B.) (this case also held that the phrase 'any like means' was not overly vague to render it unconstitutional) [*Royal Lepage*].
546. See Hutton & Macdonald, *supra* n. 523 at 97-98.
547. *Competition Act*, *supra* n. 26 at s. 76(5-6).
548. *Ibid.*
549. *Sony*, *supra* n. 548.
550. Under the former s. 61 it was held that this element required evidence that the product was sold at or below cost (see *R v. H.D. Lee of Canada Ltd.* (1980), 57 C.P.R. (2d) 186 (Que. Ct. Sess. P.)).
551. *Competition Act*, *supra* n. 26 at s. 76(9).
552. *Ibid.*, at s. 76(4).

> practice of refusing a customer, or a person seeking to become a customer, delivery of an article at any place in which the supplier engages in a practice of making delivery of the article to any other of the supplier's customers on the same trade terms that would be available to the first-mentioned customer if his place of business were located in that place.[553]

Delivered pricing would normally arise in a situation where a supplier provides products on a base price system that includes the cost of transportation. The price offered to distributors in different locations should vary based on the transportation distance between the supplier and distributor. These sections preclude the supplier from charging a higher price to a distributor who is willing to take delivery at a closer location, and thus eliminate at least some of the transportation costs involved (i.e., the distributor cannot charge for unnecessary extra delivery costs). The provisions exist to prevent oligopolistic price coordination whereby sellers quote all buyers the same delivered prices, eliminating location advantages between sellers.[554]

292. If the Tribunal finds that 'delivered pricing is engaged in by a major supplier of an article in a market or is widespread in a market with the result that a customer, or a person seeking to become a customer, is denied an advantage that would otherwise be available to him in the market',[555] the Tribunal can make an order prohibiting any or all suppliers in a market from engaging in delivered pricing. The Act provides two defences to delivered pricing. First, the Tribunal will not make an order if the supplier cannot accommodate additional customers at the proposed location without significant capital investment.[556] Second, there is an exception where the distributor sells the product in association with the seller's trademark. In this second case, if the practice of delivered pricing is necessary to maintain a standard of quality in respect to the article then the Tribunal will not prohibit it.[557] For example, in the case of a perishable product it may be necessary for the seller to deliver the product in the seller's special refrigerated trucks. There have been no 'delivered pricing' cases to date.

II. Discrimination

293. Previously, discriminatory pricing was a criminal offence under the former sections 50–51 of the Act, but the legislature repealed these sections as part of the 2009 reforms. Egregious forms of discrimination that would previously have resulted in criminal prosecution will presumably now draw scrutiny as abuses of dominance. Discrimination may constitute an anti-competitive act reviewable under section 79 of the Act. Section 76 of the Act also provides for Tribunal review of

553. *Ibid.*, at s. 80(1).
554. Wakil, *supra* n. 439 at 227.
555. *Competition Act*, *supra* n. 26 at s. 81(1).
556. *Ibid.*, at s. 80(2).
557. *Ibid.*, at s. 80(3).

discrimination because of a person's low resale pricing policy (see discussion of resale price maintenance under 'Excessive/Unfair Pricing', above).

294. Discrimination, although not explicitly listed as an anti-competitive act in section 78, can constitute anti-competitive behaviour. For example, in *Tele-Direct* the Tribunal found that Tele-Direct had discriminated against customers who sought the services of consultants. The Tribunal identified several anti-competitive acts, including:

> [S]uspicious errors, last minute contact resulting in confusion for the advertiser about what must be done to have the new advertising run or resulting in missed deadlines, identifying errors or problems in the advertising that would not otherwise be a problem and informing customers that their orders might not be processed.[558]

Although Tele-Direct did not have to deal directly with consultants, it could not actively discriminate against consultants and customers who used consultants. However, the Tribunal rejected the Commissioner's argument that the company had discriminated in its treatment of advertising agents, finding that there was insufficient evidence to show that the alleged discrimination had led to a substantial lessening of competition. Agents still represented a majority of the market share, and there was no evidence that their market share was dropping.

295. As discussed above, section 76 prohibits a producer from engaging in price maintenance by refusing to supply or discriminating against a seller because of the seller's lower pricing policy. The former section 61 (which criminalized price maintenance) was originally applied to require the low pricing policy to be the sole and effective cause of the refusal to supply, but more recently it was held that a violation of the section could occur if the low pricing policy was one of a number of proximate causes.[559] No clear judicial interpretation of discrimination ever emerged under the former section 61, but presumably discriminatory behaviour under section 76 could include '[d]elays in filing orders, charging higher prices to discounters than to premium price distributors, refusing to grant widely available discounts or rebates to discounters, imposing different payment terms or the more strict enforcement of stated credit policies'.[560]

296. Subsection 76(8) attempts to prevent a situation where a premium-pricing distributor pressures its supplier to not supply a product to a lower pricing distributor. Section 76(8) allows the Tribunal to make a remedial order if:

> any person, by agreement, threat, promise or any like means, has induced a supplier, whether within or outside Canada, as a condition of doing business with the supplier, to refuse to supply a product to a particular person or class

558. *Tele-Direct*, *supra* n. 188 at 241–242.
559. *Royal Lepage*, *supra* n. 549.
560. Hutton & Macdonald, *supra* n. 523, 100.

> of persons because of the low pricing policy of that person or class of persons, and that the conduct of inducement has had, is having or is likely to have an adverse effect on competition in a market.

However, absent criminal enforcement or the possibility of an AMP under section 76, it is doubtful that this section will effectively prevent the pressure often exerted on suppliers by their distributors, 'although the spectre of criminal liability under section 45 for a supplier who 'aids and abets' a price-fixing cartel among its customers should still serve to limit this behaviour'.[561]

§2. Exclusionary Practices

I. Predation

297. Predatory pricing is reviewable as an abuse of dominance under section 79. The Bureau defines 'predatory pricing' as:

> deliberately setting prices to incur losses for a sufficiently long period of time to eliminate, discipline, or deter entry by a competitor, in the expectation that the firm will subsequently be able to recoup its losses by charging prices above the level that would have prevailed in the absence of the impugned conduct, with the effect that competition would be substantially lessened or prevented.[562]

Some of the anti-competitive behaviours listed under section 78 encompass elements of predatory pricing, but most relevant is section 78(i), which describes as anti-competitive the practice of 'selling articles at a price lower than the acquisition cost for the purpose of disciplining or eliminating a competitor'.[563] In *NutraSweet*, the Tribunal established that this provision applies only to the reselling of acquired products, as opposed to products manufactured by the firm that is allegedly engaged in the predatory pricing. However, in the same case the Tribunal established that pricing below the cost of manufacturing the product could constitute anti-competitive behaviour.

298. In determining whether a potentially predatory pricing practice is abusive, the Bureau engages in a two-stage analysis. First, it considers the market power and profitability of the firm. Second, it engages in a cost-revenue analysis to determine whether prices are below average avoidable costs.[564] The Bureau assesses the firm's market power using its typical method, as set out in the MEGs.[565] In the context of predation, a firm's ability to recoup its losses following the predatory pricing period

561. *Ibid.*
562. PPEGs, *supra* n. 229.
563. *Competition Act*, *supra* n. 26 at s. 78.
564. PPEGs, *supra* n. 229 at 7.
565. For a discussion of how market power is assessed see 'Part 1: Chapter 4: §6 Market Power/Dominant Position'.

is particularly indicative of market power.[566] When the Bureau considers whether there are barriers to entry that will prevent other firms from joining the market and providing competition, it considers the incumbent firm's reputation and incentives for engaging in aggressive, predatory post-entry behaviour. A belief by potential competitors that the incumbent firm will engage in aggressive predatory conduct can itself constitute a barrier to entry if the belief deters potential rivals from entering the market. Relevant considerations include whether the firm competes against a number of smaller firms in different geographic markets or against a succession of firms over time; whether an entrant's financing relies on outside sources or requires ongoing profitability; whether the firm has previously responded to new or potential entry in the market by pricing below cost; and whether potential rivals are aware of this behaviour and any adverse effects experienced by rivals as a result.[567] Finally, as with any assessment of market power, market share is an important consideration. If a firm's market share is below 35%, the Bureau is generally unconcerned about predatory pricing.

299. In addition to the market power assessment, during the first phase of analysis the Bureau considers the impact of the predatory pricing on the business of the complainant firm (i.e., the firm allegedly being injured by the predatory conduct). If the complainant's business has been, or would be, reduced to the point of unprofitability, there is a reasonable prospect that the complainant may be eliminated or that competition may be diminished if the complainant raised prices after being disciplined.[568] To determine the impact on the complainant's business the Bureau asks the complainant to submit financial statements showing information on earnings and operations segregated by relevant market. If the complainant alleges that they have been prevented from entering a particular market, the Bureau asks them to create a *pro forma* projection of profitability over the time the policy has been enacted.[569] Furthermore, the Bureau considers whether the complainant relies on outside or internal sources of financing; whether the plaintiff can compete during the period of price reductions with revenues from other markets; whether the complainant possesses the resources needed to become an effective competitor; whether the complainant enjoys financial strength relative to the firm implementing the pricing; and whether the firm initiating the pricing can support it with revenues from other markets.[570] Only if the Bureau finds that the predatory pricing is being enacted by a firm with market power – and that the effect will hurt the profitability of the complainant – does the Bureau proceed to the second stage of the analysis.

300. Stage two of the analysis consists of a price and cost comparison. The Bureau measures costs based on average avoidable costs.[571] The Bureau determines avoidable costs by calculating the amount of money that a company would have saved had it not been producing a particular product during a given period of time.

---

566. PPEGs, *supra* n. 229 at 7.
567. *Ibid.*, at 11.
568. *Ibid.*, at 12.
569. *Ibid.*, at 12.
570. *Ibid.*, at 12–13.
571. *Ibid.*, at 13.

In general, avoidable costs include 'the variable costs and the product-specific fixed costs that are not sunk'.[572] Calculating costs in this way avoids a potentially complicated situation where common costs need to be allocated between several different products. Although the calculation can be quite complicated, particularly where fixed costs change over a long pricing period, the Bureau generally calculates average avoidable costs by identifying all acquisition costs and other avoidable costs, including variable costs and product-specific fixed costs. If necessary, the Bureau subtracts any revenues (such as advertising allowances) to arrive at total avoidable costs. The Bureau then divides this number by the total quantity of product produced in the relevant market to arrive at the average avoidable cost.[573]

301. Basic principles of economic rationality dictate that a firm will not sell below the average avoidable cost unless it stands to benefit, such as by increasing market power to allow for higher long-term pricing. Thus, absent a reasonable business explanation for low pricing, the Bureau considers selling below the average avoidable cost to be predatory.[574] The decision to sell below cost must amount to a policy. This point means that sales need to be ongoing or repeated, and usually a one-time sale will be insufficient to constitute a policy.[575] To justify a below cost pricing policy, a firm must advance a credible or pro-competitive business explanation, unrelated to the dominant purpose, as to why the firm engaged in the conduct.[576] For example, a firm might sell below cost to get rid of perishable or outdated products, or to persuade customers to try a new product. In *Nielsen*, the Tribunal said that it can weigh the efficiency enhancements of business justifications against their anti-competitive effects.[577]

302. As with any abuse of dominance case, to invite review the anti-competitive conduct must threaten to prevent or lessen competition substantially. In the case of predatory pricing, the Bureau is particularly concerned with whether the firm will have increased market power as a result of the conduct, to the extent that the firm can then increase prices to make up for the low pricing.[578]

303. The Tribunal has addressed predatory pricing in the context of abuse of dominance on a few occasions. First, in *NutraSweet* it failed to find predatory pricing under section 78(i) because the NSC had not been selling below its acquisition costs. The Tribunal also failed to find predatory pricing with regard to the products manufactured by the NSC because the Director failed to evince sufficient evidence

---

572. *Air Canada*, *supra* n. 524.
573. PPEGs, *supra* n. 229 at 15 (see 14–15 for a detailed outline of how the 'average avoidable cost' is determined).
574. *Ibid.*, at 15.
575. See *R v. Hoffman La Roche Ltd.* (1980), 28 O.R. (2d) 164 (H.C.J.); affirmed 33 O.R. (2d) 694 (C.A.).
576. PPEGs, *supra* n. 229 at 17.
577. *Nielsen*, *supra* n. 527 at 262.
578. PPEGs, *supra* n. 229 at 19.

on this point.[579] In *Air Canada*, the Tribunal established the framework for calculating the average avoidable cost, but never actually decided the matter because the Commissioner withdrew the case due to subsequent changes in the marketplace.[580]

304. Another provision of section 78 deals with a slightly different form of predatory pricing. Subsection 78(c) applies to freight equalization, which occurs when a supplier charges differently located customers the same price for a product, despite that fact that there are significant transportation costs involved. Freight equalization can constitute predatory pricing where the firm is earning a smaller profit or losing money on the customers located further way, and is essentially engaging in price discrimination and undercutting prices at the expense of the firms located closer to the customers. In the context of freight equalization, the practice can stabilize a cartel by dividing the cartel's profits more evenly and allowing for more transparent pricing lists.

305. Enforcement action by the Commissioner shows that certain licensing practices may constitute an abuse of dominance where the effect of such practices is to exclude access to information that is a key input in the supply of specific services. In February 2010, the Bureau filed an application with the Competition Tribunal seeking an order under subsections 79(1) and (2) of the Act that the respondent, the Canadian Real Estate Association (CREA), and its members have used their control of the Multiple Listing Service (MLS) and related trademarks to impose exclusionary restrictions on their use and thus maintain substantial or complete control of the market for the supply of residential real estate brokerage services. The Commissioner's allegation was that the exclusionary restrictions stemming from control over the MLS were having the effect of lessening or preventing competition substantially in the market for residential real estate services in Canada. This case was settled in October 2010 when members of CREA ratified a consent agreement entered into with the Bureau, which required the association to loosen the rules applicable to the use of its trademarked MLS.

306. Another case involving real estate services is currently ongoing and involves an application by the Commissioner against the Toronto Real Estate Board (TREB) alleging abuse of dominance (see *supra*, note 237). In this case, the Commissioner has alleged that TREB controls access to detailed information about properties listed on the TREB MLS such as historical prices, comparables, etc. Members of TREB, however, are not permitted to provide their customers with direct access to the complete TREB MLS, or to disseminate the more detailed information to their customers via searchable websites. The Commissioner alleges that such rules effectively prevent on-line brokerages from competing in the Greater Toronto Area, as they do in other jurisdictions. TREB, in its reply to the Commissioner's application, argues that it is exercising a legitimate proprietary right in its copyrighted database, and therefore that its conduct is sanctioned under subsection 79(5) of the Act. TREB

579. *NutraSweet*, *supra* n. 189.
580. *Air Canada*, *supra* n. 524.

has also alleged that disclosing detailed property information could raise privacy concerns.

307. In April 2013, the Tribunal dismissed the Commissioner's application on the grounds that the party alleged to have engaged in anti-competitive acts, TREB, was not a competitor in the allegedly restrained market for real estate services, and therefore paragraphs 79(1)(a),(b) and (c) of the *Act* could not apply to TREB's conduct. Having so decided, the Tribunal did not analyse the effects of TREB's conduct. The Federal Court of Appeal reversed the Tribunal's decision in February 2014, finding that, as a matter of statutory interpretation, subsection 79(1) of the *Act* could apply to conduct of the parties which are not competitors in the allegedly restrained market. The Federal Court of Appeal referred the matter back to the Tribunal for reconsideration on merits. TREB's application for leave to appeal this decision was dismissed by the Supreme Court of Canada in July 2014. As of fall 2015, the case is scheduled to be reheard by the Tribunal.

II. Tying

308. Tied selling occurs when a supply firm either requires or induces a customer to purchase one product, usually on an exclusive basis, in order to purchase a second product. Tied selling may also occur when a supplier prevents a customer from using or distributing, in conjunction with the tying product, another product that is not a brand designated by the supplier.[581] Tied selling can be an anti-competitive practice constituting an abuse of dominance under section 79.[582] Section 77 of the Act also explicitly deals with the practice. Under section 77(2), tied selling is only prohibited if – because it is engaged in by a major supplier of a product in a market, or because it is widespread in a market – it is likely to impede entry into or expansion of a firm in a market, impede introduction of a product into or expansion of sales of a product in a market, or have any other exclusionary effect in a market, with the result that competition is or is likely to be lessened substantially.[583] The Commissioner can bring applications to the Tribunal under section 77, or a private person may do so if granted leave under section 103.1.

309. In *Tele-Direct*, the Tribunal established that tied selling requires the identification of two separate product markets.[584] That is, there must be independent demand for the purchase of each product on its own. If the cost of selling the products together would be less than the benefit of selling them separately it is acceptable to sell them together, and the Tribunal does not interfere.[585] Generally, the less the products complement one another, 'consumer demand for separate products will become stronger and the efficiency justification for tying arrangements will become

581. *Competition Act*, *supra* n. 26 at s. 77(1).
582. IPEGs, *supra* n. 484 at 26-27.
583. *Competition Act*, *supra* n. 26 at s. 77(2).
584. *Tele-Direct*, *supra* n. 188 at 119.
585. *Ibid.*, at 119–120.

weaker'.[586] However, as demonstrated by *Tele-Direct*, even the tying of complementary products can be anti-competitive. Particularly for section 79, it may also be important to consider the motivation behind the seller's decision to bundle the products.

310. In *Tele-Direct*, the Tribunal found that Tele-Direct had engaged in anti-competitive tied selling contrary to sections 77 and 79. Tele-Direct, which operated a telephone advertising directory, included advertising services as part of the purchase of advertising space on non-commissionable accounts. Thus, customers would essentially have to pay twice for advertising services if they chose to obtain such services independently from another source. The Tribunal found that this pricing policy operated as a powerful inducement for customers to purchase both services and space from Tele-Direct, and consequently it constituted tied selling. The Tribunal further concluded that competition had been substantially lessened in the relevant market, as more than 50% of the commissionable advertising market was not accessible to advertising agents because of the tying practice. The Tribunal issued an order prohibiting Tele-Direct from engaging in tied selling of the two products in certain markets.

311. Tied selling can also form part of a practice of anti-competitive acts for purposes of an abuse of dominance case under section 79 of the Act. For example, in its 2010 application against CREA, the Bureau alleged that the minimum service obligations imposed on brokers for access to the trademarked MLS through which the vast majority of homes in Canada are sold, substantially lessened and prevented competition to full-service brokers from emerging. The case involved elements of tying since the allegation made by the Bureau was that CREA used its control over the MLS system to substantially prevent or lessen competition by competitive business models that provide unbundled residential real estate brokerage services to home sellers. In essence, the Bureau's theory of the case was that CREA's licensing restrictions amounted to a tying of real estate broker services with advertising of home sales through MLS.

III. Rebates

312. The Act does not expressly address rebates, but where they amount to anti-competitive conduct they can be reviewed as an abuse of dominance under section 79. In *NutraSweet*, rebates were addressed as part of a broader analysis as to whether the NSC had used its American patent to foreclose competition in the Canadian market. In that case, the NSC offered a major distributor a rebate if it would switch from a competitor. The NSC based the rebates on the different rates between Canada and the United States, and thus competitors could not know about or reasonably match the rebates. The rebates served as an example of how the NSC was willing to price below cost – without regard to how large the discounts might become – to prevent the expansion of a competitor. These rebates were one factor

586. Trebilcock, *supra* n. 152 at 451–452.

influencing the Tribunal's conclusion that the NSC had abused its dominance by using its American patent to exclude competition in Canada, which amounted to anti-competitive conduct.

313. The issue of fidelity rebates arose in the context of anti-competitive exclusive dealing arrangements, whereby customers receive discounts if they agree to purchase exclusively from the supplier. This issue first surfaced in *NutraSweet*.[587] The NSC induced customers to purchase aspartame exclusively from the NSC by providing rebates if the NSC's trademark appeared on the distributor's product. The rebates were one element of the NSC's contracts, which the NSC designed to promote exclusivity. The Tribunal assessed the exclusive contracts as a whole and found them to constitute an anti-competitive abuse of dominance.

314. Similarly, in *Canada Pipe* the Tribunal and the Court of Appeal considered whether a fidelity rebate programme was anti-competitive. The Tribunal found that there was no anti-competitive act – as required by section 79(1)(b) – because there was no negative impact on competition. The Federal Court of Appeal held that the Tribunal had erred in considering the effects on competition as part of the section 79(1)(b) analysis. Whether a practice constitutes an anti-competitive act must be determined with regard to whether its intended purpose is a predatory, exclusionary or disciplinary effect on a competitor, not with regard to the actual consequences of the action.[588] Furthermore, the Tribunal held that the rebates were not anti-competitive because they made possible the high-volume sales necessary to enable Bibby to maintain a full line of products. The Federal Court of Appeal overturned this finding, holding that this was not a pro-competitive business explanation for the conduct.[589] In part because the Tribunal had applied the wrong legal test with regard to identifying an anti-competitive act, the court remitted the issue to the Tribunal, but the dispute was later settled on consent.[590]

IV. Refusal to Deal

315. Refusal to deal constitutes an independent reviewable practice under section 75 of the Act, and the practice may also draw scrutiny as an abuse of dominance. The Tribunal addressed refusal to deal as an abuse of dominance in *Tele-Direct*.[591] Tele-Direct had a policy whereby it refused to deal with advertising consultants representing its customers. The company defended this policy on the basis that consultants had a motive to direct their customers away from directory advertising, which was antithetical to Tele-Direct's business objectives as an advertising directory. Furthermore, consultants refused to accept financial responsibility

587. *NutraSweet*, *supra* n. 189.
588. *Canada Pipe, supra* n. 226 at 278–279. The effect on competition is considered as part of s. 79(1)(c), which deals with whether 'the practice has had, is having or is likely to have the effect of preventing or lessening competition substantially in a market'.
589. *Ibid.*, at 282.
590. See *Canada Pipe* Consent Order, *supra* n. 469.
591. *Tele-Direct*, *supra* n. 188.

for the advertising payments. The Tribunal accepted the company's business justifications for the policy, and ultimately found that it was not anti-competitive for Tele-Direct to refuse to deal with consultants, as doing so would have increased Tele-Direct's operating costs. Furthermore, the alleged adverse interests to consultants were not proven, and the reputational injury they may have suffered with customers was slight at most.

316. As stated above, section 75 of the Act makes refusal to deal an independent reviewable practice. The section provides that the Tribunal, upon application from the Commissioner or an independent person granted leave under section 103.1, can make an order compelling a supplier to accept a certain customer within a specified time period on usual trade terms. For an order to be granted the Tribunal must find that:

(a) a person is substantially affected in his business or is precluded from carrying on business due to his inability to obtain adequate supplies of a product anywhere in a market on usual trade terms,
(b) the person referred to in paragraph (a) is unable to obtain adequate supplies of the product because of insufficient competition among suppliers of the product in the market,
(c) the person referred to in paragraph (a) is willing and able to meet the usual trade terms of the supplier or suppliers of the product,
(d) the product is in ample supply, and
(e) the refusal to deal is having or is likely to have an adverse effect on competition in a market[.][592]

317. Subsection 75(1)(a) first requires that the Tribunal identify the relevant market. The relevant product market relates to the refused product, and the Tribunal defines it with regard to substitutability.[593] Products are substitutes where the buyer would not be substantially affected in its business as a result of switching between the products.[594] This test requires an assessment of demand with regard to the buyer's customers, as opposed to customers generally. This approach has resulted in a more narrow definition of the product market under section 75 than under other provisions of the Act. For example, in *Chrysler* the product market consisted of Chrysler-made replacement parts, instead of replacement parts generally.[595] The Tribunal defines the geographic market in the regular way, with regard to the functional indicators that determine whether products are substitutable within a particular geographic area.[596]

---

592. *Competition Act, supra* n. 26 at s. 75(1).
593. *Canada (Director of Investigation and Research) v. Chrysler Canada Ltd.*, [1989] C.C.T.D. No. 29, 27 C.P.R. (3d) 1 (Comp. Trib.) [*Chrysler* cited to C.P.R.].
594. *Nadeau Farms* 2009, *supra* n. 537 at para. 104.
595. *Chrysler, supra* n. 597 at 10. A comparable conclusion was reached in *Canada (Director of Investigation and Research) v. Xerox Canada Inc.*, [1990] C.C.T.D. No. 18, 33 C.P.R. (3d) 83 (Comp. Trib.) [*Xerox* cited to C.P.R.].
596. *Nadeau Farms* 2009, *supra* n. 537 at para. 105. For a more extensive discussion of market identification see 'Part 1: Chapter 4: §2. Relevant Market'.

318. After identifying the relevant market, subsection 75(a) requires a determination of whether the distributor's business has been substantially affected. In *Chrysler*, the Tribunal addressed whether the effect should be assessed with respect to its impact on the distributor's entire business, or rather with respect to the more narrow line of business affected by the refusal. The Tribunal opted for the broader definition of business, holding that 'business' referred to 'the effect on the entire activity of which the refused supplies are a part'.[597] In order to be 'substantially affected' a distributor must establish that it is 'affected in an important or significant way',[598] which means more than a *de minimis* impact. The Tribunal will consider whether the product at issue accounts for a large portion of the distributor's overall business; whether another product can easily replace the product at issue; whether the capacity used by selling the product could transfer to other activities instead; and whether the product is sold in conjunction with other products or services, magnifying its impact on the business.[599] The exact thresholds for when a business is substantially affected are uncertain, but the Tribunal held that an approximate loss of 46% in sales was enough to show a substantial effect,[600] whereas an 11% loss did not meet the test.[601] Though section 75 theoretically applies to customers whom suppliers have not historically served, it is not clear how these customers would go about showing a substantial effect on their businesses.

319. To grant an order, the Tribunal must also find that the applicant could not obtain adequate supplies of a product anywhere in a market on usual trade terms. The Tribunal determines usual trade terms with respect to the relevant market, from the perspective of all distributors or customers competing to purchase the relevant product.[602] Trade terms include price, units of purchase and reasonable technical and servicing requirements.[603] If it is shown that the distributor could not purchase the product anywhere in the market on these terms, and the distributor is substantially affected in its business, subsection 75(1)(a) is satisfied.

320. Subsection 75(1)(b) requires that the inability to obtain adequate supplies has occurred as a result of 'insufficient competition among suppliers of the product in the market'.[604] The insufficient competition must be the 'overriding reason' for the inadequate supplies.[605] In the context of a single-supplier market, the Tribunal has held that a party can advance objectively justifiable business reasons for the refusal to show that insufficient competition in the market was not the cause of the inability to obtain supplies (even though there is necessarily a lack of competition

597. *Chrysler, supra* n. 597 at 18.
598. *Nadeau Farms* 2009, *supra* n. 537 at para. 131.
599. *Chrysler, supra* n. 597 at 18.
600. *Allan Morgan and Sons Ltd. v. La-Z-Boy Canada Ltd.*, [2004] C.C.T.D. No. 4, 29 C.P.R. (4th) 539, 2004 Comp. Trib. 4 CT-2003-09.
601. *Broadview Pharmacy v. Pfizer Canada Inc.*, [2004] C.C.T.D. No. 23, 2004 Comp. Trib. 23 CT-2004-006.
602. *Nadeau Farms* 2009, *supra* n. 537 at paras. 139 & 141.
603. *Competition Act, supra* n. 26 at s. 75(3).
604. *Ibid.*, at s. 75(1)(b).
605. *Nadeau Farms* 2009, *supra* n. 537 at para. 229.

in a single-supplier market).[606] Recently the Tribunal considered this element in a multiple-supplier market in *Nadeau Farms*. However, in that case, a very detailed regulatory scheme governed the supply of chickens. The Tribunal failed to find that there was insufficient competition in the market, in part on the basis that there were a number of producers in the market.[607] It is unclear how the Tribunal will assess this element in a multiple-supplier market that is not heavily regulated.

321. Subsection 75(1)(c) requires that the distributor be willing and able to meet the usual trade terms associated with the supply of the product. Relevant trade terms are the same as those discussed with regard to section 75(1)(a). In none of the major cases before the Tribunal have the respondents argued that the distributors were unwilling to meet the usual trade terms.[608] Thus, this is a generally uncontroversial part of the test.

322. The fourth element of the section requires that the product be in 'ample supply'.[609] Again, this element has been uncontested in most cases before the Tribunal. However, in *Quinlan's of Huntsville Inc. v. Fred Deeley Imports Ltd.*,[610] the Tribunal refused to grant an interim injunction, finding that if it granted an injunction then the respondent would be forced to declare a shortage of motorcycles and stop supplying to other customers. The Tribunal explained that section 75 is 'meant to deal with situations in which the product is readily available and unencumbered in the sense that it has not been sold or promised to another purchaser'.[611] More recently, in *Nadeau Farms* the Tribunal found that live chickens were not in ample supply as a result of the regulatory management system that imposed a strict quota system on suppliers. The Tribunal expanded on its earlier comments in *Quinlan*, stating that 'a product is in ample supply when its availability is not in issue when a supplier considers whether to develop its business by seeking new customers and/or new distribution channels, such as involvement in the downstream processing market'.[612] The decision of the Tribunal was upheld on appeal at the Federal Court of Appeal.[613] Situations where products might not be in ample supply include a shortage due to a strike, a scarcity of raw materials, or a supplier in the upstream market going out of business.[614]

323. Finally, for the Tribunal to make an order under section 75, it must find that 'the refusal to deal is having or is likely to have an adverse effect on competition in

606. *Xerox*, *supra* n. 599 at 115.
607. *Nadeau Farms* 2009, *supra* n. 537 at para. 246. In light of the regulatory scheme, the Tribunal also considered whether suppliers were acting independently and whether the supply management system led to insufficient competition in the market.
608. See *ibid.*, at para. 249; *Chrysler*, *supra* n. 597 at 9; and *Xerox*, *supra* n. 599 at 100.
609. *Competition Act*, *supra* n. 26 at s. 75(1)(d).
610. 2004 Comp. Trib. 28 CT-2004-009 [*Quinlan*].
611. *Ibid.*, at para. 19.
612. *Nadeau Farms* 2009, *supra* n. 537 at para. 280.
613. *Nadeau Poultry Farm Limited v. Groupe Westco Inc.* 2011 FCA 188.
614. *Ibid.*, at para. 281.

a market'.[615] 'Market' refers to the downstream market (i.e., the market in which the distributor will sell its product).[616] The Tribunal identifies the relevant downstream product and geographic markets through the hypothetical monopolist approach, as set out in the MEGs.[617] Once the Tribunal identifies the relevant market, it must assess the impact of the refusal to deal through a 'relative and comparative assessment of the market in two time frames, namely with the refusal to deal and without the refusal to deal'.[618] To find that the refusal results in an adverse effect on the market, the Tribunal must find that the remaining participants in the downstream market will have 'a position of created, enhanced or preserved market power'.[619] The assessment of market power will usually include consideration of market share and entry barriers, and may include any other relevant indicators such as price, quality and variety of product.[620] Given the limited case law on the subject, it is unclear how much the refusal to deal must affect market power to show a 'likely adverse effect'. However, the Tribunal has said that 'adverse' amounts to a lower standard than 'substantial' (which is used in several other sections of the Act, including abuse of dominance), and that 'likely' means that the adverse effects must be probable.[621]

V. Price Squeeze

324. Section 78(1)(a) of the Act recognizes vertical price squeezing as an anticompetitive act. The section describes the practice as 'squeezing, by a vertically integrated supplier, of the margin available to an unintegrated customer who competes with the supplier, for the purpose of impeding or preventing the customer's entry into, or expansion in, a market'. Vertical squeezing could occur in a few ways. Where the vertically integrated firm is operating at two levels of the supply stream, the firm could raise the price of input to a competitor operating only in the downstream market.[622] A firm in the same position could also engage in margin squeezing through a supply freeze, which occurs when a firm limits the supply available to a competitor in the downstream market.[623] If a firm operates at the manufacturing and distribution levels, it could squeeze competitors through artificially low prices at the retail level.[624] To date, there have been no reported cases applying this section.

---

615. *Competition Act*, *supra* n. 26 at s. 75(1)(e).
616. *Nadeau Farms* 2009, *supra* n. 537 at para. 294.
617. *Ibid.*, at para. 310. See also MEGs, *supra* n. 153 at 8–14; for an extensive discussion of market identification see 'Part 1: Chapter 4: §2. Relevant Market'.
618. *Nadeau Farms* 2009, *ibid.*, at para. 365.
619. *Ibid.*, at para. 379.
620. *Ibid.*, at para. 369.
621. *Ibid.*, at para. 369.
622. Trebilcock, *supra* n. 152 at 533.
623. *Ibid.*
624. Wakil, *supra* n. 439 at 213.

Chapter 3. Concentrations

325. Like other reviewable practices, the Commissioner initially conducts the review of mergers. The Commissioner may bring an application to the Tribunal in advance of a proposed merger or within one year of the completed merger.[625] The Tribunal can make remedial orders prohibiting or dissolving mergers or proposed mergers, or ordering other structural changes such as the divestiture of assets. The test for determining whether the Tribunal will make an order is whether the merger 'prevents or lessens, or is likely to prevent or lessen, competition substantially'.[626] The MEGs provide a detailed overview of the factors that the Bureau considers when assessing the competitive effects of a merger. However, the MEGs do not bind the Bureau or the Tribunal.

326. Recall from the introductory treatment of 'mergers' (Part I, Chapter 4, §7) that the Act defines 'merger' broadly to include 'the acquisition or establishment, direct or indirect, by one or more persons, whether by purchase or lease of shares or assets, by amalgamation or by combination or otherwise, of control over or significant interest in the whole or a part of a business of a competitor, supplier, customer or other person'.[627] The Act defines 'control' to mean de jure control, which amounts to holding more than 50% of the voting shares in a corporation, provided those shares are sufficient to elect a majority of the board of directors.[628]

327. The Act does not define 'significant interest'. However, in the MEGs the Bureau explains that it considers whether there is a significant interest with regard to both quantitative and qualitative factors.[629] Its qualitative assessment focuses on whether the person has the ability to materially influence the economic behaviour of the business, including decisions related to pricing, purchasing, distribution, marketing, investment, financing, and the licensing of IPRs. As outlined in the MEGs, the Bureau considers many specific factors in assessing whether a particular minority shareholding, an interest in a combination, agreement or other relationship or interest confers material influence (for a full list, see Chapter 4, § 7 'Concentrations (Mergers)').[630] In the specific context of share acquisitions, when assessing whether someone has acquired a significant interest in a corporation, the Bureau considers whether the person could obtain a sufficient level of representation on the board of directors of the corporation to materially influence the board, or to block ordinary resolutions of the corporation. Generally, less than a 10% ownership of voting interest is not considered significant. Voting interests of between 10%–50% may be significant depending on the facts, but generally, larger shareholding is needed to show

625. The limitation period is set out in s. 97 of the Act. Prior to 2009 the limitation period was three years.
626. *Competition Act*, *supra* n. 26 at s. 92.
627. *Ibid.*, at s. 91.
628. *Ibid.*, at s. 2(4).
629. MEGs, *supra* n. 153 at 1.5.
630. *Ibid.*, at 1.6.

a significant interest in a private company, as opposed to a widely held public company.[631]

328. It is possible to acquire a significant interest in a firm – meaning that a merger has occurred – in a number of different ways. A merger can occur through the acquisition of convertible securities or through the exercise of the rights therein. In the latter case, the exercise of the rights triggers the merger notification provisions. The acquisition of certain assets constitutes a merger. The MEGs provide that the acquisition of a significant interest occurs with the purchase or lease from the target company of an unincorporated division, plant, distribution facilities, retail outlet, brand name or IPRs.[632] Furthermore, where someone already holds an interest in a business, the acquisition of a greater interest may constitute a merger if the person obtains a significant interest or control as a result of the acquisition. Mergers can also arise through shareholder agreements, management contracts, franchise agreements and other contractual arrangements involving corporations, partnerships, joint ventures, combinations and other entities, depending on the terms of the arrangements.[633] Regardless of the nature of the transaction, the key consideration is whether someone has acquired a newfound control over or a significant interest in the business.

329. Once it is established a merger has occurred (or will occur), it is necessary to determine whether the merger will prevent or lessen competition substantially. This determination takes place with regard to whether the merger will create or enhance market power. The Bureau's primary concern is how market power affects price and output, but it may also consider the effect of the merger on other dimensions, such as quality, product choice, service, innovation and advertising.[634] These qualitative factors are more important in markets with significant levels of non-price competition. A party or parties may exercise market power in two ways. First, a party can unilaterally exercise market power, meaning that the merged entity can sustain higher prices (or a change to another important dimension, such as output, service, etc.) than it could have prior to the merger. Second, parties can coordinate their behaviour to exercise market power. In this situation, competitive vigour diminishes, competitors having accommodated responses to each other's price increases or changes in other relevant dimensions, such as service or product choice.

330. Whether a firm is able to exercise unilateral market power varies based on whether it is differentiated from competitors by its product or by its capacity. A merged entity that is differentiated by its products may exercise unilateral market power – and by extension substantially lessen competition – if the product offerings of the merging parties are close substitutes for one another. In such a situation, the

631. *Ibid.*, at 1.10.
632. *Ibid.*, at 1.13.
633. *Ibid.*, at 1.18.
634. *Ibid.*, at 2.2.

Bureau evaluates how the merger may change the pricing incentives of the individual firms.[635] If firms are differentiated by capacity, a merged entity can exercise market power if competing firms would not have the capacity to absorb demand that would be diverted from the merged entity if it raised prices.[636]

331. Changes in market dynamics may lessen competition substantially if the changes lead to coordinated market power or increase the level of coordinated power already present in a market. The Bureau considers that coordinated market power is only possible in concentrated markets with barriers to entry.[637] Parties can exercise coordinated market power in a number of ways, including through tacit or express understandings, or through a recognition that firms can benefit by competing less vigorously with one another. The Bureau considers that this coordination is sustainable, and therefore problematic, in the following circumstances: (i) when firms have the ability to individually recognize mutually beneficial terms of coordination, monitor each other's conduct to detect deviation, and punish competitors who deviate from the terms; and (ii) this coordination is relatively unthreatened by external factors, such as by other competitors or by the reaction of buyers.[638] The market conditions determine whether coordinated marker power is sustainable, but generally the problem is more likely to occur in markets with undifferentiated products. Transactions that are large and infrequent (relative to market demand) make coordinated behaviour less likely, as does a lack of transparency in the market.[639]

332. It is possible to characterize some mergers as 'preventing' competition, rather than lessening it. Competition is prevented if a firm can sustain higher prices by hindering the development of anticipated future competition. This occurs most often where there is no direct overlap between the businesses of the merging parties, but direct competition was expected to increase absent the merger.[640] The Bureau looks at the likelihood of entry or expansion by either merging party and at the market power held by the merging parties. Mergers that may give rise to a substantial prevention of competition include: acquisition of a potential entrant or vigorous competitor; acquisition by the market leader, pre-empting acquisition by another competitor; acquisition of an existing business by a firm that would likely have entered the market but for the merger; acquisition that prevents expansion into new geographic markets; acquisition that prevents the pro-competitive effects of new capacity; or acquisition that prevents or limits the introduction of new products.[641]

333. In *The Commissioner of Competition v. CCS Corporation et al.* which represents the first contested challenge to a merger by the Commissioner since 2005, the Tribunal found that a completed merger between CCS Corporation (CCS) and

635. *Ibid.,* at 6.13.
636. *Ibid.*, at 6.20.
637. *Ibid.*, at 6.28.
638. *Ibid.*, at 6.26.
639. *Ibid.*, at 6.31–6.32.
640. *Ibid.*, at 2.10.
641. *Ibid.*, at 2.12.

Complete Environmental (Complete) substantially prevented competition and ordered a divestiture of the hazardous waste landfill assets acquired by CCS.[642] By way of background, CCS acquired Complete Environmental Inc. and its wholly owned subsidiary Babkirk Land Services in 2011. At the time of the merger, CCS owned and operated the only two active hazardous waste landfills in north-eastern British Columbia. Babkirk owned land in the same region and held a permit to operate a hazardous waste landfill. However, Complete intended to run the site as a bioremediation business, with only an incidental landfill. The Tribunal accepted Complete's evidence of their intention not to compete with CCS. However, the Tribunal applied a 'but for' test and found that 'but for' the merger, CCS would have faced market competition. To arrive at this conclusion, the Tribunal found that Complete's bioremediation business would have failed, forcing Complete either to compete in the hazardous landfill business or to sell to a third party who would compete. Accordingly, the Tribunal was of the view that the merger substantially prevented potential future competition and ordered CCS to divest itself of its acquired assets. CCS (now called 'Tervita') and the other parties involved in the transaction appealed the Tribunal's decision to the Federal Court of Appeal. The Federal Court of Appeal upheld the Tribunal's decision.[643] CCS appealed the Federal Court of Appeal's decision to the Supreme Court of Canada.[644] In over-turning on other grounds the Court of Appeal's decision, the Supreme Court held that a two-part test applies to determine if a firm with market power will use a merger to prevent competition that would otherwise arise in a contestable market. First, the Tribunal must identify the firm or firms the merger would prevent from independently entering the market. Although this will likely be one of the merging parties, the Supreme Court did not exclude the possibility that the potential entry may come from a third party. Second, the Tribunal must examine the 'but-for' market condition, to see if the potential competitor would have entered the market absent the merger, and if so, whether the effect of that competitor's entry on competition in the market would have been substantial.[645]

334. What constitutes 'substantial' prevention or lessening of competition in the context of mergers? The Bureau considers that competition will be 'substantially' prevented or lessened if the merged entity, either alone or in coordination with other firms, could materially influence price. This assessment takes place with regard to the magnitude and duration of any price increase. Generally, the Bureau considers the prevention or lessening of competition substantial if: (i) 'the price of the relevant product(s) would likely be materially higher in the relevant market than it would be in the absence of the merger';[646] and (ii) 'sufficient new entry would not occur rapidly enough to prevent the material price increase, or to counteract the effects of any price increase'.[647] In the CCS decision, the Tribunal found that the

642. *Supra* note 118.
643. *Tervita,* supra n. 119.
644. *Tervita, supra* note 38.
645. *Ibid.*
646. MEGs, *supra* n. 1523 at 2.13.
647. *CCS, supra* n. 118.

merger effectively prevented at least a 10% decrease in landfill tipping fees, an effect it considered material. In this respect, the Tribunal found:

> [t]he degree of market power used in assessing whether competition is likely to be prevented or lessened substantially must be recalibrated downwards. That recalibrated degree of market power is a level of market power required to maintain prices *materially* higher, or to depress one or more forms of non-price competition to a level that is *materially* lower, than they likely would be in the absence of the merger. As a practical matter, in the case at bar, this distinction between 'material' and 'significant' is of little significance, because the Panel has found that prices are likely to be significantly (i.e., at least 10%) higher than they would likely have been in the absence of the Merger.[648]

335. Analysing the prevention or lessening of competition begins with identifying the product market and the geographic market. Market identification occurs through the hypothetical monopolist approach. As discussed above, the concept of substitutability determines the smallest product and geographic markets in which a hypothetical monopolist could impose a significant and non-transitory price increase above levels that would exist in the absence of the merger.[649] The next step is to identify the participants in the relevant market and to calculate their market share.[650] The Act provides that the Tribunal cannot prevent a merger solely on the basis of market share.[651] However, the Bureau takes an absence of high post-merger market shares as evidence that the merger is unlikely to enhance market power. Consequently, the Bureau generally does not challenge a merger on the basis of concerns related to unilateral exercise of market power when the post-merger market share of the merged entity would be less than 35%.[652] The Bureau also does not generally challenge a merger on the basis of concerns related to a coordinated exercise of market power if the four largest firms in the post-merger market would have a market share of less than 65%, and if the merged entity would have a market share of less than 10%.[653]

336. If the concentration thresholds exceed these limits (and sometimes even if it does not), the Bureau proceeds to a competitive effects analysis, in which it assesses various factors to determine the merger's likely effect on competition. Section 93 of the Act lists relevant factors that the Tribunal may consider in deciding whether to make an order (the Bureau considers the same factors in deciding whether to challenge the merger).[654] These include:

---

648. *Ibid.*, at para. 377.
649. For a detailed discussion of how product and geographic markets are defined see 'Part I: Chapter 4: §2. Relevant Market'.
650. For a detailed discussion of how participants in the market are identified, and how market share is calculated see 'Part I: Chapter 4: §3. Market Power/Dominant Position'.
651. *Competition Act*, *supra* n. 26 at s. 92(2).
652. MEGs, *supra* n. 153 at 5.9.
653. *Ibid.*
654. *Ibid.*, at 3.4.

(a) the extent to which foreign products or foreign competitors provide or are likely to provide effective competition to the businesses of the parties to the merger or proposed merger;
(b) whether the business, or a part of the business, of a party to the merger or proposed merger has failed or is likely to fail;
(c) the extent to which acceptable substitutes for products supplied by the parties to the merger or proposed merger are or are likely to be available;
(d) any barriers to entry into a market, including:
  (i) tariff and non-tariff barriers to international trade;
  (ii) interprovincial barriers to trade; and
  (iii) regulatory control over entry;
and any effect of the merger or proposed merger on such barriers;
(e) the extent to which effective competition remains or would remain in a market that is or would be affected by the merger or proposed merger;
(f) any likelihood that the merger or proposed merger will or would result in the removal of a vigorous and effective competitor;
(g) the nature and extent of change and innovation in a relevant market; and
(h) any other factor that is relevant to competition in a market that is or would be affected by the merger or proposed merger.[655]

Although conceptually one must define a relevant market in order to analyse the impact on competition therein, in practice market definition and the assessment of likely competitive effects may proceed simultaneously. Particularly in cases where the Bureau considers there will be no substantial prevention or lessening of competition regardless of how markets are defined, precise market definition may not be necessary.

337. Subsection 93(f) of the Act provides that the Tribunal may consider the likelihood that a merger will eliminate a vigorous and effective competitor. The MEGs explain that the class of vigorous and effective competitors may include firms that have a history of not following price increases or market stabilization initiatives; firms that provide unique services or warranties; firms that have recently expanded capacity, or plan to do so; firms that have recently made gains in market share, or are positioned to do so; or firms that have recently acquired, or will acquire, IPRs that enhance their ability to compete in the market.[656] Similarly, the elimination of a 'maverick' may also be problematic. A maverick is a firm that has 'a disproportionate incentive to deviate from coordinated behaviour'.[657]

338. Another important factor the Bureau considers when assessing a merger's impact on competition is the presence of barriers to market entry. A lack of significant barriers to entry diminishes a firm's ability to exercise market power, since competitors are more likely to enter the market and compete, preventing the firm

655. *Competition Act*, *supra* n. 26 at s. 93.
656. MEGs, *supra* n. 153 at 6.5.
657. *Ibid.*, at 6.38.

from raising prices beyond a sustainable level.[658] According to the Bureau, for entry to effectively constrain market power, its effects must occur within a reasonable period of time.[659]

339. Barriers to entry can take various forms. Subsection 93(d) states that the Tribunal may consider regulatory barriers to entry, including interprovincial trade barriers and international trade tariffs. Another important barrier to entry, though not explicitly mentioned in section 93, is the amount of sunk costs required to enter the market. Sunk costs are those that a firm cannot recover if it subsequently exits the market. The greater the sunk costs, the lower the likelihood of new competitors entering the market. Examples of sunk costs include start-up costs, such as acquiring market information, developing and testing product designs, installing equipment, engaging personnel and setting up distribution systems.[660] Sunk costs can also include costs required to overcome incumbents' head starts, such as their product-differentiation advantages.[661]

340. Subsection 93(h) empowers the Tribunal to consider any other factors that may be relevant to the lessening of competition. One such factor discussed in the MEGs is the ability of buyers to exert countervailing power. Countervailing buyer power may occur where buyers can self-supply through vertical integration into the upstream market; where the promise of substantial orders can motivate the expansion of an existing seller or the entry of a new seller; where buyers can refuse to buy other products produced by the seller; where buyers can refuse to purchase the seller's products in other geographic markets with different competitive conditions; and where buyers can impose costs on the seller (e.g., by giving less favourable retail placement to the merged entity's products).[662] In these cases, the countervailing power may prevent the lessening of competition.

341. Section 93(b) allows the Tribunal to consider whether a merging party's business has failed, or is likely to fail. The failure of one party does not provide a defence to a merger that will substantially lessen competition. Rather, section 93(b) is a recognition that 'the loss of the actual or future competitive influence of a failing firm [should not be] attributed to the merger if imminent failure is probable and, in the absence of a merger, the assets of the firm are likely to exit the relevant market'.[663] According to the MEGs, a firm is failing if it is insolvent or is likely to become insolvent; if it has initiated or is likely to initiate voluntary bankruptcy proceedings; or if it has been, or is likely to be, petitioned into bankruptcy or receivership.[664]

---

658. *Director of Investigation and Research v. Hillsdown Holdings (Canada) Limited* (1992), 41 C.P.R. (3d) 289, 324.
659. MEGs, *supra* n. 153 at 2.11.
660. *Ibid.*, at 7.11.
661. *Ibid.*
662. *Ibid.*, at 8.1.
663. *Ibid.*, at 13.2.
664. *Ibid.*, at 13.3.

342. Once it is established that a firm is failing, the Bureau considers whether there are any alternatives that are likely to provide a greater level of competition than the proposed merger would. First, the Bureau searches for a competitively preferable purchaser whose purchase of the firm would likely result in a materially higher level of competition in a substantial part of the market. If this alternative is not available, it is necessary to determine whether the failing firm would likely remain in the market through retrenchment or restructuring, and if so whether this would provide greater competition. Where neither of these scenarios is likely, the Bureau considers whether liquidation is the competitively preferable option. For example, liquidation may allow other potential competitors to buy the firm's assets and enter the market.[665] The Bureau may allow the merger if none of these options are viable means of maintaining competition in the market.

343. Even if the Tribunal finds that a merger or proposed merger will substantially prevent or lessen competition, the Tribunal may allow the merger if it would promote gains in efficiency. Section 96(1) of the Act provides that the Tribunal shall not make an order where it finds that gains in efficiency 'will be greater than, and will offset, the effects of any prevention or lessening of competition that will result or is likely to result from the merger or proposed merger and that the gains in efficiency would not likely be attained if the order were made'.[666] The Federal Court of Appeal has said that this assessment must involve a balancing of weights approach, in which the effects of the prevention and lessening of competition are weighed against all quantitative and qualitative efficiencies deriving from the merger.[667] This approach means that the Tribunal has wide latitude to consider all factors that are relevant in any given case. However, the Act requires the Tribunal to consider whether the merger will lead to a significant increase in the real value of exports, or a significant substitution of domestic products for imported products.[668] Furthermore, the Act explicitly states that a redistribution of income between parties cannot alone constitute a gain in efficiencies.[669]

344. One of two leading cases on efficiencies is *Superior Propane*.[670] The case involved the merger of two companies that marketed propane and related services. In its initial review of the merger in 2000, the Tribunal held that there would be a lessening of competition, but allowed the merger nonetheless based on the efficiencies exception. The Commissioner appealed the ruling, and the Federal Court of Appeal overturned the Tribunal's decision, holding that the Tribunal had applied the wrong efficiencies test. The Tribunal had taken the total surplus approach, in which it applied a purely quantitative approach, considering the deadweight loss (i.e., the loss to the economy as a result of the merger) as the only effect on competition to measure against the efficiency gains. The Court of Appeal held that this approach was wrong, and that section 96 required the Tribunal to take a more qualitative

665. *Ibid.*, at 13.8.
666. *Competition Act*, *supra* n. 26 at s. 96(1).
667. *Superior Propane* FCA 2001, *supra* n. 151.
668. *Competition Act*, *supra* n. 26 at s. 96(2).
669. *Ibid.*, at s. 96(3).
670. *Superior Propane* FCA 2001, *supra* n. 151.

approach and consider all negative effects of the merger, having regard to the four purposes of the Act as set out in section 1.1. This holding meant that the Tribunal had erred by not considering the effect of the merger on the redistribution of wealth and resources, and by failing to properly consider the impact that allowing a monopoly might have on the market. Consequently, the court overturned the decision and remitted the matter to the Tribunal for reconsideration.

345. In its second determination, rendered in 2002, the Tribunal reached the same conclusion: although the merger would lessen competition, it was saved by the efficiencies defence. In reaching its decision, the Tribunal applied the weight balancing approach described by the Federal Court of Appeal, paying particular attention to the transfer of wealth caused by the merger. In addition to a CAD 6 million dead weight loss caused by the merger, the Tribunal identified a wealth transfer of CAD 40.5 million per year from consumers to the merged entity's shareholders. However, the Tribunal held that only the 'socially adverse' portion of this transfer should count as a negative effect in the balancing of efficiencies. The Tribunal found that it should only consider the transfers involving low-income households – which had no alternative but to use propane – to be socially adverse. This number amounted to only CAD 2.6 million of the larger sum. Even if this amount was doubled (based on the premise that the interests of low-income households should be weighted more heavily than those of shareholders) and combined with the deadweight loss, the loss would only have amounted to just over one-third of the efficiencies gained. Thus, the Tribunal once again concluded that the efficiency gains would outweigh and offset the impact on competition. Again, the decision was appealed to the Federal Court of Appeal, but this time the court upheld the Tribunal's holding.

346. The decision in *Superior Propane* indicates that different efficiency tests may be contextually applied. As discussed in more detail below, *Tervita* recently clarified that quantifiable anti-competitive effects must be quantified and are given precedence; however, in practice the manner in which anti-competitive effects are calculated remains somewhat amorphous. Given the paucity of case law applying section 96 of the Act, its application remains a source of considerable uncertainty. The MEGs however, give merging parties some guidance as to the factors that the Bureau, and potentially the Tribunal, considers when applying the efficiencies defence. Of note, the onus of proving the elements of section 96 is on the merging parties, with the exception of the anti-competitive effects of the merger, which the Commissioner must prove.[671]

347. The MEGs describe three general categories of efficiencies that the Bureau considers: (i) allocative efficiency, meaning the degree to which resources available to society are put to their most valuable use; (ii) technical or productive efficiency, meaning the creation of a given volume of output at the lowest possible resource

671. *Superior Propane* FCA 2001, *supra* n. 151 at 329. See also, *Tervita*, supra note 123.

cost; and (iii) dynamic efficiency, meaning the optimal introduction of new products and production processes over time.[672] The Bureau does not consider gains that accrue outside of Canada.[673] As per the decision in *Superior Propane*, the Bureau makes clear in the MEGs that it considers all anti-competitive effects, including price effects (such as loss of allocative efficiency and redistributive effects) and non-price effects (such as reductions in service, quality and choice, loss of productive efficiency, and loss of dynamic efficiency).[674]

348. The Supreme Court's decision in *Tervita* (*CCS*) sheds more light on the efficiencies defence. The Supreme Court held that, in determining whether quantitative or qualitative efficiencies 'offset' the quantitative and qualitative effects of any prevention or lessening of competition, although merging parties bear the burden of proving cognizable efficiencies, the Commissioner bears the burden of proving, and where possible, quantifying, the anti-competitive effects, so they can be balanced against the claimed efficiencies. The Supreme Court found that '[e]ffects that can be quantified should be quantified, even as estimates, provided such estimates are grounded in evidence that can be challenged and weighed'. To minimize subjectivity, failure to at least estimate effects that are realistically measurable will result in those effects being assigned a weight of zero. In this regard, the Supreme Court clarified that application of the efficiencies defence will be framed as a two-step inquiry: (1) the quantitative efficiencies of the merger (adduced by the merging parties) should be compared to the quantitative anti-competitive effects (adduced by the Commissioner); if the anti-competitive effects outweigh the efficiencies, the defence will not apply, and (2) if quantitative efficiencies are larger, then the Tribunal must balance qualitative anti-competitive effects (those that are not capable of measurement), to determine whether total efficiencies offset the total anti-competitive effects. In this regard, the Supreme Court held that as long as the efficiencies exceed the proven anti-competitive effects (even if by a very small amount), the merger must be cleared. The Supreme Court also distinguished between 'early mover efficiencies' (those that a merging party would be able to realize faster as a result of the merger), and 'order implementation efficiencies' (those that could be realized sooner than a competitor only because the competitor would be delayed because of legal proceedings associated with a divestiture order). Though 'early mover efficiencies' count, 'order implementation efficiencies' do not. Lastly, the Supreme Court clarified that properly quantified environmental anti-competitive effects could be considered in the efficiencies analysis.[675]

672. *MEGs, supra n. 153* at 12.4.
673. *Ibid.*, at 12.2.
674. *Ibid.*, at 12.25–12.31.
675. *Tervita, supra* n. 123. The Supreme Court of Canada in *Tervita* over-turned the Federal Court of Appeal and the Tribunal's efficiencies holdings in that case, finding that the lack of evidence from the Bureau as to the elasticity of demand (it had led evidence only as to the estimated price increase) meant that the Bureau had failed to prove any quantifiable anti-competitive effects and therefore failed to resist the efficiencies defence in that case. A relatively negligible amount of proven efficiencies therefore was held to be sufficient to 'offset and outweigh' the anti-competitive

§1. Horizontal Mergers

349. Horizontal mergers are mergers between competitors operating in the same market. For horizontal mergers, the main concern is whether the merged entity can sustain higher prices because of diminished competition. This concern usually arises where there is a direct or existing overlap between the operations of the merging parties.[676] The MEGs, discussed throughout the beginning of this chapter, focus primarily on horizontal mergers.[677] Furthermore, all of the provisions of the Act discussed in the previous section apply to horizontal mergers.

350. In *CCS (Tervita)*, a horizontal merger was at issue. For parties contemplating such a merger, two important lessons emerge from the case. First, the transaction was non-notifiable. This implies that parties cannot assume that because they are below the size-of-transaction threshold, the transaction will not be subject to review by the Competition Bureau. Second, the Tribunal ordered divestiture of the monopoly-creating subsidiary or assets rather than dissolution of the merged entity, stating that dissolution was intrusive, overbroad, and might compromise the timely opening of the prospectively competitive facility; whereas divestiture was an available and effective remedy.[678] Since the Commissioner had sought dissolution, the Tribunal's decision in *CCS* suggests that completed mergers are unlikely to be dissolved where divestiture is an alternative, effective remedy. *CCS* was overturned on other grounds (see paragraph 62).

§2. Vertical Mergers

351. Vertical mergers are mergers between firms that produce products at different levels of a supply chain – as between a supplier and a customer, for example. Thus, vertical mergers generally involve firms that compete in different markets, such that they do not cause an increase in market concentration. In practice, the Commissioner rarely challenges vertical mergers. However, the merger provisions of the Act do not explicitly differentiate between types of mergers. As such, all the provisions discussed at the beginning of this chapter apply to vertical mergers if they are relevant. The MEGs also apply generally, and they outline some considerations specific to vertical mergers.

352. Vertical mergers can lessen competition in two ways: they can increase barriers to entry, or they can facilitate coordinated effects. A merger may create barriers to entry if it eliminates an independent upstream supply source or downstream distribution outlet, such that only a small amount of unintegrated capacity remains

effects. The Supreme Court recognized that the outcome of the case was surprising, given its holding that the merger was anti-competitive and the relatively small amount of proven efficiencies, but that the failure of the Bureau to lead sufficient evidence as to quantifiable anti-competitive effects was dispositive.

676. MEGs, supra n. 153 at 2.9.

677. *Ibid.*, at 1.21.

678. *CCS*, supra n. 118 at paras. 341–342.

at either stage. If the amount of unintegrated capacity is small enough, a firm wishing to enter the market may need to enter both the primary and secondary markets. If such dual entry involves greater sunk costs than entering the primary market alone, the Bureau recognizes the creation of a barrier. The MEGs refer to a vertically merged entity's ability to affect rivals in this way as 'foreclosure'.[679] In evaluating a vertical merger, the Bureau looks at four main categories of foreclosure:

- total input foreclosure, which occurs when the merged firm refuses to supply an input to rival manufacturers that compete in the downstream market;
- partial input foreclosure, which occurs when the merged firm increases the price it charges to supply an input to rival manufacturers that compete with it in the downstream market;
- total customer foreclosure, which occurs when the merged firm refuses to purchase inputs from an upstream rival; and
- partial customer foreclosure, which occurs when the merged firm is a distributor and can disadvantage upstream rivals in the distribution/resale of their products.[680]

353. Vertical mergers may also prevent or lessen competition if they create or increase the degree to which firms in the upstream market are able to coordinate their behaviour. This result would occur if a high level of vertical coordination makes it easier for firms to monitor the prices charged by their competitors in the upstream market. Vertical mergers could also facilitate coordinated behaviour by firms in a downstream market by increasing transparency – that is, by enabling firms to observe increased purchases of inputs – or by allowing additional ways to discourage or punish deviations (by limiting the supply of inputs).[681]

§3. MARKET/PRODUCT EXTENSION MERGERS

354. Market extension mergers are mergers between firms that sell the same products in different geographic markets. Product extension mergers are mergers between firms that are selling different product lines in the same geographic market. These mergers could fit within the Bureau's definition of conglomerate mergers, as discussed in the following section. They may also be examples of mergers that the Bureau assesses as 'preventing' competition. For example, the MEGs indicate that a merger may result in the prevention of competition in the event of an acquisition that prevents or limits the introduction of new products, or which prevents the expansion into new geographic markets.[682] *Superior Propane* provides an example of competition being lessened due to prevention of expansion into a new geographic market. Although the merging parties were competitors in some markets (making the merger a horizontal one), one of the parties had plans to expand its

679. MEGs, *supra* n. 153, at 11.4.
680. *Ibid.*, at 11.7.
681. *Ibid.*, at 11.9.
682. *Ibid.*, at 2.12.

activities to the geographic market of Eastern Canada. Because the merger would have prevented this expansion, the Tribunal held that the merger would substantially prevent competition.[683] The same analysis could apply in the case of a pure market or product merger. The *CCS* (and on appeal, *Tervita*) case is the leading case on prevention of competition, however, having been addressed by the Supreme Court of Canada in 2015. See paragraph 333 above for a detailed discussion. In brief, the Commissioner must be able to prove that the merger will prevent entry by one of the merging firms that is likely, timely and substantial. Specifically, the Supreme Court of Canada held that the time-frame for when a merging party, in absence of the merger, is expected to enter the market must be, through the use of evidence, discernible. However, a determination of what is an acceptable time-frame shall be considered on a case-by-case basis. Furthermore, the likelihood of the merging party's future entry must be 'likely' on a balance of probabilities and the pro-competitive effect must be substantial, taking into consideration price, output, marketplace effects and other competition-related dimensions.

§4. Pure Conglomerate Mergers

355. The Bureau defines 'conglomerate merger' broadly, as a merger between parties whose products do not compete and are not vertically related.[684] The Bureau may assess these mergers in the same way as a merger that would 'prevent' competition, as discussed above. Generally, conglomerate mergers involving no overlap only create concern when one of the parties to the merger would likely have entered the other party's market, but for the merger.

§5. Joint Ventures

356. The definition of 'merger' in section 91 of the Act refers to the acquisition or establishment of control or a significant interest by 'combination'. This term encompasses joint ventures. Thus, most joint ventures are reviewable in accordance with any of the relevant principles discussed throughout this chapter. However, section 95 provides a limited exception whereby certain joint ventures are not subject to an order by the Tribunal under section 92.[685] The exception applies only to joint ventures that are formed through a non-corporate means to undertake a specific project or a programme of research and development. Furthermore, the agreement must provide for the termination of the joint venture at the end of the project, and the project must not likely have been undertaken absent the joint venture. There is also a requirement that the joint venture prevent or lessen competition only to the extent that is reasonably necessary to undertake the project. This section has not been considered by the Tribunal to date, so it is uncertain how this test would operate in practice.

683. *Superior Propane*, *supra* n. 151 at 45–51.
684. MEGs, *supra* n. 153 at 11.1.
685. Nor are these joint ventures subject to pre-merger notification requirements (s. 112).

Part III. Administrative Procedure

Chapter 1. Administrative Investigations before the Antitrust Authority

§1. Initiative

357. The Commissioner is the administrative authority responsible for investigations under the Act. The Commissioner must initiate a formal inquiry under section 10 of the Act if there is reason to believe that: (i) someone has violated an order made pursuant to the Act; (ii) someone has or will commit a criminal offence under the Act; or (iii) grounds exist for making an order under one of the reviewable practice sections of the Act. Furthermore, the Commissioner must initiate a formal inquiry if there is a complaint made by a group of at least six Canadians pursuant to section 9, or if the Minister of Industry orders the commencement of an inquiry. In practice, the Bureau also initiates informal investigations based on complaints from members of the public and based on publicly available information, before deciding to 'go on inquiry'.

I. General Sectors Inquiries

358. Unlike the old *Combines Investigation Act*, the *Competition Act* does not provide the Commissioner or any other body with official authority to conduct formal sector inquiries. Over the past decade, there has been some political discussion about adding these powers to the Act. In 2003, national public consultations took place on the issue, but to date the legislature has not made any changes.[686]

359. In practice, the Bureau may initiate informal inquiries into sectors of the market. In such situations, the Bureau cannot rely on any formal investigatory tools, so the investigation proceeds based entirely on publicly available information or information offered voluntarily by participants in the sector. The Act allows the Commissioner to hire 'temporary, technical and special assistants',[687] and these people may conduct the informal inquiries. An informal inquiry might produce

686. For an overview of the investigatory power under the *Combines Investigation Act* and the reform discussions see S. Legault & E. Melrose, *Market Studies: A Contextual Overview* (Competition Bureau 2006).

687. *Competition Act*, *supra* n. 26 at s. 25.

information that would lead the Commissioner to believe that an offence had occurred under the Act, or that an order could be made pursuant to one of the reviewable practice provisions of the Act. At this point, the Commissioner could commence a formal inquiry under section 10; however, a formal inquiry must target specific people and/or businesses, rather than the general sector.

II. Ex Officio Investigations

360. As discussed above, the Commissioner must begin a formal inquiry if she has reason to believe that: (i) someone has violated an order made pursuant to the Act; (ii) someone has or will commit a criminal offence under the Act; or (iii) that grounds exist for making an order under one of the civilly reviewable practice sections of the Act.[688] The Commissioner's belief may flow from an informal investigation instigated of the Bureau's own accord. The Minister of Industry may also order the initiation of an inquiry.[689]

III. Complaints

361. Section 9 of the Act provides an official mechanism whereby a group of at least six Canadians can submit a complaint to the Commissioner. The complainants must believe that: (i) someone has violated an order made pursuant to the Act; (ii) someone has or will commit a criminal offence under the Act; or (iii) grounds exist for making an order under one of the reviewable practice sections of the Act.[690] The complaint must include the nature of the alleged contravention or offence, or the grounds alleged for making the order. The complaint must also describe the evidence supporting the opinion.[691] Upon receipt of a complaint, section 10 requires the Commissioner to launch an inquiry. However, the manner in which the Commissioner conducts the investigation is subject to her discretion. The court does not grant orders of *mandamus* requiring the Commissioner to complete inquiries.[692] Beyond providing complainants with confirmation that a complaint has been received, the Bureau cannot provide information about a possible or ongoing investigation. Inquiries are conducted in private, and section 29 of the Act imposes confidentiality restrictions with regards to complaints received and examined.[693]

362. In addition to this formal complaint procedure, the Bureau also invites members of the public to submit complaints through its website or by telephoning its information centre. The Bureau looks into these complaints and, if warranted, may launch an informal or formal inquiry. Furthermore, the Bureau also has in place an Immunity Programme and a Leniency Programme to encourage individuals with

688. *Ibid.*, at s. 10(1)(b).
689. *Ibid.*, at s. 10(1)(c).
690. *Ibid.*, at s. 9(1).
691. *Ibid.*, at s. 9(2).
692. *Ashley, supra* n. 270.
693. *Competition Act, supra* n. 26 at s. 29.

knowledge of cartel activity to come forward and provide the Bureau with information that may lead to an investigation or help in an ongoing investigation.[694]

§2. Powers

I. Requests for Information

363. Often during the course of an informal inquiry, the Bureau sends a Request for Information (RFI) to the complainant, other stake-holders, or in the case of a non-criminal matter, to the targeted party. RFIs are modelled on the formal information or documentation orders issuable under section 11 of the Act. Even in the case of a formal inquiry, the Bureau has sometimes opted to proceed by RFI instead of making use of its formal powers.[695] The targets of RFIs are not legally bound to disclose any information to the Bureau, but doing so may allow the target more opportunity to control the scope of the information and documentation sought by the Bureau.

II. Investigatory and Search Powers

364. Only when a formal investigation has commenced under section 10 can the Bureau make use of its investigatory and search powers. These powers derive in part from the Act, as well as from the *Criminal Code* (though the powers stemming from the *Criminal Code* only apply to criminal investigations). Section 11 of the Act allows the Commissioner to seek a court order for the production of documents or to conduct an oral examination if someone is likely to have information relevant to the section 10 inquiry. Section 15 of the Act allows the Commissioner to seek a court order for the issuance of a search warrant if there are reasonable grounds to believe that there has been a violation of the Act, or that the reviewable conduct sections have been engaged, and if there are reasonable grounds to believe that the premises contain records or other evidence related to the violation or the reviewable conduct. The *Criminal Code* provides the Commissioner with the authority to conduct judicially authorized wiretaps during the investigation of criminal conspiracies (section 45), –bid-rigging (section 47) and deceptive telemarketing (section 52.1(3)).[696] For a detailed discussion of these provisions, see above in 'Part 1: Chapter 5: §1 Administrative Enforcement: B. Investigating Powers'.

365. It is a criminal offence to interfere with an investigation of the Commissioner.[697] Likewise, it is an offence for a party to fail to comply with orders compelling the production of evidence under section 11 or granting a search warrant

694. For a detailed discussion of these programmes see 'Part 1: Chapter 5: §3. Criminal Enforcement: I. Criminal Sanctions for antitrust violations'.
695. Royal, *supra* n. 269 at 24.
696. *Criminal Code*, *supra* n. 19 at s. 186(1).
697. *Competition Act*, *supra* n. 26 at s. 64(1).

under section 15.[698] In the case of section 11 orders obtained on an ex parte basis, it is possible to appeal the decision to the Federal Court.[699] The Court can set aside an order on the grounds that a matter arose or came to light subsequent to the order's issuance, or on the basis of fraud. In *Labatt Breweries*,[700] the court set aside a section 11 order because the record upon which it had been obtained by the Commissioner on an ex parte basis had been 'misleading, inaccurate and incomplete', such that it would not have been granted had the Commissioner provided full and accurate disclosure initially.[701] The Court can either set aside or vary an order. The Bureau does not independently vary orders.

366. In the case of a search warrant issued under section 15, there is no opportunity to challenge the initial order. However, the targeted party may challenge the admissibility of evidence obtained as a result of the order in the subsequent proceeding. For example, if the Commissioner did not have reasonable grounds to believe the information offered in support of the warrant, the target of the search could argue that there was a violation of section 8 of the *Charter* (unreasonable search and seizure), and consequently the evidence could be deemed inadmissible under section 24(2) of the *Charter*. Note that this scenario is more likely to arise in the criminal context, as the Bureau more rarely uses search warrants in civil investigations.

III. Cooperation with Other State Institutions

367. Section 29 governs the extent to which the Bureau can cooperate with other state institutions to share information. The section provides that the Bureau cannot communicate broad categories of information obtained pursuant to the Act to any other person except 'a Canadian law enforcement agency or for the purposes of the administration or enforcement of this Act'.[702] The Bureau interprets 'law enforcement agency' broadly to include 'any federal or provincial authority that enforces acts or regulations that provide for criminal, civil, or administrative sanctions'.[703] This interpretation allows the Bureau to cooperate with other government agencies in a wide range of circumstances, including when the Bureau receives information pertinent to the mandate of another agency; when there is a potential violation of another statute; when the Bureau needs the assistance of another agency, such as a police agency; when the Bureau works in coordination with another agency on a

698. *Ibid.*, at s. 65.
699. See *Federal Court Rules*, SOR/98-106, s. 399.
700. *Labatt Breweries, supra* n. 272.
701. *Ibid.*, at para. 3.
702. *Competition Act, supra* n. 26 at s. 29(1). The following information is protected by this section: '(*a*) the identity of any person from whom information was obtained pursuant to this Act; (*b*) any information obtained pursuant to section 11, 15, 16 or 114; (*c*) whether notice has been given or information supplied in respect of a particular proposed transaction under section 114; (*d*) any information obtained from a person requesting a certificate under section 102; or (*e*) any information provided voluntarily pursuant to this Act'.
703. Competition Bureau, *Information Bulletin on the Communication of Confidential Information under the Competition Act*, 5 (Competition Bureau 2013).

particular matter; or when a Canadian law enforcement agency requests the information to fulfil its mandate.

368. The Bureau interprets 'administration or enforcement' to include cooperation with foreign state institutions. Accordingly, the Bureau shares otherwise confidential information with other states when appropriate to its cooperative activities with foreign authorities.[704] In 2002, the legislature amended Part III of the Act to allow the government to enter into civil Mutual Legal Assistance Treaties (MLATs). In this context, MLATs are agreements with foreign governments for reciprocal assistance in civil competition matters. Section 30.01 of the Act sets out the minimum requirements for any such treaty. For example, the foreign laws that address conduct similar to that addressed in the Act must be substantially similar to Canada's laws, and the information provided must be subject to privacy laws similar to Canada's. Under such an agreement, the foreign state could make a request to the Minister of Justice. The Minister could then apply to a court for a search warrant; an order to permit evidence gathering for use in the foreign state; an order to compel someone to participate in teleconferencing with the foreign state; or an order permitting the lending of evidence previously used in a Canadian proceeding. There is no requirement that a parallel investigation into the conduct occur in Canada. All of the procedural rules and protections that apply under section 15 (dealing with search warrants), section 16 (dealing with searching computers) and section 19 (providing protections with regard to information covered by solicitor-client privilege) apply to the foreign proceeding, unless a provision in Part III provides otherwise. So far, Canada has not entered into any civil MLATs.

369. Although Canada has yet to enter into any formal treaties under Part III, the Federal Government and Commissioner have entered into cooperation agreements with several state governments and foreign competition authorities.[705] Section 30.3 of the Act confirms the preservation of all arrangements, even in light of Part III. Although these cooperation agreements vary, they generally provide that the countries agree to notify one another if certain circumstances arise that are relevant to the other party. For example, relevant circumstances that may require notification include the review of a merger that involves a firm controlled by a person or corporation in the other state, or the ordering of a remedy that expressly requires or prohibits conduct that would take place in the other state. The agreements also recognize that it is in the enforcement bodies' mutual interest to cooperate and work together. In the case of treaties between the Canadian federal government and foreign governments, agreements typically specify methods of cooperation in some detail.[706] In contrast, agreements between the Commissioner and foreign competition bodies tend to be less detailed, with the parties merely agreeing that they will

---

704. *Ibid.*, at 7. See also M. Sullivan & J. Filion, *The Basics of International Cartel Enforcement in Canada* 9 (Competition Bureau 2004).

705. Canada has cooperation agreements with the United States, the European Community, the Republic of Korea, the Republic of China, Japan, Mexico, Great Britain, Australia, New Zealand, Brazil, Chile, Taiwan, and India (see International Efforts, *supra* n. 64).

706. See e.g., *Agreement Between The Government of Canada and the European Communities Regarding the Application of their Competition Laws*, 17 Jun. 1999, Can. T.S. 1999 No. 38.

endeavour to cooperate where possible.[707] In addition, most such agreements provide for the possibility of periodic meetings to consult and exchange information and feature provisions to safeguard the confidentiality of information exchanged between the parties. Furthermore, some of Canada's free trade agreements feature sections dealing with competition policy and include similar cooperation obligations.[708]

370. In addition to these competition-specific agreements and provisions, the *Mutual Legal Assistance in Criminal Matters Act*[709] allows the Canadian government to enter into criminal MLATs (whereas Part III of the Act discussed above allows for civil MLATs).[710] Drafters of Part III of the *Competition Act* largely modelled the statute after the *Mutual Legal Assistance in Criminal Matters Act*. Thus, the type of cooperation possible under criminal MLATs is very similar to that discussed above with regard to civil MLATs. In recent years, the Bureau has used criminal MLATs in cartel cases to request information located in other jurisdictions and to request assistance in compelling witnesses.[711]

371. Canada also participates in international discussions and consultations on the development of competition law through the OECD, the International Competition Network and the International Consumer Protection and Enforcement Network.[712]

§3. Right of Defence

372. Individuals charged under the criminal provisions of the Act enjoy the full complement of legal rights provided by the *Charter*. As well, accused individuals face trial in accordance with the principles of ordinary criminal procedure. For example, the prosecution has the onus of proving guilt beyond a reasonable doubt, and the defendant has a right to full disclosure of the prosecution's evidence. Given that the proceedings before the Tribunal are civil in nature, and given that the defendant does not face the risk of criminal sanctions (though the defendant may incur significant AMPs for certain conduct), the *Charter* and other legal rights applicable to criminal proceedings do not apply to the same degree to proceedings before the

707. See e.g., Canada, Australia & New Zealand, 'Cooperation Arrangement Between the Commissioner of Competition (Canada), the Australian Competition and Consumer Commission and the New Zealand Commerce Commission Regarding the Application of their Competition and Consumer Laws' http://www.competitionbureau.gc.ca/eic/site/cb-bc.nsf/eng/01595.html (25 Oct. 2000).
708. See e.g., *Free Trade Agreement between the Government of Canada and the Government of the State of Israel*, 31 Jul. 1996, Can. T.S. 1997 No. 49 (entered into force 1 Jan. 1997).
709. R.S.C. 1985, c. 30 (4th Supp.).
710. To access a current list of Canada's MLATs visit: Canada Treaty Information, 'Search', http://www.treaty-accord.gc.ca/search-recherche.aspx.
711. Sullivan, *supra* n. 708 at 11.
712. See International Efforts, *supra* n. 64.

Tribunal.[713] The discussion in this section deals with contested civil proceedings before the Tribunal. The main source of procedural rules for the Tribunal is the *Competition Tribunal Rules.*[714] The *Federal Court Rules*[715] supplement any gaps in the *Tribunal Rules.*[716]

I. Content and Notification of Opening Decisions

373. At any point during an investigation the Commissioner may decide that the case warrants bringing an application before the Tribunal. Contentious proceedings under the Act, both when initiated by the Commissioner or when initiated by a private party who has been granted leave under section 103.1, commence through a Notice of Application.[717] Within five days of filing the Notice of Application, all respondents must receive service.[718] In addition to some basic procedural information, the Notice of Application must contain the sections of the Act that enable the application; a concise statement of the grounds for the application and of the material facts that the applicant relies upon; a concise statement of the economic theory of the case, if relevant, and except in the case of an application pursuant to Part VII.1 of the Act (Deceptive Marketing); and the particulars of the order sought.[719]

374. A person who has been served with a Notice of Application may oppose the application by serving a response within 45 days of receiving service of the notice.[720] The response must provide an admission or denial of each allegation in the Notice of Application; a concise statement of the grounds for opposing the application and of the material facts that the person opposing the application relies upon; and a concise statement of the economic theory of the case, if relevant, except in the case of an application pursuant to Part VII.1 of the Act (Deceptive Marketing).[721] The Commissioner or private applicant then has the opportunity to file a reply admitting or denying any allegations in the response.[722] If the respondent fails to reply to the service, the applicant may move for the Tribunal to issue the order sought. If the Tribunal has heard sufficient evidence to justify the order, the Tribunal will then issue the order.[723]

713. The legal protections applicable to criminal proceedings are set out in s. 11 of the *Charter*. Note that the Act as a whole is still subject to the *Charter*, so while the procedural rights don't necessarily apply in administrative proceedings, a respondent is still free to challenge the constitutionality of any given provision of the Act.
714. *Tribunal Rules*, *supra* n. 73.
715. *Federal Court Rules, supra* n. 703.
716. *Tribunal Rules*, *supra* n. 73 at s. 34(1).
717. *Ibid.*, at s. 36.
718. *Ibid.*, at s. 37(2).
719. *Ibid.*, at s. 36(2).
720. *Ibid.*, at s. 38.
721. *Ibid.*, at s. 38(2).
722. *Ibid.*, at s. 39.
723. *Ibid.*, at s. 41.

II. Proceedings: Hearings, Access to File, Briefs

375. Proceedings before the Tribunal are subject to rules of disclosure similar to other civil proceedings. This point means that the Commissioner (or private person bringing the application) and the person under review must each provide full disclosure of any relevant information. This requirement is different from criminal proceedings under the Act, in which the accused has a right to silence and, consequently, no disclosure obligations. Once service of the pleadings is complete, the parties must deliver each other an affidavit of documents containing a list of all documents 'relevant to any matter in issue' that are, or were ever, in the possession, power or control of the party.[724] The parties must then make these documents available for inspection to the other party.[725]

376. Either party can claim that a document is privileged, meaning that disclosure of the contents of the document is not required. However, a party cannot rely on privileged documents during the proceedings unless they subsequently disclose the documents. In the event of a challenge to privilege, the Tribunal can assess the document to determine the validity of the privilege claim.[726] The Commissioner's ability to claim privilege is a second way in which civil disclosure varies from criminal disclosure. In criminal cases the Crown must provide full and ongoing disclosure, and its ability to claim privilege is extremely limited.

377. The most important forms of privilege are solicitor-client privilege and litigation privilege. Solicitor-client privilege applies to any communications between a client and their lawyer or their lawyer's agent, provided that the client made the communications for the purpose of seeking legal advice and intended confidentiality.[727] Solicitor-client privilege applies to external counsel, as well as in-house counsel. It applies if the Commissioner or other members of the Bureau seek legal advice, as from the Department of Justice. Litigation privilege applies to documents that have been prepared for the dominant purpose of litigation.[728] Thus, once litigation is within contemplation, it may apply to a wide variety of information that has been created. For example, it applies to interview notes made by the Bureau staff during the course of a formal inquiry, because a formal inquiry demonstrates that litigation is within contemplation.[729]

378. The Commissioner has also successfully invoked another important form of privilege called public interest privilege. Public interest privilege may apply if there is a strong public interest in protecting the information that outweighs the interest in disclosure. The four conditions for public interest privilege are: (i) the

724. *Ibid.*, at s. 60(2).
725. *Ibid.*, at s. 65.
726. *Ibid.*, at s. 61.
727. See *Solosky v. The Queen*, [1980] 1 S.C.R. 821.
728. See *General Accident Assurance Company v. Chrusz* (1999), 45 O.R. (3d) 321, 180 D.L.R. (4th) 241.
729. *Canada (Director of Investigation & Research) v. NutraSweet* (1989), Comp. Trib. CT-8902-79, 1989 CarswellNat 1074 at para. 17.

communications must originate in confidence; (ii) the element of confidentiality must be essential to maintain the relationship between the parties; (iii) the relationship, in the opinion of the community, ought to be sedulously fostered; and (iv) the injury to the relationship by disclosure must be greater than the benefit to be gained by the correct disposal of the litigation.[730] The Commissioner has successfully invoked public interest privilege to avoid disclosing the contents and identities of informers and the content of interviews with them. In *Nielsen*, the Federal Court of Appeal upheld the then-Director's right to refuse disclosure of certain complaints and correspondence received by the Bureau, as well as notes and materials prepared by Bureau staff in their meetings with various industry members. The decision states:

> [T]he Director has to be able to obtain information from the relevant industry in performing his functions under the *Competition Act*. To gain the cooperation of people in the industry he must be able to gather information in confidence, his informants not being identified unless of course they are called as witnesses in a proceeding before the Tribunal.[731]

The decision has since been followed by the Tribunal in more recent cases.[732]

379. Finally, dispute settlement privilege applies to communications made during attempts to settle a litigious matter through negotiation or mediation. It exists to allow parties to freely negotiate with the aim of settling disputes before trial. There are three elements of dispute settlement privilege: (i) litigation is underway or is being contemplated; (ii) communications are made for the purpose of attempting settlement; and (iii) there is an express or implied intent that the material will be kept confidential if negotiations fail.[733] Thus, if the Commissioner and a party unsuccessfully attempt to reach a Consent Agreement and the negotiations fail, the information disclosed by either party is likely inadmissible against the other at subsequent proceedings.

380. If a party claims that the information in a document is confidential, the Tribunal can inspect the document and, if appropriate, issue a confidentiality order with regard to its disclosure.[734] Unlike a claim of privilege, a confidentiality order does not exempt the document from disclosure; rather a confidentiality order may place limits on the disclosure, such as a prohibition against copying the document or a restriction on who may see it.

---

730. These factors are known as the Wigmore criteria, and were first cited by the Supreme Court in *Slavutych v. Baker*, [1976] 1 S.C.R. 254 at 260.

731. *D & B Co. of Canada Ltd. v. Canada (Director of Investigation & Research)* (1994), 176 N.R. 62 (sub nom. *Director of Investigation & Research, Competition Act v. D & B Cos. of Canada*) 58 C.P.R. (3d) 353, 1994 CarswellNat 1849 at para. 2.

732. See e.g., *United Grain Growers, supra* n. 364; and *Canada (Commissioner of Competition) v. Sears Canada Inc.*, [2003] C.C.T.D. No. 16, 28 C.P.R. (4th) 385 (Comp. Trib.); and *Commissioner of Competition v Air Canada*, 2012 CACT 21 (CanLii).

733. See *Tele-Direct, supra* n. 188.

734. *Tribunal Rules, supra* n. 73 at s. 66.

381. The Ontario Superior Court of Justice reviewed the legal principles underlying sealing orders as they relate to the reviewable matters provisions of the *Competition Act* in the *Commissioner of Competition v. Chatr Wireless Inc.*, which involved a motion related to the Commissioner's application against Rogers for alleged misleading advertising of its Chatr brand of discount wireless telecommunications services. The Court issued a partial confidentiality (or sealing) order with respect to certain information used by the Commissioner in her application.[735] As part of its investigation into the allegations against Rogers and Chatr, the Bureau collected information from recent discount wireless carrier entrants Public Mobile, Wind Mobile and Mobilicity. In its motion, the Bureau argued that its ability to access information required in enforcement proceedings, and its duty not to release information that could frustrate the goals of the *Competition Act*, required it to maintain the confidentiality of confidential business records supplied to it for investigatory purposes. In determining whether the information at stake was confidential, the Court relied on the two part test developed in the Supreme Court's decision in *Sierra Club of Canada v. Canada (Minister of Finance):*

(a) The order is necessary to prevent a serious risk to the proper administration of justice because reasonably alternative measures will not prevent the risk; and
(b) The salutary effects of the publication ban outweigh the deleterious effects on the rights and interests of the parties and the public, including the effects on the right to free expression, the right of the accused to a fair public trial and the efficacy of the administration of justice.[736]

In view of the foregoing factors, the Court allowed the motion to seal various marketing information but refused it in respect of 'dropped call' rates – which it found were at the heart of the Commissioner's case against Rogers and therefore ought to be disclosed.

382. Sixty days prior to the hearing the Commissioner (or private applicant) must provide pre-hearing disclosure – including a complete list of the documents to be relied on during the hearing (noting any waivers of privilege) – and a witness statement that sets out the evidence that will be provided by any lay witness.[737] The respondent must provide the same pre-hearing disclosure within thirty days of the hearing. The applicant may then respond within fifteen days of the hearing with any additional documents or witness statements it intends to rely upon at the hearing.[738] Unless the Tribunal orders otherwise, a party cannot introduce at the hearing any document that is not disclosed in the affidavit of documents or pre-hearing disclosure, or any document for which privilege is not waived.[739] Similarly, the applicant must serve any reports by expert witnesses at least sixty days in advance of the hearing. The respondent must serve expert witness reports at least thirty days in advance

735. 2011 ONSC 3387.
736. [2002] 2 S.C.R. 522, 2002 SCC 41.
737. *Tribunal Rules*, *supra* n. 73 at s. 68.
738. *Ibid.*, at ss 69 and 70.
739. *Ibid.*, at s. 71.

of the hearing, and the applicant must serve a reply report at least fifteen days in advance of the hearing.[740] In practice, the parties typically will confer on and the Tribunal will make a scheduling order addressing the timing for pre-hearing disclosure.

III. Statement of Objections

383. The Canadian equivalent of a 'Statement of Objections' is the Notice of Application to the Tribunal, discussed above. The Bureau generally reveals its theory of harm to potential respondents before filing a Notice of Application and typically attempts to settle the matter consensually but it is not statutorily required to do so.

IV. Final Hearing and Decision

384. Final hearings take place before a panel of three to five members of the Tribunal, with the panel including at least one judicial member and one lay member.[741] Hearings are generally open to the public, but they can take place in camera in circumstances involving confidential information.[742] Both parties have the opportunity to provide arguments, present lay evidence and expert evidence, and cross-examine the opposing side's witnesses. The onus is on the Commissioner or private applicant to prove, on a balance of probabilities, that the facts warrant an order.

385. Private parties can apply for leave to intervene in a proceeding before the Tribunal for a matter involving any reviewable practice except for Deceptive Marketing under Part VII.1 of the Act.[743] To obtain leave, an applicant must show: (i) that the matter allegedly affecting them is within the Tribunal's jurisdiction; (ii) that they are directly affected by the conduct; (iii) that their intended representations are relevant to an issue raised by the Commissioner; and (iv) that they bring a unique or distinct perspective that will assist the Tribunal in determining the issues before it.[744] If the case has been brought by a private applicant the Commissioner may also intervene.[745] Provincial Attorneys General can intervene to make representations on behalf of their provinces if an order is being sought under section 92, which deals with mergers.[746] Intervening parties may file documents with the Tribunal and have access to information filed by the parties.

740. *Ibid.*, at s. 77.
741. *Competition Tribunal Act*, *supra* n. 27 at s. 10(1).
742. *Tribunal Rules*, *supra* n. 73 at ss 29 and 30.
743. *Competition Tribunal Act*, *supra* n. 27 at s. 9(3).
744. *United Grain Growers*, *supra* n. 364.
745. *Competition Act*, *supra* n. 26 at s. 103.2.
746. *Ibid.*, at s. 101. Provincial Attorney Generals can also intervene in the case of applications to file or amend specialization agreements (s. 88).

386. The Tribunal makes its decisions on a majority basis. If there is an equal split between the members, the presiding member makes the decision. The presiding member is a judicial member appointed by the Chairman of the Tribunal to preside over a particular case.[747] Only judicial members can determine questions of law.[748] Upon reaching a decision, the Tribunal issues an order, if warranted, in accordance with the relevant section of the Act. Failure to comply with an order by the Tribunal, except for an order to pay an AMP, is a criminal offence punishable by fine or imprisonment.[749] The exception for AMPs is necessary for constitutional reasons, as the courts have held that the possibility of imprisonment for non-payment of an administrative fine violates section 7 (the right to life, liberty and security) of the *Charter*.[750]

747. *Competition Tribunal Act*, *supra* n. 27 at ss 10 and 12.
748. *Ibid.*, at s. 12.
749. *Competition Act*, *supra* n. 26 at s. 66.
750. See *R. v. Gray*, [1989] 1 W.W.R. 66, 44 C.C.C. (3d) 222, 66 C.R. (3d) 378, 44 C.R.R. 6 (Man. C.A.); and *R. v. Burt*, [1988] 1 W.W.R. 385, 38 C.C.C. (3d) 299, 60 C.R. (3d) 372 (Sask. C.A.).

Chapter 2. Voluntary Notifications and Clearance Decisions

§1. MERGER CONTROL

387. In 1986, anti-competitive mergers became a civilly reviewable practice under the Act, and the notification process became established. The Bureau administers notification and review of mergers, and the Bureau can bring an application to the Tribunal if it believes a merger will substantially prevent or lessen competition. Prior to the 2009 amendments, the Act contained separate notification requirements and time periods for complex and non-complex mergers. In 2009, the legislature streamlined the notification requirements to be the same for all mergers and to include a uniform thirty-day initial notification period (extendable by issuance of a supplementary information request by the time the parties take to respond fully to the request plus an additional thirty days). In addition, the 2009 amendments raised the transaction-size thresholds for pre-merger notification and established a formula for automatic annual adjustment of the thresholds based on Canada's GDP. The changes also reduced the time that the Commissioner has to challenge a completed merger from three years to one year, as well as introducing AMPs and injunctive relief to more effectively enforce compliance with the waiting periods. The *Notifiable Transactions Regulations*[751] also underwent amendment to reflect these changes to the Act. A series of *Interpretation Guidelines* provide additional detailed procedural information regarding compliance with notification requirements. In January 2012, the Bureau published revised Merger Review Process Guidelines[752] (MRPG) outlining how it operates in light of the new process.

§2. PRELIMINARY FILING OBLIGATIONS

388. The scope of transactions falling within the notification requirements is very broad, with the Act providing only limited exceptions. Notification thresholds are based on the size of the target in Canada as well as, the size of the parties' Canadian-related business. The target entity can exceed the thresholds on its own, even without the acquiring party having a presence in Canada. The exception is for corporate amalgamations, which require at least two parties to the transaction to have a significant presence in Canada. If the merger consists of the acquisition of shares or an interest in an unincorporated business combination, control and interest thresholds must be met to trigger the notification requirement. Of note, the Bureau retains the right to review a transaction even if the thresholds are not met (and thus notification is not required).[753]

751. *Notifiable Transaction* Regulations, *supra* n. 72.
752. Competition Bureau, *Merger Review Process Guidelines* (Competition Bureau 2012).
753. See e.g., Competition Bureau, *Technical Backgrounder: 'Superior Plus' Acquisition of Certain Propane Assets in Western and Central Newfoundland from Irving Oil and Irvin Oil Marketing* (Competition Bureau 2009), in which the Bureau initiated an investigation of a non-notifiable transaction, and concluded that the transaction would likely substantially prevent or lessen competition in the retail supply of propane in Central and Western Newfoundland for commercial and industrial use.

389. If a proposed transaction's size exceeds the thresholds (discussed in more detail below), the parties to the transaction must notify the Commissioner of the proposed merger.[754] In the case of an acquisition of shares, the parties to the transaction are the person or persons seeking to acquire the shares and the corporation whose shares are to be acquired. Section 16 of the *Notifiable Transactions Regulations* sets out the information that the Bureau requires. The parties must include descriptions of their principle businesses and the business objectives underlying the transaction. The parties must also provide background information on their businesses and that of their affiliates, including a summary description of each of the principal categories of products they or their affiliates supply, sell or distribute; a list of the twenty most important current suppliers and customers for each of those principle categories of products; a statement identifying the total annual volume or dollar value of purchases from and sales to all suppliers and customers for each principle product; and a summary of the geographic regions of sales for its principal businesses and the principal businesses of its affiliates. In addition, the parties must provide the following information pertinent to the transaction: a copy of each legal document, or the most recent draft of that document, that is to be used to implement the proposed transaction; a list of the foreign competition or antitrust authorities that have been notified of the proposed transaction by the parties and the date of each authority's notification; and all studies, surveys, analyses and reports that an officer or director of the corporation prepared or received for the purpose of evaluating the merger. A CAD 50,000 filing fee must accompany the notification and can be paid in whole or in part by either party.[755]

I. Criteria and Thresholds

390. Sections 109 and 110 stipulate the notification requirements for the acquisition of assets, the acquisition of shares, proposed corporate amalgamations, proposed non-corporate combinations, and the acquisition of an interest in an unincorporated business combination. In all cases, the parties to the proposed transaction, including their respective affiliates,[756] must together have assets in Canada greater than CAD 400 million, or they must have gross revenues flowing in, into or out of Canada greater than CAD 400 million.[757] In addition, the following target-specific conditions, if met, give rise to a notification requirement:

More recently, the *CCS* (on appeal, *Tervita*) case involved an application filed post-closing against a non-notifiable transaction. See discussion at paragraph 62 above.

754. *Competition Act, supra* n. 26 at s. 114(1).

755. Competition Bureau, Competition Bureau Fees and Service Standards Handbook for Mergers and Merger-Related Matters, November 2010 (Competition Bureau, 2010) [Service Standards].

756. Affiliate is defined in s. 2(2) of the Act to include corporations where one is a subsidiary of the other, corporations where both are subsidiaries of the same corporation, corporations each affiliated with the same corporation, or partnerships or sole proprietorships both controlled by the same person.

757. *Competition Act, supra* n. 26 at s. 109.

(a) *Acquisition of assets (section 110(2)):* In the case of a proposed acquisition of any of the assets in Canada of an operating business,[758] the aggregate value of those assets or the gross revenues from sales in or from Canada generated from those assets must exceed the transaction threshold established in section 110(7)-(8), which was CAD 86 million for transactions completed in 2015 (indexed annually).[759]

(b) *Acquisition of shares (section 110(3)):* In the event of a proposed acquisition of voting shares of a corporation that carries on an operating business or controls a corporation that carries on an operating business the following two conditions must be met:
   - the aggregate value of the assets in Canada that are owned by the corporation or by corporations controlled by that corporation (other than assets that are shares of any of those corporations), or the gross revenues from sales in or from Canada generated from those assets must exceed the transaction threshold established in section 110(7)-(8), which was CAD 86 million for transactions completed in 2015 (indexed annually); and
   - the person or persons acquiring the shares, together with their affiliates, must own voting shares of the corporation that in the aggregate carry more than 20% of voting shares if the corporation's voting shares are publicly traded; more than 35% of voting shares if none of the corporation's voting shares are publicly traded; or more than 50% of voting shares if the person or persons already owned more than 20% (for a publicly traded company) or 35% (for a private company) of the company's voting shares.

(c) *Amalgamation (sections 110(4) and (4.1)):* In the case of a proposed amalgamation of two or more corporations, there is a size of the parties' requirement and a target-size requirement. At least two parties to the amalgamation, including their respective affiliates, must have assets in Canada or gross revenue from sales in, from or into Canada exceeding the threshold established in section 110(7)-(8), which was CAD 86 million for transactions completed in 2015 (indexed annually); and the continuing corporation would have assets in Canada or gross revenues from sales in or from Canada exceeding the threshold established in section 110(7)-(8).

(d) *Non-corporate combinations (section 110(5)):* In the case of a combination, which is an agreement between two or more persons to carry on business through a non-corporate method, the value of the assets in Canada of the continuing business, or the gross revenue from sales in or from Canada generated from those assets must exceed the threshold established in section 110(7)-(8),

758. The Act defines operating business to include 'a business undertaking in Canada to which employees employed in connection with the undertaking ordinarily report for work'. Interpretation Guideline No. 1 of the Bureau's Notifiable Transactions Interpretation Guidelines, *supra* n. 149, provides a broad interpretation of operating, stating that '[a] company that is engaged in the business of holding investments, whether passive or otherwise, may be an operating business if it satisfies the remainder of the definition of that term'.

759. The threshold may be indexed each year to change in accordance with Canada's GDP. Subsec. 110(8) provides the formula to calculate the change in the notification requirements. The new threshold is generally announced in January of each calendar year.

which was CAD 86 million for transactions completed in 2015 (indexed annually).

(e) *Acquisition of an interest in a non-corporate combination (section 100(6)):* In the case of an acquisition of an interest in a combination that carries on business other than as a corporation, the following two conditions must be met:
  - the aggregate value of the assets in Canada that are subject to the combination, or the gross revenues from sales in or from Canada generated from those assets must exceed the transaction threshold established in section 110(7)-(8), which was CAD 86 million for transactions completed in 2015 (indexed annually); and
  - as a result of the acquisition, the person or persons acquiring the interest, together with their affiliates, would hold an aggregate interest in the combination entitling them to at least 35% of the profits or 35% of the assets upon dissolution. If the person already holds this much interest, they must then be entitled to receive 50% of profits or assets.

II. Turnover Calculation

391. The calculation of aggregate assets and revenues is generally fairly straightforward. The determination relies on the most recently available audited financial statements, which must date to within fifteen months of the date of notification.[760] The *Notifiable Transactions Regulations* provide some technical guidance as to how to calculate assets and revenues. In the case of assets, the Bureau should deduct the following amounts: any amount that represents duplication arising from transactions between affiliates; any amount that represents duplication arising from an ownership interest of one person in another person, whether or not those persons are affiliated; and any amount provided for depreciation or diminution of value.[761] With regard to revenue, the Bureau should include the following sums in the calculation: the amounts accruing from the sale or lease of goods, other than those amounts not properly constituting revenue; and the amounts accruing from the rendering of services. The Bureau does not deduct expenses or other amounts incurred or provided for in relation to the sale or lease of goods or the rendering of services other than for duplication arising from transactions between affiliates.[762] The *Notifiable Transactions Regulations* also provide some other section-specific requirements, so they should always be consulted when calculating assets and revenues.

392. In cases where the calculation is complicated, the parties may wish to bring an application under section 124 seeking written guidance from the Commissioner. Section 124 allows a party to apply for a written opinion from the Commissioner

760. See *Notifiable Transaction Regulations, supra* n. 72, ss 4-7.
761. *Ibid.*, s. 4.
762. *Ibid.*, s. 5.

with regard to any provision of the Act or its regulations. If the written facts submitted by the applicant are accurate, the decision binds the Commissioner.[763] In practice, parties often seek and rely upon informal advice from the Bureau's Merger Notification Unit.

III. Market Share Calculation

393. Market share is not relevant to determining whether a transaction is notifiable. As a matter of practice, the Bureau considers market share when determining the complexity of a merger for the sake of providing timelines under its Service Standard policy, as discussed below.[764]

IV. Other Relevant Notions

394. The aforementioned notification threshold categories are broad enough to catch most transactions. However, sections 111–113 of the Act establish several narrow classes of transactions which are exempt from the notification requirements. Section 111 applies to certain acquisitions of voting shares, assets or interests. For example, acquisitions of shares or interests solely for the purpose of underwriting are exempt, as are acquisitions of shares or interests received through gifts, intestate successions or testamentary dispositions. Section 112 applies to joint ventures. Just as certain non-corporate joint ventures are exempt from substantive merger review under section 92, the same transactions are exempt from notification requirements.[765] Section 113 exempts transactions all the parties to which are affiliates of one another from notification requirements, and also provides some procedural-type exceptions. For example, parties do not need to file pre-merger notification if the Commissioner has issued an Advance Ruling Certificate (ARC) under section 102 or has waived the requirement under section 113(c) because the parties have already provided substantially similar information in an application for an ARC. A more detailed discussion of ARCs follows below.

§3. Structure of Proceedings

395. As discussed in the introduction of this chapter, the legislature streamlined the structure and proceedings under the notifiable transaction provisions in 2009. As a result of the changes, the initial notification requirements and waiting periods are the same for all notified transactions.

763. *Competition Act*, *supra* n. 26, s. 124.1(2).
764. See Service Standards, *supra* n. 759.
765. Section 112 does not explicitly state that the combination must be non-corporate, but the Bureau's position is that this requirement should be read into the section. See Notifiable Transactions Interpretation Guidelines, *supra* n. 149 at Interpretation Guideline No. 4.

I. Preliminary Assessment and Full Investigation

396. If a transaction meets notification thresholds and thereby triggers the requirement to notify the Commissioner of the proposed merger, an automatic thirty-day waiting period applies to the transaction. This rule means that the transaction cannot close until the expiration of at least thirty days, unless the Bureau notifies the parties sooner that it does not intend to challenge the transaction (i.e., issues a 'no-action letter').[766] During this initial waiting period, the Bureau conducts its initial investigation into the competitive effects of the merger. The Bureau may also ask the parties to voluntarily provide more information, which would potentially pre-empt the Bureau from invoking the formal 'supplementary information request' (SIR) process (discussed below).[767] The Bureau has indicated that it clears the 'vast majority' of notified mergers during this thirty-day waiting period.[768] All of the parties to the transaction must provide notice. However, any of the parties required to give notice under the Act may give notice and supply information on behalf of and in lieu of other parties (if duly authorized to do so by those parties). Parties may also give notice or supply information jointly.[769]

397. If the Bureau believes that a proposed transaction raises competition issues and may require a remedy it may issue an SIR. An SIR has the effect of extending the waiting period for another thirty days from the time that the parties comply with the SIR.[770] The SIR is an information-gathering tool that the Bureau can use to formally request that the parties produce certain information. Because the second thirty-day period does not start running until the additional information has been provided, a failure to comply with the SIR precludes the parties from legally closing the deal, unless the Bureau issues a no-action letter under section 123(1), clearing the transaction (with or without conditions). Section 116 limits the scope of filings and responses to SIRs. The Bureau cannot require parties to provide information that is not known or reasonably attainable; information that is privileged or otherwise required by law to remain confidential; or information that could not, on any reasonable basis, be considered relevant to a lessening or prevention of competition.

398. The Bureau may also make voluntary requests to third parties for information, or if necessary the Bureau may invoke its investigative power under section 11 to compel the production of certain information. However, the Bureau has said that if the parties cooperate with the SIR it rarely needs to resort to section 11 to gather information from the parties.[771]

399. At any point, the Bureau may stop either waiting period by issuing a no-action letter, indicating that the Commissioner does not currently intend to

766. *Competition Act*, *supra* n. 26 at s. 123(1).
767. Merger Review Process Guidelines, *supra* n. 756 at 2.
768. *Ibid.*, at 1.
769. *Competition Act, supra* n. 26 at s. 114(4).
770. *Ibid.*, at ss 114(2) and 123(2).
771. Merger Review Process Guidelines, *supra* n. 756 at 4 n. 14.

challenge the proposed transaction. The parties then become free to close the transaction; however, the possibility remains that the Commissioner could challenge the transaction in the future. The same is true when the initial thirty-day waiting period and/or the additional thirty-day waiting period imposed by the SIR – if one was sought – expire. Section 92 allows the Commissioner to challenge a completed merger for up to one year after its closing, unless an ARC was issued in respect of the transaction and circumstances have not materially changed.[772] However, if the relevant waiting period expires or the no-action letter is granted along with a waiver of the requirement to notify, the parties can close the transaction without fear of the Commissioner applying for an order under section 123.1. Section 123.1 applies when the court determines that a person, without good and sufficient cause, has completed or is likely to complete a proposed transaction before the end of the applicable waiting period. A court has broad authority to grant any remedy it considers appropriate – including an AMP of up to CAD 10,000 per day – for failure to comply with the waiting periods set out under section 123. A court can also order the provision of information pursuant to an SIR; issue an interim order prohibiting the completion of a transaction; or issue an order dissolving a merger or ordering the divestiture of assets.

400. If the Tribunal grants an injunction under either section 100 or section 104, the parties may be prevented from closing the transaction despite the expiration of the waiting periods. When the Commissioner believes that a proposed transaction may give rise to competition issues, but has yet to challenge the merger under section 92, he or she may seek an interim order from the Tribunal forbidding any person 'from doing any act or thing that it appears to the Tribunal may constitute or be directed toward the completion or implementation of a proposed merger'.[773] When the Commissioner has made an application under section 92, he or she can apply for an injunction under section 104 of the Act. Section 104 is a general section allowing the Tribunal to issue injunctive relief if an application has been brought in relation to any reviewable practice. For detailed discussions of both of these provisions, see 'Part I: Chapter 5: §1 Administrative Enforcement: VI. Interim measures'.

II. Time Framework

401. In addition to the basic legally binding timelines imposed by the notifiable transaction provisions of the Act (discussed in the previous section), the Bureau has published non-binding service standards indicating the (informal) timelines within which it aims to review transactions, depending on their complexity. These are discussed in the Fee and Service Standards Handbook for Mergers and Merger-Related Matters (Service Standards).[774] The Service Standards provide that all transactions subject to an ARC or notification are classified as either 'non-complex'

772. Section 97 of the Act provides the one year limitation period.
773. *Competition Act*, *supra* n. 26 at s. 100.
774. Service Standards, *supra* n. 759.

or 'complex'.[775] The Bureau determines complexity based on a number of factors, including product market, geographic market, market share and barriers to entry. The Bureau's timeframe for reviewing mergers depends on the complexity classification.

402. Generally, the Bureau classifies a merger as non-complex if there is an absence of competition issues, and no or minimal overlap between the two parties. The Bureau defines 'minimal overlap' as a post-merger market share of less than 10% in any relevant market. Transactions may also be non-complex if there is a combined post-merger market share of between 10% and 35%, but lacking any of the factors indicative of complex mergers. Between 2002 and 2010, the Bureau classified about 88% of merger filings as non-complex.[776]

403. The Bureau is likely to classify a transaction as complex if it is between competitors or between customers and suppliers, and if there are indications that the transaction *may*, or are likely to, create, maintain or enhance market power. Generally, if the post-transaction market share of the parties exceeds 35%, the Bureau considers the transaction to be complex. If the post-transaction market share is below 35%, the Bureau may still classify the deal as complex if one of the following complicating factors obtains: the definition of relevant markets is challenging; the merger is between participants in a concentrated industry; the post-merger incremental increase in market share is not de minimis; the existence of barriers to entry; there are few effective remaining competitors; the evaluation of the effectiveness of remaining competition or the assessment of potential sources of new competition is difficult; the existence of credible complaints or competitive concerns; an efficiency exception or failing firm claim requires analysis; and cooperation and coordination with one or more foreign competition authorities is required. Between 2002 and 2010, the Bureau classified about 12% of proposed transactions as complex or 'very complex' (a designation it no longer uses – applicable to complex transactions for which a SIR was issued).[777]

404. The Bureau had previously distinguished between 'complex' and 'very complex' mergers. Between 2002 and 2010, the Bureau only classified about 2% of reviewable transactions as very complex.[778]

405. The Service Standards set out the maximum amounts of time that the Bureau takes to provide a response, assuming cooperation from the parties: 14 days for a non-complex notification filing or ARC request; 45 days for a complex notification filing or ARC request; and 30 days following the receipt of a complete response to an SIR.[779]

---

775. *Ibid.*, at 3.
776. *Ibid.*, at 4.
777. *Ibid.*, at 5.
778. *Ibid.*
779. *Ibid.*, at 11.

406. In certain cases complex mergers, there may be circumstances where the Bureau's review is not completed within the initial thirty-day waiting period and the Commissioner elects not to issue an SIR. In these circumstances, the Merger Review Process Guidelines state that the Bureau will proceed to complete its investigation beyond the expiration of the initial waiting period and, may enter (before or after expiration of the initial thirty-day waiting period) into a 'timing agreement' with the parties in order to address key issues, including commitments regarding closing of the proposed transaction and possible further production requirements.[780]

407. The revised Merger Review Process Guidelines note that the Bureau will require parties to produce 'refreshed' information where the period between the date of issuance of an SIR and the date of certification of a complete response exceeds (typically) ninety days. In such cases, the Bureau will require responsive records to be current to within thirty days of the certification of a party's response.[781]

408. Subject to commitments made to the Bureau by the parties to a proposed transaction, or orders obtained under section 100 or 104 of the Act, parties are legally permitted to close their transaction upon expiry of the initial thirty-day waiting period if no SIR has been issued. However, without an ARC or no-action letter, the parties have no assurances from the Commissioner that the proposed transaction will not be challenged.[782]

409. The Bureau has also said that during the review process it may attempt to work with the parties to voluntarily establish a timing agreement. A timing agreement sets target dates for key events in the process. For example, it might include a date for when the Bureau will inform the parties which employees or agents it would like to interview; commitments on the parties' rolling production of documents to comply with Bureau requests; timing for status updates, interim reports, and the Bureau's final assessment; and a time for the closing of the transaction.[783]

410. The revised Merger Review Process Guidelines contain information on timing requirements during hostile transactions.[784] In the context of a hostile transaction, a target is not able to affect (e.g., delay) the commencement of the relevant waiting periods by delaying its pre-notification filing or its response to an SIR. The revised Guidelines note that the Bureau – in order to ensure receipt of SIR responses from targets on a timely basis – will typically issue an SIR in combination with a timing agreement (to certify compliance on or before a specified date) and/or a court order obtained pursuant to section 11 of the Act, which compels the target to provide information to the Bureau. In the context of a hostile transaction, the Bureau

780. Merger Review Process Guidelines, *supra* n. 756 at 3.
781. *Ibid.*, at 7.
782. *Ibid.*, at 3.
783. *Ibid.*, at 13.
784. *Ibid.*, at 3.

may also request that a bidder provide a timing commitment (not to certify compliance before a specified date) to ensure that the Bureau has sufficient time to obtain and analyse information from all parties.[785]

III. Right of Defence

411. If the parties believe that the scope of an SIR is inappropriate, or if the parties believe they have fully complied with an SIR that the Bureau claims is incomplete, they can contact the responsible Assistant Deputy Commissioner and attempt to resolve the issue. If a resolution proves unattainable, parties may submit a written notice of appeal to the Senior Deputy Commissioner of the Mergers and Monopolistic Practices branch. The complaint is then forwarded to another Senior Deputy Commissioner or Deputy Commissioner, who reviews the matter and, if warranted, modifies the scope of the SIR or declares that the parties have complied with the SIR. If the parties continue to oppose the SIR or claim they have complied, the Commissioner may choose to bring an application under section 123.1 arguing that the party has completed or is likely to complete a proposed transaction in non-compliance of the waiting period. No order is made if the party had or has 'good and sufficient cause'. The onus falls on the party to demonstrate good and sufficient cause. If the court or Tribunal finds that the party should have complied with the SIR (or complied more extensively), it may order compliance or invoke any of the other remedies available under section 123.1, as discussed above.

§4. Clearance and Conditional Clearance

412. Technically speaking, once the initial thirty-day waiting period and the thirty-day SIR extension (if applicable) expire, the parties are legally clear to close the transaction, provided the Commissioner has not sought an interim order under section 100 or 104. However, as discussed above, the Commissioner can challenge the transaction for up to one year after the closing date. The Commissioner can explicitly clear the transaction in two ways: by providing an ARC or a no-action letter. An ARC binds the Commissioner, whereas a no-action letter does not. Thus, only the ARC provides complete assurance that a merger will not be challenged (and even then, it can be challenged for up to one year after closing on the basis of information which is materially different from that upon which the ARC was based).

413. A party to a proposed merger can apply to the Commissioner for an ARC guaranteeing that the Commissioner will not challenge the proposed transaction under section 92.[786] If obtained, the Certification binds the Commissioner provided that the transaction closes within one year, and there are no substantive changes in the information the parties submitted in regard to the ARC request.[787] The issuance

785. *Ibid.*, at 14.
786. *Competition Act*, *supra* n. 26 at s. 102(1).
787. *Ibid.*, at s. 103.

of an ARC exempts the parties from the requirement to file pre-notification materials.[788]

414. If the Commissioner is unwilling to issue an ARC, but does not intend to immediately challenge the merger, it is common for the Commissioner to issue a no-action letter. Generally these letters state that the Bureau has completed its investigation, and no immediate competition issues have been identified, meaning that the Bureau currently does not intend to challenge the transaction. Unlike an ARC, no-action letters do not bind the Commissioner, who reserves the right to challenge the merger if competition issues subsequently emerge. Furthermore, a no-action letter does not officially exempt parties from filing obligations, though the Commissioner may (and frequently does) waive those filing obligations as long as the information provided pursuant to the ARC request was substantially similar to that which would have been provided under the section 114 filing requirements.[789] The Commissioner can also issue a no-action letter at any point during the post-filing investigation period. The legal effects of the letter are the same regardless of the date of issuance.

415. Alternatively, if a merger gives rise to possible competition issues, clearance may only come when the parties and the Commissioner have agreed to a Consent Order. The majority of anti-competitive mergers resolve through Consent Orders. If a Consent Order proves unattainable, and the Commissioner brings a contested application to the Tribunal, clearance could come in the form of a Tribunal decision. The Tribunal may either find that no prevention or lessening or competition has, is, or is likely to occur, or the Tribunal may make an order under section 92 (see below). In these cases, the Consent Order or Tribunal order could include conditions that must be met in order for the merger to proceed.

I. Conditions and Undertakings

416. Section 92 of the Act provides that, if the Tribunal finds that a merger or proposed merger substantially prevents or lessens competition, or is likely to substantially prevent or lessen competition, it can issue any of the following orders:

- In the case of a completed merger, the Tribunal can order any person to dissolve the merger in such manner as the Tribunal directs; to dispose of assets or shares designated by the Tribunal in such manner as the Tribunal directs; or, with the consent of the Commissioner and the person subject to the order, to take any other action.
- In the case of a proposed merger, the Tribunal can order the person pursuing the merger not to proceed with the merger; order the person not to proceed with part

788. *Ibid.*, at s. 113(b).
789. *Ibid.*, at s. 113(c).

of the merger; prohibit the person, should the merger or part thereof be completed, from doing any act or thing the prohibition of which the Tribunal determines to be necessary to ensure that the merger or part thereof does not prevent or lessen competition substantially; or, with the consent of Commissioner and the person subject to the order, take any other action.

Thus, the Tribunal can order structural remedies, but can only issue behavioural remedies with the consent of the Commissioner and the party involved. Consent Orders must be registered with the Tribunal and it must be possible for the Tribunal to have ordered the content of the agreements. Thus, the content of Consent Orders must fit the aforementioned provisions, though the residual 'any other action' category catches most agreements since the parties necessarily consent to the content. A registered Consent Agreement has the same legal force and effect as an order of the Tribunal.[790]

417. After the filing of a Consent Agreement with the Tribunal, the agreement can only be amended by application to the Tribunal. It can be amended if both the Commissioner and parties to the agreement consent to the amendment.[791] It can also be amended without the consent of all the parties if the Tribunal finds that the circumstances that led to the agreement have changed, such that under the current circumstances the agreement would not have been made or would be ineffective in achieving its purpose.[792] A third party may also apply to the Tribunal to have a Consent Agreement rescinded or varied. The third party must demonstrate that they are 'directly affected', and that the terms of the agreement could not have been made as an order of the Tribunal.[793] The Tribunal has held that, for a party to be directly affected, that party must establish the following relationship:

> [It] experiences firsthand a significant impact on a right which relates to competition or on a serious interest which relates to competition. The impact must be definite (i.e. not speculative or hypothetical) and must be caused by the consent agreement and not by another agreement or obligation.[794]

418. Further light was shed on consent agreement challenges brought under section 106(2) of the Act in *Kobo Inc. v. The Commissioner of Competition.*[795] In *Kobo*, the Commissioner investigated certain book publishers' activities related to

---

790. *Ibid.*, at s. 105(4). It is a criminal offence to violate most orders of the Tribunal (s. 66).
791. *Ibid.*, at s. 106(1)(b).
792. *Ibid.*, at s. 106(1)(a).
793. *Ibid.*, at s. 106(2).
794. *Burns Lake Native Development Corp. v. Commissioner*, [2006] C.C.T.D. No. 16 at para. 81 (Comp. Trib.).
795. *Kobo*, *supra* n. 286. Although Kobo appealed the Tribunal's decision to the FCA, the appeal was dismissed and the Tribunal's decision was upheld (see *Rakuten Kobo Inc. v Canada (Commissioner of Competition)*, 2015 FCA 149). Kobo filed an application for leave to the SCC to appeal the FCA's decision on 13 Aug. 2015. Kobo also seeks an order suspending the subsection 106(2) proceeding pending the SCC decision regarding its leave application and, if leave is granted, pending the disposition of its appeal (see *Kobo Inc. v. The Commissioner of Competition* (14 Aug. 2015)

digital books and entered into a consent agreement with several publishers, other than *Kobo*. The agreement impacted many of Kobo's Canadian digital book contracts and Kobo challenged the agreement under section 106(2) of the Act. The Competition Tribunal's decision limited the scope of a potential challenge under section 106(2). More specifically, the Tribunal decided that its jurisdiction on a section 106(2) application is limited to assessing the following:

1. Whether the terms of a consent agreement are not within the scope of the type of order(s) that the Tribunal is permitted to issue in respect of the reviewable trade practice in question.
2. Whether the consent agreement (a) identifies each of the substantive elements of the reviewable trade practice in question; and (b) contains either (i) an explicit agreement between the Commissioner and the respondent(s) that each of those elements has been met, or (ii) a statement that the Commissioner has concluded that each of those elements has been met, together with a statement by the respondent(s) that they do not contest that conclusion.
3. Whether the terms of the consent agreement are unenforceable or would lead to no enforceable obligation, for example, because they are too vague.[796]

A. Content

419. The content of consent agreements reached between the Commissioner and the parties varies on a case-by-case basis, as the agreements are akin to contracts negotiated between the parties. One of the most common elements of a consent agreement is that the parties must divest certain assets.[797] Often agreements also include 'hold separate' clauses, which prevent the co-mingling of assets and business information until the competition issues have resolved.[798] Behavioural components can also, however, be included

---

(Motion record to suspend subsection 106(2) proceeding). According to Kobo, suspending the subsection 106(2) proceeding is 'in the interests of justice' under the three-part *RJR-Macdonald Inc. v. Canada (Attorney General)'s* injunction test (see *Kobo v The Commissioner of Competition* (13 Oct. 2015) CT-2014-002 (Memorandum of Fact and Law of Kobo (Motion to Suspend s. 106(2) proceeding). As of 13 Oct. 2015, both parties have filed their respective memorandum of fact and law.

796. *Ibid.*, at para 3.

797. See e.g., *Commissioner of Competition v. Novartis* (6 Aug. 2010), CT-2010-008 (Comp. Trib.), in which one party had to divest three medical products, and all related interests in the products, including intellectual property rights, manufacturing material, product marketing materials and customer lists.

798. See e.g., *Commissioner of Competition v. IESI-BFC Ltd.* (30 Jun. 2010), CT-2010-005 (Comp. Trib.), in which a hold separate agreement was instituted for the period starting with the closing of the transaction and ending when certain assets had been divested in accordance with the agreement.

B. Timing

419.1. Like the content of consent agreements, the timing of any conditions or undertakings required in Tribunal orders or consent agreements varies on a case-by-case basis. There are no provisions in the Act requiring specific timelines.

§5. RELATIONS WITH OTHER MERGER CONTROL AUTHORITIES

420. The Bureau generally cooperates with other authorities when there is overlap between the Bureau's mandate and that of another Canadian authority, or when there is overlap between investigations. As discussed above, section 29 of the Act deals with the ability of the Bureau to share confidential information it obtains in the course of its investigations. The section has been interpreted to allow the sharing of information not only with other Canadian authorities, but also with international authorities. The sharing of information with regard to certain specialized transactions – namely those involving transportation or financial institutions – is explicitly provided for in the Act.[799]

I. Other Authorities within the Local Jurisdiction

421. The *Canada Transportation Act* provides that, if a transportation-related transaction is notifiable under the *Competition Act*, the Minister of Transport must also receive notification.[800] The Minister of Transport then decides within forty-two days whether the transaction raises public interest concerns. If the Minister of Transport has concerns related to the public interest an investigation commences, and the Commissioner has 150 days from the original notification period to report any competition-related concerns to the Minister of Transport. The Minister of Transport considers the Commissioner's views in her decision as to whether to grant approval of the transaction. If the Minister of Transport approves a transaction, the Tribunal cannot make an order challenging the decision.[801] In deciding whether a transportation-related transaction would be in the public interest, the Minister of Transport considers economic factors, environmental factors, safety concerns, security concerns and the social impact of the proposed transaction.[802]

422. The Minister of Finance may generally review mergers involving financial institutions. In these cases, if the Minister of Finance finds that the transaction is in

799. See *Competition Act*, *supra* n. 26 at ss 29.1 (Communication to Minister of Transport) and 29.2 (Communication to Minister of Finance).
800. *Canada Transportation Act*, *supra* n. 91 at s. 53.1(1).
801. *Competition Act*, *supra* n. 26 at s. 94(c).
802. See Transport Canada, *Guidelines for Mergers & Acquisitions involving Transportation Undertakings* (Transport Canada 2008).

the public interest the Tribunal cannot make an order challenging the transaction.[803] Similarly, these transactions are exempt from notification requirements.[804]

423. As discussed in 'Part 1: Chapter 1: §1. National Sources', large transactions by foreign investors in Canada may be subject to review under the *ICA*. In these cases, the Minister of Industry conducts the review. The Minister of Canadian Heritage conducts the review if the investment has a cultural component. This review does not replace the Commissioner's review. Thus, foreign investment transactions may be subject to two review processes if the deal meets all relevant thresholds. In practice, the Commissioner usually communicates with the relevant Minister, such that clearance under the *ICA* is not usually possible until the Commissioner has first cleared the transaction from a competition perspective.[805]

II. International Coordination

424. Although the Bureau's overriding concern is with the competition effects of transactions in the Canadian market, the Commissioner sometimes communicates with foreign authorities if a particular merger will have a cross-jurisdictional effect.[806] The Commissioner has said that '[w]here appropriate, the Bureau will agree to support and/or use as a starting point, the remedies agreed to in other jurisdictions, provided that the Bureau is satisfied that a sufficient remedy is implemented to address any Canadian issues'.[807] As discussed in 'Part III: Chapter 1: §2 Powers: III Cooperation with Other State Institutions', the Commissioner and/or Canadian government have cooperation agreements with several other states, including the United States and the EU.

---

803. Section 94(b) of the Act provides that the exemption applies to: 'a merger or proposed merger under the *Bank Act*, the *Cooperative Credit Associations Act*, the *Insurance Companies Act* or the *Trust and Loan Companies Act* in respect of which the Minister of Finance has certified to the Commissioner the names of the parties and that the merger is in the public interest – or that it would be in the public interest, taking into account any terms and conditions that may be imposed under those Acts'.

804. *Competition Act*, *supra* n. 26 at s. 113(a.1).

805. Anthony F. Baldanza, *Fundamentals of Canadian Competition Law 2015* 281 (J. Musgrove, J. Macneil & M. Osborne eds., Thomson Carswell 2007).

806. See e.g., Competition Bureau, *Competition Bureau Requires Divestitures in Herbicide Merger*, http://www.competitionbureau.gc.ca/eic/site/cb-bc.nsf/eng/03264.html (28 Jul. 2010), in which:

> [t]here was extensive international cooperation leading to the resolution of [the] case … The Competition Bureau worked closely with FTC staff throughout the investigation to arrive at a proposed settlement order that restores competition in both Canadian and U.S. markets for MCPA. Throughout their respective investigations, staff from various international partners and the FTC coordinated their enforcement efforts under the terms of relevant cooperation agreements and the OECD recommendation on cooperation among its members.

807. Competition Bureau, *Competition Bureau Clears Dow Chemical's Acquisition of Rohm and Haas*, http://www.competitionbureau.gc.ca/eic/site/cb-bc.nsf/eng/02954.html (23 Jul. 2009).

425. If the Bureau sends the parties an SIR, it may be willing to accept information that the parties submitted to a foreign competition authority provided that: (i) the parties provided appropriate confidentiality waivers to the foreign antitrust agency to permit sharing of information with the Bureau; (ii) the parties do not impose unreasonable restrictions with regard to the Bureau's use of the data; and (iii) for all purposes the Bureau may treat the data and records received as if the parties provided the materials directly to the Bureau.[808] When appropriate, the Bureau may be willing to obtain this information directly from the foreign authority, though the parties must provide the Bureau with an index clearly indicating which documents satisfy each component of the SIR.

808. MEGs, *supra* n. 153.

Chapter 3. Challenging of the Administrative Decision

§1. Competent Courts

426. On questions of law, decisions of the Tribunal are, as a matter of right, subject to judicial review by the Federal Court of Appeal. The Federal Court of Appeal may also consider decisions on questions of fact, but only if the Court grants leave to appeal. From the Federal Court of Appeal, decisions are appealable to the Supreme Court of Canada only with leave to appeal. The Supreme Court grants leave to appeal only if a panel of three Supreme Court judges concludes that the issue is of sufficient public importance or raises important enough questions of law to warrant granting leave.

§2. Time Limits

427. The limitation period for bringing an application for judicial review from a Tribunal decision to the Federal Court of Appeal is thirty days from when the Tribunal first communicated the decision or order.[809] For appeals to the Supreme Court, notice of appeal must be served on all parties to the case and filed with the Supreme Court Registrar within thirty days of the Federal Court of Appeal having issued its decision.[810]

§3. Scope of Judicial Review

428. As discussed above, decisions of law are reviewable as of right, while decisions of fact require leave to appeal. Generally, the principles of judicial review dictate that the courts review decisions of administrative bodies on either a reasonableness standard or a correctness standard.[811] Questions of law are more likely to require the correctness standard, while questions of fact mitigate in favour of a lower reasonableness standard. The expertise of the administrative body is also an important consideration. In *Southam*, the Supreme Court held that, on a question of mixed law and fact, the Tribunal's decision was subject to a test of reasonableness.[812] Thus, a decision did not necessarily need to be the one the appeal court would have chosen, so long as it was an outcome reasonably available to the Tribunal. This decision regarding the appropriate standard represents deference to the Tribunal's significant expertise in economics.

---

809. *Federal Courts Act*, R.S.C. 1985, c. F-7, ss 18.1(2) and 28(2).

810. *Supreme Court Act*, RSC 1985, c S-26 at s. 58(1)(b).

811. *Dunsmuir v. New Brunswick*, 2008 SCC 9, [2008] 1 S.C.R. 190.

812. *Southam*, *supra* n. 161 at 427. Note that this decision was based on a three standards of review approach; correctness, reasonableness and patent unreasonableness. In *Dunsmuir* the Supreme Court instituted a two standard of review approach, eliminating the patent unreasonableness standard.

429. Subsequently, the Federal Court of Appeal held that decisions of the Tribunal on questions of law are subject to a correctness standard.[813] In the 2001 case of *Superior Propane*, the Federal Court of Appeal found that the correctness standard was appropriate due to section 13(1) in the *Competition Tribunal Act*, which states that a decision of the Tribunal can be appealed 'as if it were a judgment of the Federal Court – Trial Division'. Furthermore, the Tribunal's judicial member alone (a Federal Court judge) decides questions of law. This consideration led the Court to conclude that the judicial member's expertise was not sufficiently greater than that of the Court of Appeal to justify a deferential approach.[814]

430. Most recently, the Court of Appeal used the same reasoning to conclude that a decision of the Tribunal – decided by a judicial member sitting alone – should not be reviewed based on administrative principles, but rather should be reviewed like lower court decisions.[815] Thus, the Court applied the standard of review articulated by the Supreme Court in *Housen v. Nikolaisen*.[816] In *Housen*, the Supreme Court established that decisions of law are subject to review on the correctness standard, whereas decisions of fact or mixed law and fact are subject to a reasonableness review. The Court of Appeal again held that the decision of the Tribunal was subject to correctness, as it was a question of law.

431. Thus, it is evident from past decisions that questions of law are subject to review on a correctness standard. Hence, if the Tribunal does not decide the issue as the Court would have done, the Court may overturn or vary the outcome, and will often remit the case to the Tribunal for reconsideration.[817] It is somewhat less clear how the Court will review decisions of fact or mixed law and fact. Based on *Southam* and the principles articulated in *Dunsmuir*, it is very likely that the Tribunal's factual decisions will receive some level of deference. However, the degree of leeway that the Court will give to decisions of the Tribunal remains to be seen.

---

813. See *Superior Propane* FCA 2001, *supra* n. 151; *Air Canada v. Canada (Commissioner of Competition)*, 2002 FCA 121, [2002] 4 F.C. 598; and *Canada Pipe*, *supra* n. 226.
814. *Superior Propane* FCA 2001, *supra* n. 151 at 311–312.
815. *Commissioner of Competition v. Premier Career Management Group Corp.*, 2009 FCA 295.
816. 2002 SCC 33, [2002] 2 S.C.R. 235.
817. The Federal Court of Appeal recently applied the correctness standard in reviewing the Tribunal's decision on the interpretation of subsection 79(1) of the Act in the TREB case, *supra* n. 238. The Court of Appeal substituted its own interpretation of the Act, reversed the Tribunal's decision and remitted the matter back to the Tribunal for reconsideration on the merits.

Selected Bibliography

Brown, D.J. (eds.). *2015 Competition Act and Commentary*. Markham: LexisNexis Canada Inc., 2014.

Facey, B. & Assaf D. *Competition & Antitrust Law: Canada & the United States*. Markham: LexisNexis Butterworths, 2006.

Musgrove, J., J. Macneil & M. Osborne (eds.). *Fundamentals of Canadian Competition Law 2015*. Toronto: Thomson Carswell, 2015.

Trebilcock, M. et al. *The Law and Economics of Canadian Competition Policy*. Toronto: University of Toronto Press Incorporated, 2002.

Wakil, O. *The 2015 Annotated Competition Act*. Toronto: Thomson Reuters, 2014.

Selected Bibliography

Index

The numbers here refer to paragraph numbers.

Index

www.ingramcontent.com/pod-product-compliance
Lightning Source LLC
Chambersburg PA
CBHW071340230926
51846CB00002B/397
9789041166401